CINEMA '62

CINEMA '62

The Greatest Year at the Movies

STEPHEN FARBER AND
MICHAEL McCLELLAN

FOREWORD BY BILL CONDON

RUTGERS UNIVERSITY PRESS

New Brunswick, Camden, and Newark, New Jersey, and London

Library of Congress Cataloging-in-Publication Data

Names: Farber, Stephen, author. | McClellan, Michael, author.
Title: Cinema '62: the greatest year at the movies / Stephen Farber and
Michael McClellan.
Other titles: Cinema sixty-two | Cinema nineteen sixty-two
Description: New Brunswick: Rutgers University Press, 2020. | Includes
bibliographical references and index.
Identifiers: LCCN 2019021236 | ISBN 9781978808829 (cloth: alk. paper)
Subjects: LCSH: Motion pictures—United States—History—20th century.
Classification: LCC PN1993.5.U6 F347 2020 | DDC 791.430973—dc23
LC record available at https://lccn.loc.gov/2019021236

A British Cataloging-in-Publication record for this book is available from the
British Library.

♾ The paper used in this publication meets the requirements of the American
National Standard for Information Sciences—Permanence of Paper for Printed
Library Materials, ANSI Z39.48-1992.

www.rutgersuniversitypress.org

Manufactured in the United States of America

In memory of Judge Daniel L. Brenner, whose wit and wisdom are sorely missed.

Stephen Farber

In memory of my mother, Dolores McClellan, an avid movie fan, who inspired me to be one, too.

Michael McClellan

CONTENTS

FOREWORD

Choosing the best year in movies has always been fun sport, for film critics and fans alike. The year 1939 was a popular favorite for decades, with 1999 recently emerging as a credible rival. But I've found that a cineaste's "greatest year" more often than not lines up with the early years of his or her adolescence. (Martin Scorsese, a prodigy in this as in all things, is the exception that proves the rule—he seems to have discovered the joys of cinema at age seven, and his golden age takes him into his late teens.) So I'll admit I was intrigued but skeptical when Mike McClellan told me that he and Stephen Farber were writing a book about the films of 1962, with the immodest title *Cinema '62: The Greatest Year at the Movies.* Was this just another case of immortalizing the thrill of first discovery? (I'll admit that it took me some time to acknowledge that, despite its glories, my personal year of discovery—1971—wasn't a central moment in the history of cinema.) Well, I'm happy to report that this fascinating and hugely enjoyable book dispelled my doubts, making a very convincing case for both its premise and that very cheeky title.

In this lovingly detailed work of scholarship and criticism—don't worry, there are also healthy dollops of gossip and scandal—a powerful argument emerges. It's Farber and McClellan's bold perception that, in an art form well into its second century, 1962 represents the inflection point—both a summation of everything that had come before and a harbinger of all that would follow.

The studio system, though teetering, had not yet collapsed, and the year's roster of directors includes such Golden Age giants as John Ford, Howard Hawks, Orson Welles, Vicente Minnelli, George Cukor, Leo McCarey, Lewis Milestone, John Huston, and Busby Berkeley (admittedly not all in top form). The international cinema is represented by an equally impressive list of masters: Satyajit Ray, Akira Kurosawa, Luchino Visconti, Jean Renoir, Roberto Rossellini, Luis Buñuel, Ingmar Bergman, Michelangelo Antonioni, and Federico Fellini. The nouvelle vague is possibly in its fullest flowering, with major works by Alain Resnais, Claude Chabrol, François Truffaut, Eric Rohmer, Jean-Luc Godard, and Agnes Varda. Tony Richardson represents the British kitchen sink movement, while a crop of young American directors—Robert Mulligan, John Frankenheimer, Blake Edwards, Arthur Penn, Frank Perry, Sidney Lumet, and Sam Peckinpah—graduates from television with honors.

Old and young; past, present, and future—all live side by side. Veteran critic Bosley Crowther may still reign at the *New York Times,* but Andrew Sarris and Pauline Kael are making noise. To say nothing of Stanley Kubrick, John Cassavetes, and Roger Corman, three unclassifiable iconoclasts who will change the landscape of cinema before the decade ends.

This is the story brought to vivid life in this book. The authors' thesis reaches its climax in a brilliant examination of David Lean's *Lawrence of Arabia,* a film that in this telling holds up a mirror to the tensions and complexity of this most remarkable year.

I hope that—as with most hit movies—this wonderful book inspires the authors to write a sequel, a second "Greatest Year at the Movies." 2020, anyone?

Bill Condon

PREFACE AND ACKNOWLEDGMENTS

We met at a screening in the summer of 2001 through a mutual friend, writer-director Bill Condon. As we began to discuss favorite and least favorite movies past and present, we made a surprising discovery: each of us considered 1962 the greatest year in film history. This was not a rash judgment. By 2001 both of us had seen thousands of movies: Michael McClellan as a film buyer for national movie chains, and Stephen Farber as a critic and journalist. The following year, in 2002, McClellan decided to mount a weeklong retrospective of the films of 1962 at Landmark Theatres, where he was working as vice president. To coincide with that program, Farber, a longtime contributor to the *New York Times* and other publications, wrote an article for the *Times,* "1962: When the Silver Screen Never Looked So Golden." That article and the Landmark retrospective stirred a lot of enthusiastic response, including a segment on NPR. We first thought of following up with a documentary film, but we became enmeshed in our careers.

Time went by, but the idea never completely went away, and we ultimately decided to make our case in a book. The histories written about Hollywood in the twentieth century have, for the most part, ignored the early 1960s. Film historians and critics usually dismiss this period as the tail end of the studio era, after the Golden Age had passed. The chronicles of the rise and fall of the studio era (the 1930s through the 1950s) have been mostly conventional narratives, with movie star and filmmaker biographies (some more tell-all than others) added to the mix. The New Hollywood that rose in the late 1960s and flourished in the 1970s has been the subject of recent works. But when the early 1960s are mentioned, it is usually in terms of the "calcified" Hollywood studio system, the aging stars, and the "recycled" picture plots. While those elements did exist, they were not the whole story—far from it in fact.

Our research provided the book's eventual structure, which is an extended essay combining film history, pop culture, and critical analysis. We offer a thematic approach (rather than chronologically or by genre), looking at scores of films released in the United States in 1962. In revisiting these movies, we came across some previously overlooked gems and rediscovered a cinematic mother lode, one even larger than we had first thought. Many of these films were critical and commercial hits. Some failed at the box office and have been undeservedly forgotten. We showcase the acclaimed and the underappreciated, the hidden and neglected. The stories behind the making of select films illuminate the social, cultural, economic, and political currents of the times and expose the tumultuous studio politics, but the films are always the main focus, and we sought out many of the survivors of that remarkable year to help tell the tale.

Unfortunately, as the years passed, many of our firsthand sources for the book passed away as well. Some filmmakers and actors made in-person appearances at the Landmark screening series in 2002, but by the time we began working on the book, Janet Leigh (costar of *The Manchurian Candidate*), directors Ken Annakin (*The Longest Day*) and Hubert Cornfield (*Pressure Point*), and producer Martin Manulis (*Days of Wine and Roses*) had died. However, James B. Harris, the producer of *Lolita,* who appeared at the theater in 2002, was still very much with us fifteen years later, and blessed with a remarkable memory and unflagging energy.

We managed to track down several of the other survivors of that banner year, including actors Shirley Knight (*Sweet Bird of Youth*), Mariette Hartley (*Ride the High Country*), Mary Badham (*To Kill a Mockingbird*), Barrie Chase (*Cape Fear*), Susan Kohner Weitz (*Freud*), Gina Gillespie (*What Ever Happened to Baby Jane?*), and David McCallum (*Freud, Billy Budd*); director-producer Terry Sanders (*War Hunt*); researcher Lillian Michelson (*The Manchurian Candidate*); and the Oscar-winning film editor of *Lawrence of Arabia,* Anne V. Coates, who gave us her final interview before her death in 2018. Burt Lancaster's daughter, Joanna Lancaster, remembered some vivid anecdotes from her father's production of *Birdman of Alcatraz*. Our time with Angela Lansbury (*The Manchurian Candidate*), still vibrant at the age of ninety-three, was particularly notable. We are grateful to all these individuals and several others for sharing their memories of working on these landmark films of 1962. Although we benefited from the memories of these surviving filmmakers and from many other research sources, our chief purpose in writing this book was to provide an appreciation of as many of these films as possible—films with the scope and substance that had gone missing from contemporary movies. We hoped to share our enthusiasm with readers and give a sense of the vibrancy of cinema '62.

One point of clarification: in compiling our list of the films of 1962, we used as our criterion the dates that these films were released in the United States. This includes a number of international releases that opened in their country of origin in 1961 (in some cases even earlier) but were not given a regular release in the United States until 1962. Then, as now, there were films made in other countries that never made it to our shores. We focus instead on the films that played in American theaters, which included an abundance of foreign films, far more than could be found in most cities today. We aim to evoke the moviegoing experience of 1962 for American audiences, in an era when all movie theaters in the United States were single screens or drive-ins, years before the advent of the multiplex. We have relied on release dates as listed in the *New York Times* and trade papers like *Variety*.

Additionally, however, our survey is necessarily extended into the first quarter of 1963. The Academy Awards, a component of the story, were held in April that year, and some nominated films from 1962 were released nationwide in the first months of 1963 at the height of "Oscar season." This was and continues to be common industry practice. In fact, *Gone with the Wind,* the top film of the heretofore-hallowed year, 1939, was not widely seen until 1940.

In identifying what we believe to be the most important films of 1962, we borrow the criteria of the Library of Congress and its National Film Registry, those films selected for their "historical, cultural, or aesthetic significance." We ended up writing at length about fifty films from that year and included mentions of a couple dozen more. It is hard to imagine any other year, including 1939 or any recent year, offering as much material for detailed critical appreciation.

The authors wish to thank the following individuals for their contributions and support in writing this book: our current editor Nicole Solano, who rescued the project after our original publisher went out of business; original editor Stephen P. Hull for his guidance in shaping the book; Dan Gvodzen and Tyler Smith for their expert technical assistance; our enthusiastic agent, Eric Myers; Jane Dystel, Dayna Hagewood, Michael Blaha, Jack and Janet Ratcliffe, Richard Abramowitz, R. Wayne Case, Ann Bayer, Evelyn Renold, Marlene McCampbell, Paul Weitz, Barry Sandler, Kristine Krueger, Tony Guzman, and the staff of the Margaret Herrick Library, and the late Dan Ireland, whose early enthusiasm and encouragement are not forgotten.

"Where were you in '62?" That intriguing question adorned all the advertising for George Lucas's smash hit comedy, *American Graffiti,* when it opened in 1973. For the moviegoers who yearn for more than the empty, sterile films that clog the modern multiplex, we extend an invitation to become immersed in an extraordinary movie year. Our hope is that those who still remember where they were in '62 will relish the journey into the past, and other, younger readers will come to wish they were there, too.

CINEMA '62

INTRODUCTION

At the end of the studio era and before the full-blown emergence of the New Hollywood, 1962 stands out as a pivotal year in film history. Many movie buffs have anointed 1939—the year of *Gone with the Wind* and *The Wizard of Oz*—as the greatest in cinema history. Other critics have enshrined other years or decades as their personal favorites. But the honor should really belong to 1962, a single year that saw an explosion of provocative cinema that has never been equaled. Although 1939 may have been the golden year of the Hollywood studio era, with a plentiful number of high-quality entertainments, the output that year did not come close to matching the breadth and depth of movies released in 1962.

In her memoirs, Academy Award–winning actress Sophia Loren describes the era succinctly: "It was the Fabulous Sixties, which were to change the world forever. The years of the Beatles and JFK, of *8½* and James Bond, of the popularity of nightclubs and the nonviolent protests of Martin Luther King, Jr."[1] All of the elements highlighted by Loren were part of the story of 1962.

Loren herself benefited from a thriving foreign film movement in 1962 that did not exist in 1939, and which has faded in the twenty-first century. After World War II ended, many European countries experienced a cinematic rebirth, and American art houses boomed. Most of the great foreign auteurs of the 1950s and 1960s—including Fellini, Antonioni, Bergman, Truffaut, Buñuel, Kurosawa, Visconti, De Sica, and Resnais—had important films released in 1962. One of the first important female directors outside the United States, Agnes Varda, made her breakthrough film, *Cleo from 5 to 7*, in 1962.

But even the American movies of that year were far more sophisticated than they had been in earlier decades. Young directors Sidney Lumet (*Long Day's Journey into Night*), John Frankenheimer (*The Manchurian Candidate, Birdman of Alcatraz*), Arthur Penn (*The Miracle Worker*), and Sam Peckinpah (*Ride the High Country*) mingled with master auteurs from another era—John Ford (*The Man Who Shot Liberty Valance*), Howard Hawks (*Hatari!*), John Huston (*Freud*), and David Lean (*Lawrence of Arabia*). Legendary stars Bette Davis, Joan Crawford, Barbara Stanwyck, Katharine Hepburn, John Wayne, James Stewart, and Cary Grant were working alongside contemporary favorites Doris Day, Paul Newman, Jack Lemmon, and Marlon Brando, along with brand-new faces Jane Fonda, Peter O'Toole, Steve McQueen, and Warren Beatty.

It was a fascinating transitional period in Hollywood. The art of black-and-white cinematography had a last hurrah; for the final time, black-and-white films constituted more than 60 percent of the movies nominated for the year's Academy Awards, before the virtual disappearance of the format by the late 1960s. The TV networks had dictated the change by demanding films shot in color, and the studios capitulated. And there was another Oscar milestone— for the first time in Academy history, the majority of films eligible for awards were made overseas. Italy and Japan each produced more films annually at this time than the American movie industry.

In Hollywood most of the moguls who had created the film business were either dead or deposed. Of the legendary studio founders, only Walt Disney and Jack Warner were still in charge of their fiefdoms in 1962. Agency Music Corporation of America (MCA) completed its buyout of Universal-International that year, foreshadowing the corporate-conglomerate takeovers of the Hollywood studios that would occur later in the decade. Universal, now the most profitable of all the studios with its focus on limited production and distribution deals with independent producers, became the paradigm for the New Hollywood. The newly ensconced executives at the reconstituted studios were desperate to reclaim a lost audience, and that meant they were willing to take chances on adult material and risky subjects that would have been unthinkable a few years earlier.

The Production Code that had constricted films for decades was beginning to crumble, and in 1962, audacious directors tackled subjects that had once been taboo. Otto Preminger's *Advise and Consent* and Edward Dmytryk's *Walk on the Wild Side* were among the first Hollywood pictures to mention the subject of homosexuality. MGM gingerly agreed to release a film of Vladimir Nabokov's controversial novel, *Lolita,* with Stanley Kubrick at the helm. These films, combined with frank international films on domestic screens, were so disturbing to American bluenoses that they tried to reinstate state and local censorship laws that had lain dormant. One censorship battle even landed in the White House on the desk of President John F. Kennedy, who scotched the moralizing fervor.

Not all of the movies that shocked audiences in 1962 were sexual in nature. *The Manchurian Candidate* dealt with the terrifying subject of political assassination, and it was also the first film to satirize the McCarthy era excesses that had paralyzed the country and divided the Hollywood community just a few years earlier. In addition, the film's fictional plot of foreign intervention in American politics now seems eerily prophetic. Other hot topics inflamed the screen. Two films that have fallen into obscurity, Stanley Kramer's *Pressure Point* and Roger Corman's *The Intruder,* dealt with the problems of virulent racism and white supremacy. The flawless adaptation of Harper Lee's novel *To Kill a Mockingbird,* along with *The Intruder,* protested the bigotry bred into Southern culture, and the enormous popularity of *Mockingbird* helped to inspire civil rights legislation that occurred just two years later.

The impression that this was a sleepy time in American history, an extension of the quiescent Eisenhower era of the 1950s, is far from the truth. Confrontations over civil rights, including the landmark battle to admit James Meredith to the University of Mississippi, shook the country. The Cuban missile crisis of October brought the United States closer to the brink of nuclear war than any event before or since. Partly because of the perceived Communist threat, President Kennedy quietly increased the number of American troops in Vietnam. Conflicts that would mushroom later in the 1960s were foreshadowed in these events of 1962.

Looming social and political protest was also previewed in popular music. Folk singer-songwriter Pete Seeger had two of his activist anthems hit the charts during the year: "Where Have All the Flowers Gone" by the Kingston Trio and "If I Had a Hammer," a top ten hit for Peter, Paul and Mary. And consider some of the major publishing events of that year, which also gave hints of brewing cultural changes. Rachel Carson's best seller, *Silent Spring,* helped to launch the environmental movement. Anthony Burgess's dystopian novel, *A Clockwork Orange,* foreshadowed the youth revolt. And an even more seminal book, Ken Kesey's *One Flew Over the Cuckoo's Nest,* was published in 1962. Film versions of the Burgess and Kesey novels did not appear until a decade later, but these widely admired books testified to a growing antiestablishment spirit that was also reflected in the work of some of the enterprising filmmakers of the early 1960s.

Despite all the challenges facing the motion picture industry in that period, 1962 produced near-record theatrical grosses, as the box office boasted its best performance since the peak year of 1946. And largely because of the explosion of international cinema, there was a rising film culture that flourished in major cities and universities. As movie producer John Houseman (later an Oscar-winning actor) noted, "What people are talking about now, whether it's in New York or Rome or Paris, is the cinema."[2] Adults in a national Gallup poll once again listed moviegoing as their number one leisure activity.

Some critics and historians have identified the 1970s as the second golden age of American film, and indeed many important directors emerged during that decade. Critic and journalist Charles Taylor, in *Opening Wednesday at a The-ater or Drive-In Near You,* his blunt account extolling the overlooked B movies of the 1970s, boldly calls that decade "the last great period in American mov-ies." For us the 1960s are a less heralded but more intriguing era, with 1962 unequivocally the last great year at the movies—a rare confluence of art, stu-dio craftsmanship, and commerce that has never been surpassed.

The youth audience had not yet been fully discovered, so Hollywood was not trying to pander to teenagers. Of course there were films aimed at the family audience, with a version of the Broadway smash *The Music Man* and Walt Disney pictures most prominent, while Elvis Presley vehicles, "twist" movie musicals, and a few horror films were directed at teen moviegoers. Youngsters from age ten to nineteen happened to be the most frequent ticket buyers. But for the most part, these younger audiences were expected to go to the same thoughtful, serious movies that engaged adults; there was none of the narrow niche marketing that began to dominate in the 1970s. Realism was the keynote of most films made in the United States and abroad in 1962. The reliance on fantasy-franchise filmmaking began with *Star Wars* in 1977 and has come to overwhelm Hollywood today. Also, the movies of the 1970s often had an aggressively self-important tone, whereas filmmakers in the 1960s were not working so stridently to create masterpieces; they simply wanted to make good movies on meaningful subjects, and the industry of that period supported them.

One other failing of 1970s movies was the relegation of women to narrow, stereotypical roles. It was the age of the buddy movie, and although there were a few exceptions—Robert Altman's *3 Women,* Paul Mazursky's *An Unmarried Woman*—most important films by directors like Francis Ford Coppola, Michael Cimino, and William Friedkin were completely male-oriented. This trend was a continuation of Hollywood's gender bias since the 1950s; many of the successful genre films produced in the postwar era—war movies and westerns—were directed at the male audience. But there were still great roles for actresses in such 1962 films as *The Miracle Worker, Days of Wine and Roses,*

All Fall Down, Long Day's Journey into Night, Sweet Bird of Youth, Lolita, Gypsy, The Manchurian Candidate, and *What Ever Happened to Baby Jane?* Hollywood in the 1970s did not offer such a strong gallery of vibrant female characters.

Whether they revere the films of the 1960s or the 1970s, most critics would agree that the quality of American movies has deteriorated over the past three decades. Charles Aidikoff, the operator of a popular Beverly Hills screening room that previewed thousands of films for movie industry professionals and movie stars for nearly fifty years, testified to that decline a number of years before his death (in 2016 at the age of 101). He lamented to the *Los Angeles Times*, "Nowadays the proportion of 'lousy' to 'good' films is about 10-to-1," and he fondly recalled a far different proportion in earlier decades. Reminded by his son that the "lousy" films paid the bills, Aidikoff responded sarcastically, "You're right, we don't want to alienate the lousy filmmakers."[3]

What had changed? In Hollywood, costs have risen astronomically, and so major studios produce fewer movies, a trend that was already emerging in the early 1960s. When the budgets are so high, risks are also going to be kept to a minimum. The reason that movies like *Freud, Long Day's Journey into Night,* and *Billy Budd* got made in 1962 was that these "highbrow" projects didn't represent much of a financial risk. The studios simply couldn't go broke by producing them. The prestige they accumulated by tackling these arty subjects was worth the minimal financial losses they might incur.

Of course the main reason these projects came to fruition is that writers, directors, and producers were passionate about the stories. The star directors of 1962 were witty, well-educated, adventurous artists like Billy Wilder, William Wyler, John Huston, Joseph L. Mankiewicz, Sidney Lumet, John Frankenheimer, Arthur Penn, Richard Brooks, Stanley Kramer, and David Lean. They were drawn to high-quality literary and theatrical material, and indeed, many of the movies of 1962 came from great writers like Ernest Hemingway, F. Scott Fitzgerald, Vladimir Nabokov, and Herman Melville, as well as playwrights Eugene O'Neill, Tennessee Williams, and Arthur Miller. Nowadays filmmakers rarely turn to literature or theater for inspiration; most acclaimed novels and plays are never turned into movies. It's hardly a surprise that the literacy of contemporary films has declined.

Filmmakers of the 1960s were attuned to the social changes transforming America during the Kennedy era. They also were committed to probing the motivations of fascinating, complex characters. Movies of 1962 were psychologically astute and often starkly uncompromising. It is remarkable that many of them—*The Manchurian Candidate, Days of Wine and Roses, Lolita, Ride the High Country, Lonely Are the Brave, Mutiny on the Bounty, Sundays and Cybele,*

Jules and Jim, What Ever Happened to Baby Jane?—had dark, unflinching endings. Even *Lawrence of Arabia,* the year's expensive, Oscar-winning epic, ended with the hero broken and defeated.

The year 1962 was also when independent productions began to have a real impact. *David and Lisa,* the story of two gifted, disturbed teenagers who meet in a mental hospital, scored a surprising box office success and earned Academy Award nominations for its director, Frank Perry, and screenwriter, Eleanor Perry. John Cassavetes, who had made his first independent feature, *Shadows,* a couple of years earlier, had another film released in 1962, *Too Late Blues. The Connection,* a controversial drama about drug-addicted jazz musicians, roused the censors and even attracted the attention of the White House. It was helmed by a woman director, Shirley Clarke, a key figure in the New American indie cinema. A low-budget antiwar movie, *War Hunt,* produced by newcomers Terry and Denis Sanders, introduced Robert Redford in his first screen role. New companies like Seven Arts provided the financing for several volatile movies (including *Lolita* and *What Ever Happened to Baby Jane?*) that the major studios agreed to release. It was the beginning of a brand-new style of filmmaking.

At the same time that young filmmakers were testing the waters and creating a model for independent film that would flourish in later decades, the studios continued to produce expensive epics that would be unimaginable today. When television boomed in the 1950s, the moguls decided that if they wanted to lure audiences away from home, they needed to provide spectacular experiences that were impossible to duplicate on the small screen. This led to new formats like Cinemascope and Cinerama and to exclusive reserved-seat engagements of big-budget movies. This trend was still going strong in 1962. *West Side Story* had opened as a special roadshow event at the end of 1961, and after winning ten Oscars in April 1962, it continued to draw audiences, scoring the year's highest grosses. *The Longest Day, Mutiny on the Bounty,* and *The Wonderful World of the Brothers Grimm* (the first narrative film produced in the Cinerama format) all opened in roadshow engagements, complete with intermission and souvenir programs, and drew large audiences despite sometimes mixed reviews.

Of course the peak of the year's epic moviemaking was David Lean's Oscar-winning masterpiece, *Lawrence of Arabia.* To achieve absolute verisimilitude in re-creating T. E. Lawrence's Arabian campaign, Lean sought out desert locations in Jordan and Morocco and spent more than a year filming under arduous conditions. This was a time when filmmakers did not have the benefit of computer technology to enhance their shooting; everything was filmed live, and the result turned out to be one of the most visually dazzling accomplishments of the era. The *New Republic* film critic Stanley Kauffmann praised the extraordinary "visual experiences that almost touch the other senses."

The kind of dedicated perfectionism that Lean championed has not entirely disappeared from today's cinematic universe. One of the most honored films of 2015 was Oscar winner Alejandro G. Iñárritu's *The Revenant*, a nineteenth-century survival tale that was filmed over a period of nine months in various rugged and remote locations. When the director needed to complete the film, and the elements did not cooperate, he moved the entire company to Argentina, the only place where he could find the wintry landscapes that matched the original settings in Canada. No one questioned the director's dedication or the visual splendors of the finished film. But there was one thing missing from *The Revenant*—a literate and nuanced screenplay. *Lawrence of Arabia*, by contrast, had a script that was completed by award-winning playwright Robert Bolt, and it benefited from brilliant dialogue as well as multilayered characterizations. The contrast of these two magnificently photographed, wide-screen epics illustrates the impoverishment of storytelling since the landmark year of 1962.

Similarly, one of the most acclaimed films of 2017 was Christopher Nolan's 70mm epic, *Dunkirk*. Unlike most other contemporary directors, Nolan tries to avoid CGI and film as much as possible with cast members on real locations. The logistical effects he achieved in the scenes of soldiers trapped on the beach and evacuated by a flotilla of boats are indeed impressive. But the dialogue is minimal (and often inaudible), and most of the individual characters are so sketchily drawn that they never come alive. Technically, movies may be as dazzling as ever, but some of the depth that they achieved in 1962 has gone missing.

In 2013, after the death of *Lawrence*'s star, Peter O'Toole, best-selling author Joseph Wambaugh recalled an incident from his days as a vice cop in Los Angeles. In the fall of 1962, Wambaugh was working outside an after-hours drinking spot, with the aim of busting late-night offenders. One night his superiors stopped two men getting out of a taxi outside the club; the police found a bag of marijuana and some pills on the back seat. One of the men was a recognizable face—scabrous stand-up comic Lenny Bruce. The other was described by Wambaugh as "a tall, fair-haired young man with an upmarket Brit accent." At that time the drugs they possessed could have landed them in jail with a felony conviction. The young Brit pleaded with the officers to let him go. He told them that he was in Los Angeles to promote a soon-to-be-released movie, which he described as "a role of a lifetime" that would make him known throughout the world. Then he held up his fist and said, "This hand isn't working properly. I was bitten by a camel while we were filming."

The officers had never heard of the man or the movie he described, but his Irish surname won him a bit of sympathy from the cop in command, and they grudgingly agreed to let the two passengers off with a warning. Bruce died of a drug overdose four years later. "As to the obscure actor," Wambaugh wrote in his reminiscence, "everything he said that night came true. And we were all better off for having him in bars rather than behind them. R.I.P., Mr. O'Toole."[4] If many of the blazing talents of 1962 have died, their achievements live on to inspire us all.

1 · OVERSEAS EXPLOSION

On April 9, 1962, the Academy of Motion Picture Arts and Sciences awarded the year's best actress Oscar to Sophia Loren for her performance in Vittorio De Sica's Italian drama *Two Women* (1961). With the win, the Italian actress, who had risen to worldwide prominence in the late 1950s, became the first player in Academy history to be honored for a foreign-language role. Several foreign-born actors had been nominated (and a few had won), but never for a role in a foreign-language movie. Loren's victory was a milestone and a telling marker of a profound change in the world of cinema. Later that year, Loren would also be seen in the omnibus import *Boccaccio '70,* a film that would generate as much box office and critical heat as its voluptuous star and newly respected artist. But the unexpected Oscar for "this wildly beautiful and talented girl," as Greer Garson declared when she accepted the absent Loren's award at the ceremony, embodied more than just a previously perceived sexpot showing off her acting abilities. Her victory was emblematic of the new internationalization of old Hollywood and underlined the sheer abundance of foreign films on American screens in 1962.

There were, of course, important films being made in other countries as far back as the silent era and into the 1930s. In 1939, the year that many film buffs have trumpeted as a watershed in film history, Jean Renoir made a film that may be his most impressive achievement, *The Rules of the Game.* Renoir was probably the most revered foreign director of the period. In 1938 his antiwar opus, *Grand Illusion,* was the first foreign-language film ever to be nominated for best picture, a feat that was not repeated until 1969. But audiences did not see Renoir's version of *The Rules of the Game* in 1939. The distributor cut the film before its release in Paris, and then it was cut even more drastically because of poor audience reaction. To compound the problem, the negative was destroyed when the Allies bombed studios in Boulogne near the end of World War II.[1] It was not until the late 1950s that the film was reassembled and restored to the version that Renoir had originally intended. In 1962 the British magazine *Sight and Sound* conducted an international critics' poll to rank the greatest films ever made. *The Rules of the Game* came in third, right behind *Citizen Kane* and *L'Avventura*.

By that time, of course, an explosion of international cinema had radically changed the provincial cinematic landscape that existed in 1939. In 1938 brothers Kurt and Max Laemmle, cousins of Universal Studios founder, Carl Laemmle, bought their first movie theater in Los Angeles; Max changed the programming to specialized and foreign fare in the postwar years. But the foreign film market was extremely limited in those days. The French film *Children of Paradise* was an art-house hit in 1946–1947, and a startling wave of Italian neorealism began to reach these shores after World War II. In 1947 the Academy gave a special award to Vittorio De Sica's *Shoeshine,* the first foreign film to be so honored.

It was not until 1956 that the Academy inaugurated a competitive category for foreign-language submissions. Federico Fellini's *La Strada* won that first award, and during the next few years, American audiences were introduced to the work of a new cadre of international directors, including Ingmar Bergman, Alain Resnais, and Jean-Luc Godard, as well as Fellini. Partly these films appealed to audiences because they were bolder and more sexually explicit than Hollywood movies straitjacketed by the censorious Production Code. Moviegoers were stimulated (in more ways than one) by adult subject matter that had to be treated far more gingerly in American films. But it wasn't simply the sensual appeal of foreign films that mesmerized art-house patrons. These films were intellectually provocative and stylistically daring, stirring comparisons to the most innovative twentieth-century works of literature and drama.

Until the postwar years, the studios owned the majority of American movie houses, and foreign films had been largely unwelcome except at a handful of independent theaters. When the studios were forced to divest their movie theaters by the federal government's Paramount consent decrees of 1948, many theaters, now under new ownership, were available for more diverse programming. As foreign films found more receptive patronage, a nascent specialty audience emerged; it was the beginning of a golden era for art houses.

By 1962, the year that *The Rules of the Game* soared to the top of the critics' list of favorites, this foreign film renaissance was in full bloom. It is hard to think of any other year that presented such a diverse collection of masterpieces from abroad. Besides new works from directors Bergman, Akira Kurosawa, Resnais, Luis Buñuel, Fellini, and others, François Truffaut released two bittersweet classics, *Shoot the Piano Player* and *Jules and Jim,* in America in 1962. Rising Italian auteur Michelangelo Antonioni also saw two films, *La Notte* and *Eclipse,* open in American theaters. And England's Tony Richardson, the leading figure in the "angry young man" school of British cinema, also had two movies on American screens: *A Taste of Honey* and *The Loneliness of the Long Distance Runner.*

Of the 707 films released in the United States in 1962, 280 were foreign films.[2] More adventurous mainstream exhibitors embraced foreign films to fill their screens as studio production declined. The majority of these movies were now handled by independent distributors that were not encumbered by the restrictive Production Code. The resulting proliferation of foreign films with adult themes, nudity, and frank sexuality was unprecedented.

The studios didn't miss a beat, however, and climbed aboard the international bandwagon by releasing select films through separate art divisions (which conveniently didn't require Code approval). These subsidiaries included Lopert (United Artists) and Davis-Royal (Columbia); by the end of the year, Twentieth Century-Fox also invested in a specialty division (a distant ancestor of Fox Searchlight). The other majors followed a similar pattern of acquiring, and in some cases financing, select product but on a more limited basis, accompanied by studio cofinancing of overseas production.

The proliferation of foreign films was expedited by the increasing practice of offering both subtitled and dubbed-in-English versions of the same movie, if it found box office success. This led to simultaneous showings in some cities in two different theaters, catering to both the art crowd and the mass market. Thereby, foreign films reached the widest possible audience in an era before the advent of the cinema multiplex.

Just as the foreign film invasion of American movie screens left a cultural imprint on Hollywood, reverberations were also felt internationally. When *Sundays and Cybele* opened in New York on November 12, 1962, it marked the rare occasion when a foreign-language film premiered in the United States ahead of the release in its country of origin. (Paris opened nine days later.) It was decidedly a gamble, as nearly all international films' U.S. openings were delayed for several months, and sometimes a year or more, after their original overseas release, in order to build critical consensus and audience awareness.

Thus *Divorce Italian Style, Last Year at Marienbad, Through a Glass Darkly, Yojimbo, La Notte, Viridiana,* and *A Taste of Honey* all premiered in 1961 in their respective countries, while *Devi, Shoot the Piano Player,* and *Peeping Tom* were from 1960. But they would not reach their full international impact until they opened in the United States in 1962. The creative power brokers of Hollywood certainly took notice of these pictures. For the second year in a row, the majority of the Oscar nominees in the original screenplay category were foreign-language films—*Divorce Italian Style, Last Year at Marienbad,* and *Through a Glass Darkly,* with *Divorce* securing bonus nods for best actor (Marcello Mastroianni) and best director (Pietro Germi). Even more remarkably, it was *Divorce* that won the screenwriting Oscar that year, the first foreign-language feature film winner in the writing categories.[3]

Screenwriters of foreign-language films had already been recognized in the post–World War II period with nominations for *Children of Paradise, Open City, Shoeshine, The Bicycle Thief, Mr. Hulot's Holiday, The 400 Blows, Wild Strawberries,* and *La Dolce Vita,* among others. But it was not until the early 1960s that foreign-language actors and directors began to make inroads into the Academy ranks of nominees and winners. Frederico Fellini was nominated for best director of 1961, and Sophia Loren's win confirmed Academy recognition of top-tier foreign artists outside the writing categories. While hosting the Oscar ceremony in April 1963, Frank Sinatra acknowledged the ascendancy of overseas cinema, stating, "Even though we like to think of Hollywood as the film capital of the world, we know that motion pictures [are] an international art."

New York City was the gateway for all foreign films, which premiered there before expanding their release to the rest of the country—a pattern largely unchanged in the twenty-first century. In 1962, 280 foreign films opened in Manhattan (everything from erotica to esoterica). Elsewhere the emerging markets of Albuquerque, Kansas City, and Denver exemplify both the reach of international films and the potential for art-house audience development by 1962. Albuquerque boasted two art houses, as well as once-a-week showings of foreign films by the University of New Mexico film society (with similar organizations found on college campuses nationwide). Additionally, a proliferation of specialized film societies helped spread the flourishing film culture beyond the metropolitan areas and universities. The American Federation of Film Societies estimated that more than 3,000 groups devoted to the art of cinema were operating nationwide.[4]

Enterprising exhibitors introduced the foreign film culture to even smaller markets. One management executive of the Stanley-Warner theater chain identified the audience that he felt should not be overlooked, positing, "Each town, no matter its size, has a population of professional people, teachers, and others of highly developed taste who may not want the ordinary run of film fare but will come out for the art picture."[5] Hamlets such as Lima, Ohio, and Punxsutawney, Pennsylvania (the setting for Bill Murray's popular 1993 movie, *Groundhog Day*), which had shown promise with British pictures and dubbed prints of the top foreign films, were now deemed ready for the likes of Ingmar Bergman. But one particular French film and nouvelle vague sensation, *Last Year at Marienbad,* proved very difficult to market in smaller towns and was a real "puzzler" there. Those less worldly art-film patrons, however, were not alone in their bafflement.

The enigmatic *Last Year at Marienbad,* directed by French filmmaker Alain Resnais (who had received international acclaim with 1959's *Hiroshima Mon Amour*), and based on an original screenplay by avant-garde novelist Alain Robbe-Grillet, is one of the most discussed and dissected films in cinema history. The very nature of the film, with its elliptical, fragmented structure, had already provoked debate upon its European debut. The *Hollywood Reporter* noted that the "offbeat arty [*Marienbad*] provided more food for controversial comment in the Continental press than any motion picture in years." Initially French distributors thought it "too difficult" for the audience and declined to release it, but the film became more commercially viable after winning the Golden Lion at the Venice Film Festival. Soon after that, it broke box office records in Paris, in advance of its U.S. release in 1962 to equally divided critical reception.

Set in a luxury hotel, the film deals with three principal unnamed characters (identified in the script as X, A, and M): a narrator, X (Giorgio Albertazzi); a woman, A (Delphine Seyrig), with whom he claims he had an affair the year before at another resort, Marienbad; and another man, M (Sacha Pitoeff), who may or may not be A's husband. The film begins with voice-over narration that is repeated while the camera glides through the ornately decorated corridors, chambers, and landscaped grounds of a baroque château. The rest of the film consists of scenes that take place in the rooms of the hotel and outside in the gardens, with Albertazzi trying to convince Seyrig that not only did they have an affair but that they had agreed to rendezvous one year later and run off together. Seyrig does not recall the alleged affair or ever having met Albertazzi before. Meanwhile, Pitoeff engages Albertazzi in a game of chance, which Albertazzi always loses. At one point in the fractured narrative, there are scenes in which Seyrig may or may not have been raped by Albertazzi and killed by Pitoeff, but that is left ambiguous.

Resnais filmed in black and white, photographed by Sacha Vierny in the Dyaliscope wide-screen format, which emphasizes the geometric, stylized mise-en-scène, even though the actors depict their characters naturalistically.

FIGURE 1.1 The garden setting from *Last Year at Marienbad*. (Photofest)

The interiors are often filled with other characters, but they rarely interact with the principals and are often frozen artificially as background props. The most famous setting, the exterior garden with geometrically shaped trees and bushes (some painted one-dimensionally to enhance the illusion) and larger than life-size statuary, utilizes actors as décor, with the conversing principals in the foreground.

Robbe-Grillet wrote a very detailed script with specific direction, adhered to for the most part by Resnais. The director considered himself the coauthor of the film. The film's nonlinear story is definitely reminiscent of his hit *Hiroshima Mon Amour*. The film also strongly echoes Robbe-Grillet's works of fiction, with their repetitive descriptions and fractured timelines and plots. But the author and director could not agree on whether the characters had actually met at Marienbad. Robbe-Grillet asserted, "One must remember the man is not telling the truth. The couple did not meet the year before." Resnais countered, saying, "I could never have shot this film if I had not been convinced that their meeting had actually taken place."[6]

Some critics seized on this disagreement as a chance to deride the picture. Detractors called the film pretentious and incomprehensible, and it would be widely satirized. One dissenter was on-the-rise critic Pauline Kael, who dismissed it as "the snow job in the ice palace . . . a no-fun party with non-people." Andrew Sarris, the principal American proponent of the auteur theory, often disagreed with Kael, but not in this case. He sardonically noted the film "demonstrated that ambiguity was less appealing as a subject than as an attitude."

More receptive adherents included film critic Roger Ebert, who was impressed with the film's "voluptuous quality, . . . its command of tone and mood, its hypnotic way of drawing us into its puzzle, its austere visual beauty."[7] That beauty is partially personified by Seyrig, playing the woman at the center of the story, who is coolly elegant, dressed in chic couture by Coco Chanel.

Bosley Crowther, the film critic of the *New York Times* and the era's most influential reviewer in the United States, was sufficiently dazzled. He forewarned his readers, "Be prepared for an experience such as you've never had from watching a film," calling it "truly extraordinary." He further exclaimed, in his characteristic purple prose, "It may grip you with a strange enchantment, it may twist your wits into a snarl, it may leave your mind and senses toddling vaguely in the regions in between. But this we can reasonably promise: when you stagger away from it, you will feel you had delighted in (or suffered) a unique and intense experience."

So it is left for the viewer to decipher the meaning of it all. Is the film a dream, with Seyrig and Albertazzi at the center of recycled imagery and shadowy memories? Are all the characters dead, souls trapped in limbo? Here the director may also be lending a clue, with the choice of ominous, gothic organ music by composer Francis Seyrig for the film's soundtrack. So is the film, then, an existential horror story? It may be a big-screen *Twilight Zone,* a reading bolstered by its nomination as "best dramatic presentation" by the Hugo Awards, prizes given annually (since 1953) in the field of science fiction and fantasy.

Or perhaps the picture should be interpreted as a dreamlike portrayal of romantic and sexual obsession. This interpretation is strengthened by the constant repetition of dialogue and imagery, giving the feeling of someone caught in the grip of a profound romantic attraction. In this reading of the film, X would be the primary character, reliving his initial encounters with A with a vivid, almost tactile intensity that she does not share. Frequently this kind of romantic obsession is indeed one-sided, and although the film exaggerates the disparity in the two lovers' memory of their initial encounter, it captures something truthful about the disconnections in many romances.

Could the film be a more experimental version of Hitchcock's *Vertigo,* another study of one-sided romantic obsession that also employed subtly stylized visual images less radical than the experiments of Resnais and Robbe-Grillet? In the later scenes of *Vertigo,* James Stewart revisits and relives his earlier encounters with Kim Novak, much as X and A replay their romantic rendezvous. In the Hitchcock movie there was of course a diabolical murder plot that partially explained the divergent responses of Stewart and Novak, but the themes were not so dissimilar from those played out in Resnais's château. In any case, this is just one possible reading of the elusive *Marienbad*. Resnais suggested at the time that the film might be an absolute fantasy, "as when the young woman imagines in a lurid, comic way that her husband will murder her."[8] Like a cubist work of art, or a celluloid Rubik's Cube, the interpretations are multiple and varied.

Marienbad was the quintessential cocktail party and coffeehouse movie, sparking lively discussion and generating highly desired word-of-mouth advertising, as its elusive meaning was endlessly debated. Fellow French auteur François Truffaut had stated early in the year, "With *Marienbad*, Resnais carried the cinema farther than it had ever gone before without worrying about whether audiences would follow."[9] One thing that is certain is the economic and cultural impact the film had on the domestic art-house movement. Although it was not to everyone's taste, and never achieved the status of a commercial blockbuster, it played for thirty-two weeks in New York after opening in early March 1962 at the Carnegie Hall Cinema, setting a new house record. Expanding nationwide, it played deep into the summer as one of the year's solid specialized hits.

After the film's '62 domestic release the writers' branch of the Motion Picture Academy was intrigued enough to nominate Robbe-Grillet's original screenplay for an Oscar. *C'est dommage* the art directors' branch could not have been as generous, overlooking Jacques Saulnier's unique production design in favor of thoroughly conventional fare like *Period of Adjustment* in the black-and-white category. But the influence of *Last Year at Marienbad* has resonated through the years, with its fractured storytelling style widely imitated by other artists. Master directors like Stanley Kubrick, David Lynch, and Terrence Malick paid homage in their films.

Another filmmaker who fragmented time and space, Italy's Michelangelo Antonioni, who had been making films for more than a decade, emerged from the European New Wave with his international breakthrough success, *L'Avventura*, in 1960. Both of his subsequent films, *La Notte* and *Eclipse,* were released in the United States in 1962. These films form a trilogy on modern alienation and found a receptive audience with critics and art-house patrons. In making *L'Avventura,* Antonioni formed a relationship—both on screen and off—with leading lady Monica Vitti that would last throughout the 1960s. Their intense collaboration reminded critics of other great director-actress pairings, like that of Josef von Sternberg and Marlene Dietrich, Federico Fellini and Giulietta Masina, or Ingmar Bergman and Liv Ullmann.

In *La Notte,* coiffed in a black wig, Vitti had a tasty supporting role as the rich daughter of a tycoon who tempts the world-weary hero during a long, decadent party sequence that forms the climax of the movie. But in this film Antonioni also proved that he was not immune to the lure of star casting that tantalized directors on both sides of the Atlantic. Vitti was a mesmerizing screen presence but not yet an international movie star, so Antonioni cast her in a supporting role and gave the leads to Marcello Mastroianni and Jeanne Moreau. As the amoral journalist in *La Dolce Vita,* Mastroianni had risen to international stardom, and Moreau's roles in Louis Malle's *Elevator to the Gallows* and *The Lovers* and in Roger Vadim's modern-day updating of *Les Liaisons Dangereuses* had established her as a vibrant new screen presence. For all his reputation as a rarefied highbrow director, Antonioni was not above seeking a larger audience for his films by populating them with bona fide movie stars. Moreau and Mastroianni rewarded the director's trust with charismatic performances that certainly helped to bring greater attention to this demanding study of marital ennui.

Nevertheless, the nearly plotless film divided critics at the time. Antonioni's strongest American champion was *New Republic* critic Stanley Kauffmann, who was positively enraptured by *La Notte.* As he wrote in his review of February 26, 1962, "I have now seen *La Notte* three times and I speak carefully when I say that I think Antonioni is making a new art form. In this film, even more strikingly than in *L'Avventura,* he is forging a new language apposite to a changed world. . . . It is essentially as drastic a revolution as abstract expressionist painting or Beckett's litanylike dialogue." By contrast, Pauline Kael included this film, along with *Last Year at Marienbad,* in her diatribe against the arty films of the era, in her article cleverly titled "Come-Dressed-As-the-Sick-Soul-of-Europe-Parties." The party scene that Mastroianni's Giovanni and Moreau's Lidia attend consumes almost the final hour of the two-hour movie and is clearly meant to epitomize the enervation of upper-class Italian society.

Kael also objected to the main theme of the film, Antonioni's lament for the decay of love between Giovanni and Lidia. In the final scene, after they leave the party at dawn—both of them having flirted with other lovers during the long, sleepless night—Lidia reads Giovanni a love letter. He finds it completely unrecognizable but is startled when she tells him that it was a letter he wrote to her years ago, during the first flush of their romance. The melancholy of this conclusion was moving to many viewers but not to Kael. She wrote, "And isn't it rather adolescent to treat the failure of love with such solemnity? . . .

If it is the sickness of our time that married people get fed-up with each other, when was the world healthy? (Perhaps the marriage in *La Notte* just lasted too long: I don't know anybody who has stayed married for ten years— nobody except relatives.)"[10]

Kael's argument is provocative and witty, but perhaps also beside the point. The death of love may have been explored before, but it is a primal subject, which is why artists return to it. Still, it isn't primarily the theme of *La Notte* that makes it memorable. Antonioni's masterful use of sound and image enriches what might have been an overly familiar study of modern despair. In a classic sequence earlier in the film, Lidia leaves a book party, and the sights and sounds she encounters on a walk through the city crystallize the isolation of an individual in an impersonal urban wasteland. She passes a crying baby, stands by herself against a wall while a plane roars overhead, is disoriented when she encounters a seemingly meaningless fight between two thugs, then watches some other boys set off rockets. The sequence encapsulates the film's themes without a word of dialogue, themes that have continued to resonate with sophisticated viewers. In a poll of accomplished directors conducted in 1963 by *Cinema* magazine, Stanley Kubrick selected *La Notte* as one of the ten best films ever made. Decades later, at the time of a major reissue for the film's fifty-fifth anniversary, the *Los Angeles Times* acknowledged Antonioni as a master who "created a potent new language for storytelling and in the process charted a topography of modern ennui."[11]

Antonioni continued to explore these themes of urban angst in his next film, *Eclipse,* which opened at the end of 1962. *La Notte* was set in Milan, while *Eclipse* takes place in Rome. In this film Vitti has the leading role, and her costar is Alain Delon, the handsome French actor who burst into prominence in *Purple Noon* (based on Patricia Highsmith's novel *The Talented Mr. Ripley*) a couple of years earlier. As he did in *La Notte,* Antonioni helped to ensure his film's visibility by casting a rising international star in his picture, even if Delon (like Moreau in *La Notte*) had to be dubbed into Italian.

The director's command of sound and imagery remains startling. In the opening sequence, as Vitti's Vittoria breaks up with her lover, the harsh sound of a portable fan in their apartment adds to the mood of unease. In a later scene, as Vittoria walks past an empty, unfinished building, the dissonant music on the soundtrack (composed by Giovanni Fusco) intensifies her sense of isolation. But *Eclipse* adds something new to the Antonioni universe. The scenes in the Borsa, the Roman stock exchange where Delon's Piero works, are quite unlike any other sequences in the movie or in Antonioni's other work. In contrast to his characteristic images of loneliness and silence, these stock

FIGURE 1.2 Director Michelangelo Antonioni (center) on the set of *Eclipse*. (Photofest)

exchange scenes are consumed with tumult and noise. At one point the brokers observe a moment of silence for a dead colleague, but soon the frenzy
resumes, as customers and brokers scream their orders to buy and sell, and
Antonioni's camera plunges right into the chaos.

These raucous, high-energy sequences can be contrasted with the daring
finale of the film, a seven-minute wordless sequence that does not include the
principal actors. It is an almost documentary-like sequence observing Vittoria's neighborhood—fences, telephone poles, empty streets, and fountains
marked only by rustling leaves and screeching tires, then a gradual shift from
afternoon to evening as lights flicker and come on. Critics debated the meaning of this extended coda. Stanley Kauffmann offered perhaps the most sympathetic and convincing interpretation: "To me it is simply a sounding board
against which the story, now ended, resonates for a while, as a pedal may hold
the closing notes of a piano piece. . . . It is quite simple and quite daring, and it
is not a trick. It is an action in art by a self-confident artist."

Some exhibitors, however, were less indulgent than Kauffmann, and there
were reports that some of them had shortened this closing sequence or lopped
it off entirely, an indication that the experimental new foreign films were not
always to the liking of more conservative theater owners, who felt obliged to
exhibit the new art films even when they were bewildered or downright hostile to the movies' content. Today exhibitors might be inclined to edit a different
sequence of the film, a bizarre episode verging on racism, in which Vittoria

puts on a blackface performance while visiting a couple of friends, one of whom has spent time living in Africa. *La Notte* also includes a strange sequence in which Mastroianni and Moreau visit a nightclub where a black female contortionist performs. These sequences indicate surprising racial insensitivity on the part of an upper-class white filmmaker of the era. Antonioni may have made a few questionable choices in *La Notte* and *Eclipse*, but the director's cinematic innovations enthralled adventurous moviegoers.

Although there was an audience for highbrow items like *Last Year at Marienbad*, *La Notte*, and *Eclipse*, the most commercially successful international films were comedies. British amusements starring Peter Sellers (*Waltz of the Toreadors, Only Two Can Play*) and Margaret Rutherford (*Murder She Said*) were especially popular. Although these films were mostly minor diversions, the comedy mystery *Murder She Said*, featuring Agatha Christie's distaff detective Jane Marple, proved to be a surprise hit vehicle for the septuagenarian Rutherford, who was a well-known player in the art-house circuit and had been delighting audiences since the 1940s. British films, while still imports, had the obvious advantage of being English language. But the Italian laugh inducer *Divorce Italian Style* did not let the language barrier hinder it from becoming one of the biggest foreign hits of the year.

Divorce Italian Style, directed by Pietro Germi from an original screenplay by Germi with Ennio De Concini and Alfredo Giannetti, is a satirical comedy about an impoverished, bored Sicilian aristocrat (Marcello Mastroianni), who inveigles his devoted but overly amorous wife (Daniela Rocca) into an adulterous affair so that he can find an excuse to kill her. Conveniently, he would then be free to marry his young, beautiful cousin (Stefania Sandrelli), who seems to return his affections, at least up until the movie's wicked final shot.

Germi had been a director of serious social dramas since the 1940s, and this was his first return to comedy since adapting a French farce, *Mademoiselle Gobete*, in 1952. His keen observations of the mores of Italian society in those earlier films would serve him well in *Divorce Italian Style*, and he uses the neorealist style effectively in the black-and-white film (photographed by Leonida Barboni and Carlo Di Palma; Di Palma later collaborated extensively with filmmaker Woody Allen). Philip Kaufman, the director of *The Right Stuff* and *The Unbearable Lightness of Being*, remembers seeing the movie for the first time at the Esquire Theatre in Chicago in 1962. "It is a perfect movie," he declares, "so witty and mature and playful. The direction, the black-and-white cinematography: it makes you want to be in a black-and-white world and certainly to shoot black-and-white films."[12]

Utilizing a flashback structure, the film opens with Mastroianni returning from a short prison term and happily recounting his adventures in matrimony and murder. Mastroianni provides voice-over narration as he wryly assesses his situation in the context of Italian cultural habits and political traditions, all the while rationalizing his lust for his nubile cousin and his plan to dispose of his wife (divorce being forbidden in Italy). When he pushes his wife into an affair, the townspeople mock him as a cuckold, and he cunningly manipulates that scorn to his advantage. He is aided in his elaborate scheme by the tradition codified in Italian law, which would mete out light punishment for this particular brand of homicide—Article 587 of the Italian penal code, the "crime of honor."[13]

Time magazine lauded writer-director Germi for "something wildly, wickedly, wonderfully funny. He has applied a cunning hotfoot to the world's biggest boot." Bosley Crowther in his *New York Times* review thought it "a dandy satiric farce," pointing out how nimbly director and star "accomplished that very difficult and delicate thing of making murder seem an admirable ambition and the would-be murderer seem a sympathetic gent, all without violating reason or causing really serious moral offense." Crowther's own sexism, reflected in a number of his other reviews of the period, led him to gloss over the hero's murder of his inconvenient wife.

While critics of the day praised the comedy, at least one admirer, director Martin Scorsese, who is of Sicilian ancestry, finds a darker tone beneath the laughter. He states, "But to me, and my parents as well, the film didn't play as a satire—we never looked down on the situation or the characters. Every detail in *Divorce Italian Style* is so truthful and right that all Germi had to do was heighten everything a bit to make it funny."[14] Germi found the perfect player in Mastroianni, whose droll performance as the scheming Baron cemented his international reputation as one of Italy's (and the era's) finest actors.

Mastroianni had been offered the part after a number of other actors had declined, and Germi hired him reluctantly. Mastroianni related how he had to audition: "Germi's image of me as an actor was strictly limited to my image in *La Dolce Vita* and perhaps he thought I belonged to the same social class. He was a reserved man, almost rude, a misanthropist who seemed to despise anyone who had anything to do with the frivolous world of cinema . . . he certainly had no idea that I might be the right actor for his film."[15] Mastroianni began using a facial tic in his performance that he borrowed from Germi. During the production, costar Daniela Rocca, a beauty who had to be deglamorized for the role of the Baron's wife, became overly sensitive about her appearance and performance. There were also rumors about an affair between the

FIGURE 1.3 Marcello Mastroianni as the Sicilian baron in *Divorce Italian Style.* (Screen shot)

insecure actress and Germi; at one point Rocca slashed her wrists, and she was off the set for two weeks. Mastroianni recalled, "None of this did anything [good] for the tic that Germi had on one side of his face."[16]

Divorce Italian Style opened in September 1962 and quickly became an art-house smash, setting a new box office record at New York's Paris Theatre (shuttered 2019) before embarking on a national expansion. Many exhibitors were looking to fill their empty screens in the fall season (studio releases had dwindled to new lows) and wanted in on the fun, booking dubbed versions of the Italian import to great success. Mastroianni, who became the first male actor nominated for a foreign-language performance, was also on American screens in 1962 in *La Notte, Bell' Antonio,* and *A Very Private Affair* (with Brigitte Bardot), and he was thrust to even greater international stardom. But he was blasé about his Hollywood acclaim. During a publicity tour in October, he cordially told the *New York Times,* "The best films in the world are being made in Italy. Why should I go anywhere else?"[17] Unlike Germi, he didn't even bother to attend the Academy Awards. He resisted working in Hollywood for the rest of his illustrious career.

Mastroianni wasn't too far off the mark about the importance of Rome to international filmmaking. Runaway production was a continued thorn in the side of labor forces in Hollywood and a matter of concern to the Southern California economy. But the fact that it was considerably cheaper to film outside Hollywood, after post–World War II unionization and inflated star salaries helped drive up production costs, was not lost on the studios.[18]

Hollywood, attempting to come to terms with this increased globalization, found a way to make light of the situation. At the 1962 Academy Awards honoring films for 1961, host Bob Hope bantered with presenter Rosalind Russell about the topic. Hope introduced Russell as just in from Tokyo, referring to her 1961 movie, *A Majority of One,* which was set there. Russell pointed out that it was actually shot in Burbank, while chastising Hope for making *The Road to Hong Kong* in London. Hope quipped, "We had to, we couldn't get studio space in Rome."

One of the major behind-the-scenes instigators of the overseas explosion was American producer Joseph E. Levine, a former exhibitor who founded Embassy Pictures in 1954. Levine had attained box office prosperity with exploitation pictures like the Japanese import *Godzilla* (1956) and the Italian *Hercules,* a box office phenomenon in 1959. He was a major proponent of old-fashioned marketing and showmanship, contending, "I have always felt that advertising is like learning . . . a little is a dangerous thing."[19] Later he added prestige via art-house releases like *Two Women,* and he was instrumental in helping Sophia Loren net the Oscar. His show business hucksterism intrigued documentary filmmakers the Maysles brothers (*Gimme Shelter, Grey Gardens*), who profiled him in a rarely seen picture, *Showman,* in 1963. Decades later the Levine marketing playbook of saturation advertising and shrewd award season campaign tactics found new adherents among companies like Miramax, reinforcing the notion that there is often very little new in Hollywood. Subsequently, three Embassy foreign releases in 1962 reaped the benefits of Levine's brand of ballyhoo: *Boccaccio '70, Divorce Italian Style,* and *The Sky Above—The Mud Below,* all substantial hits in art houses and select regular theaters that year.

Perhaps the most surprising of Levine's successes was a film with neither scripted story, familiar actors, nor well-known director. *The Sky Above—The Mud Below* is a filmed account of a seven-month expedition into uncharted territory of then Dutch New Guinea by documentarian Pierre-Dominique Gaisseau. Upon its release in June 1962 (and decades before the advent of the National Geographic Channel), American audiences were fascinated by the thousand-mile journey of the filmmaking team as they encountered hardships battling dense jungle, leeches, steep mountains, and other natural perils like heat, hunger, and exhaustion. The native tribe they encountered, the Una, were labeled Stone Age pygmies by the explorers; hints of cannibalism and headhunting added to the piquant mix of exotic dangers.

One reason for the documentary's popularity, aside from the travelogue adventure, dubbed English narration, and an Academy Award (for best documentary feature of 1961), was the sensationalist appeal of its content. "See white men forced into intimacies with their native hosts!" was one of show-man Levine's marketing slogans that not only enticed the crowds but also awakened the local censors. Because of its depiction of bare-breasted native women and nearly naked men, both Detroit and Chicago restricted showings of the French anthropological film, with the Windy City (the original home of the Legion of Decency) banning the film outright for its depiction of "not adequately clothed" New Guinea natives.[20] All that breathless attention helped the documentary to a $2 million dollar gross, with more box office sizzle than many Hollywood studio films.

Other skirmishes with government censors and critics arose throughout the year. Foreign films and independent features with provocative adult content were under fire for offending local community moral standards. In 1962 the censors were still holding sway in such states as Virginia, Maryland, Kansas, Ohio, Texas, and New York. Major cities like Chicago, Boston, Atlanta, and Detroit required censor review, along with smaller markets like Memphis, Birmingham, and Pasadena (just outside the movie capital). The Legion of Decency, a watchdog agency since the 1930s, still held enormous sway guid-ing the nation's vast Catholic population in 1962. Studios regularly conferred with the Legion to steer clear of a Condemned rating.

The courts however, had become inadvertent allies of the motion picture industry when the U.S. Supreme Court ruled part of the New York state cen-sorship law unconstitutional in 1959. But the local censors did not surrender without a fight. Ohio was the battleground over Louis Malle's notorious film *The Lovers* (1960), when a Cleveland exhibitor was convicted of knowingly showing an "obscene" film, with other squabbles fought in Columbus and sub-urban Dayton. *The Lovers* caused such a ruckus that *Variety* reported, "It looked like Ohio, for a time, might declare war on France." The Supreme Court finally overturned the ban in 1964.

Other foreign films aroused the censors. The Italian anthology film *Boccac-cio '70* was one of fifteen foreign movies slapped with the Legion of Decency's infamous C rating (Condemned as morally objectionable for all) in 1962. But times were changing. After *Boccaccio '70* opened the brand-new art venue Cin-ema I and Cinema II in Manhattan on June 26 and settled in for a five-month run, the New York–based Loew's theater circuit booked the prestige import for fall playoff. It was the first time a Legion-condemned film ever played in that prominent movie house chain.

The movie that raised the censors' temperatures to the boiling point is a four-part omnibus production about morality and love, reimagining how the ribald Renaissance author Giovanni Boccaccio might have presented these tales if writing them in the twentieth century, as contemporary versions of his fourteenth-century *Decameron*. Conceived by the Italian screenwriter Cesare Zavattini (*The Bicycle Thief, Two Women*), and coproduced by Sophia Loren's husband, Carlo Ponti (with financial backing by Joseph E. Levine), *Boccaccio '70* seems innocuous by twenty-first-century standards. The film's reputation rests on its collection of international talents, with segments by directors Mario Monicelli, Federico Fellini, Luchino Visconti, and Vittorio De Sica, starring European beauties Anita Ekberg, Romy Schneider, and Sophia Loren. All of the film's four segments poke wittily at the hypocrisies of Italian society.

Monicelli had directed the successful caper comedy *Big Deal on Madonna Street* two years earlier. But his episode, a lighthearted tale about a young couple dealing with restrictive office (and sexual) politics in the big city, was dropped outside of Italy, presumably due to the film's excessive length (the complete version ran close to three and a half hours); it also suffered from the absence of a major star. Even attendees of the Cannes Film Festival missed out; the abridged version debuted there. Monicelli's segment bursts with vitality, establishing the rich color schematic and setting the vibrant tone maintained throughout all the film's episodes.

The international version of *Boccaccio '70* released in 1962 opens with Fellini's satirical segment, "The Temptation of Doctor Antonio," with Peppino De Filippo as a late-middle-aged prude who is a self-appointed morals gatekeeper, railing against perceived indecency and vice in Italian society. He takes umbrage over a giant billboard outside his building displaying the full-length figure of a well-endowed Anita Ekberg beckoning viewers to *bette piu latte* (drink more milk). Nino Rota (*La Strada, Romeo and Juliet, The Godfather*) provides a jaunty melody to accompany the visuals of crowds gathering to ogle the advertisement and sing the catchy jingle. Popular composer Henry Mancini, profiled in *Time* as the "hottest music man in Hollywood," was so taken with the tune that he covered it in his best-selling album of 1962's memorable movie themes. In the film Antonio soon falls under the spell of the ad, and when the image of Ekberg comes to life to pursue the moralistic crusader, his fortitude dissolves. Thin-skinned censors could apparently see themselves in Antonio, and they were not amused. Fellini's surreal comic touches, which would become a signature for his films in the 1960s and 1970s, are in early bloom here.

Fellini, one of the most acclaimed directors in motion picture history, was at a career peak in 1962. Earlier in the year his international sensation, *La Dolce Vita*, garnered him the first-ever nomination for a director of a foreign-language film; he was about to embark on another influential film that would seal his

FIGURE 1.4 Oscar-winning director Federico Fellini. (Photofest)

reputation, *8½*. *La Dolce Vita* had broken box office records in Italy but also drew the ire of the Catholic Church. "The Temptation of Doctor Antonio" segment in *Boccaccio '70* afforded the director an opportunity to target the repressive Catholic morality of his country. He stated, "I wanted to show metaphorically how man's imprisoned appetites can finally burst their bonds and bloat into an erotic fantasy that comes to life, takes possession of its creator and ultimately devours him."[21] Fellini went on a publicity tour for the U.S. premiere, and after learning that the Legion of Decency had condemned the film for "grossly suggestive concentration upon indecent costuming situations and dialogue," he told the press, "I think censorship is a horrible thing, which should not exist, because to admit the need for censorship is to admit that mankind is forever infantile."[22]

The next segment, Visconti's "The Job," depicts a young aristocratic couple (Romy Schneider and Tomas Milian) forced to deal with Milian's dalliances with prostitutes that are exposed by the press. Schneider threatens to bolt the loveless "marriage of property," as she describes it, and become an "ordinary woman" by working for a living. Her solution is to become her husband's mistress, paid for her efforts. Visconti's direction and elegant framing of the couple's power struggle, in what is basically an observant battle-of-the-sexes interior piece (with peekaboo nudity of Schneider undressing and bathing), notably enhance the viewing experience. *Cinema* magazine highlighted the film's female-centric status, noting Schneider's character as "more dominant than the male," which was an unusual phenomenon in the man's world of 1962.[23]

If the provocative images of Ekberg and Schneider were not enough ammunition for the censors, the incendiary bombshell of Sophia Loren in "The Raffle," Vittorio De Sica's contribution to *Boccaccio '70*, would make their heads explode. Loren plays a carnival worker who is the "prize" of a lottery, and her voluptuous figure in a form-fitting, flaming red outfit, which she discards at key plot moments, was more than enough fuel to set the screen ablaze. Loren exudes sensuality, but the actual story is more whimsy than taboo, with Loren's virtue intact at the end; apparently the censors could not see past their steamed-up spectacles. In her memoirs, Loren praised the director's approach: "De Sica used all the irony he could muster—which was always gentle and delicate even when it was just one step away from the grotesque." She elaborated on her performance: "I had lots of fun shooting the movie in that rural area . . . hearing the Romagnolo accent always put me in a good mood."[24] Loren's happiness also charmed the critics. It was another triumph for the actress, as Hollis Alpert in *Saturday Review* cited her "spirited performance," and *Show* magazine proclaimed Loren "one of the most accomplished comediennes in films today."

Movie impresario Levine gleefully sold *Boccaccio '70* as a female triptych, emphasizing the alluring attributes of the stars in the ads—"Three stories of the sexes, somewhat daring, somewhat different, somewhat delicious"—and undoubtedly could not believe his good fortune when the Catholic Church attacked the film. Levine had already planned a big marketing push, but this kind of free publicity was gravy, and Loew's decision to book the film circuit-wide, Condemned rating be damned, made it a regional crossover hit. With *Divorce Italian Style* and *Boccaccio '70* soon playing everywhere, American movie houses were now infused with the sights and sounds of old-world Italian culture, ribbed and flayed open for audience amusement.

Most conflicts with the censors were waged locally, but one censorship battle landed in the White House on the desk of President John F. Kennedy. In October 1962, Congress, as the capital district's legislator, passed a censorship law for Washington, DC. But the law's final disposition lay in the hands of JFK, who had been lobbied by both the Motion Picture Association of America (MPAA) and the American Civil Liberties Union (ACLU) to ax the pending statute. The outcome was not clear-cut, as Kennedy had earlier indicated apparent support for some forms of censorship. In July 1961 the *New York Times* reported that he "requested of the American Newspaper Publishers Association that information detrimental to the national interest be withheld from the American people." In the 1962 case, however, JFK sided with the motion picture industry and vetoed the DC censorship bill, foiling the bluenoses.[25]

In the meantime, the daring content of international cinema stimulated Hollywood tastemakers. The Motion Picture Academy awarded the 1961 foreign-language Oscar to Swedish auteur Ingmar Bergman for his austere, four-character chamber drama *Through a Glass Darkly*, just in time for the film's domestic release in March 1962. As an exploration of artistic and spiritual themes, the film is the first of the director's "faith trilogy," followed in subsequent years by *Winter Light* and *The Silence*. Critical and commercial success burnished his reputation as a marquee filmmaker on the American art-house circuit for the next two decades.

Bergman, like Pietro Germi, had been working in film since the 1940s. The directors of *Boccaccio '70* also began their careers during that decade. One important foreign director with a controversial film on-screen in 1962 had an even longer history. Luis Buñuel was a Spanish-born provocateur who spent most of his career working outside his home country. In the late 1920s he teamed up with Spanish surrealist painter Salvador Dalí to make two experimental short films, *Un Chien Andalou* and *L'Age d'Or*, that exploded the language of cinema at the very end of the silent era. Buñuel made those two movies in France, and after Franco seized power, the director felt he could not remain in Spain. He spent time in the United States and later migrated to Mexico, where he made several gritty films about the underbelly of urban life—including *El* and *The Young and the Damned*. He even made one American film during the 1950s—*The Adventures of Robinson Crusoe* starring Dan O'Herlihy.

But in 1961 producers persuaded Buñuel to return to Spain for the first time in thirty years. The film he made there, *Viridiana* (which reached American theaters in 1962), was suffused with his characteristic caustic wit, antireligious sentiment, and sexual boldness. It was saucy and sacrilegious enough to earn a Condemned rating from the Legion of Decency, which meant that Buñuel joined younger directors like Antonioni, Fellini, and Truffaut in provoking the ire of the Catholic Church's watchdog agency. But Buñuel had been at it longer than any of these other auteurs, and he remained unrepentant. His most famous—and characteristically wry—quote was "I'm still an atheist, thank God!"

Viridiana centers on a young woman who is about to take her vows as a nun. But when her uncle, her only living relative, asks to see her, she ventures out from the convent. Her uncle (played by one of Buñuel's favorite actors,

Fernando Rey) contemplates seducing her. In one of the scenes that undoubtedly inflamed the Legion of Decency, he persuades Viridiana to wear his dead wife's wedding dress. He drugs her and carries her upstairs to bed and begins undressing her, though he backs off before consummating their relationship. Nevertheless, the encounter spoils Viridiana on the cloistered life, and she sets up house on her uncle's estate. Soon the peasants are holding a bacchanal, in one notorious scene gathering at the dinner table in positions that parody the famous da Vinci painting of the Last Supper. No doubt this irreverence inflamed the European Catholic hierarchy; even the Vatican condemned the movie. But the film's notoriety revived Buñuel's career and placed him at the center of film culture for the rest of his life.

Like many of these other foreign directors, Akira Kurosawa directed his first film in the 1940s. In 1951 his groundbreaking movie, *Rashomon,* which introduced a whole new word and concept to the international vocabulary, was named the year's best foreign-language movie by the Motion Picture Academy. In the 1950s a series of acclaimed films—including *Ikiru,* the enormously influential *Seven Samurai,* and *Throne of Blood* (an adaptation of Shakespeare's *Macbeth*)—established the Japanese master as one of the giants of the foreign film renaissance.

However, his 1962 release *Yojimbo* found Kurosawa in a more playful mood. That tongue-in-cheek samurai western ultimately proved to be just as influential as his masterpieces, *Rashomon* and *The Seven Samurai.* Some critics of the era were disappointed when comparing *Yojimbo* to those earlier classics, and they were shocked by the movie's irreverent approach to violence. In an early scene that seemed reminiscent of the shocking images found in Buñuel's films, a dog wanders through a strife-ridden town carrying a severed human hand in its mouth.

Kurosawa's favorite actor, Toshiro Mifune, plays an amoral samurai in nineteenth-century Japan. At the start of the film he saunters into a town divided by two rival gangs. The setup is reminiscent of many classic westerns (*Shane* in particular), in which a stranger tries to reconcile a battle between two warring factions, cattle men and homesteaders or settlers and outlaws. Although Alan Ladd's Shane was a gunfighter with a shady past, Mifune's Sanjuro is a far more compromised and opportunistic figure, willing to play both sides against each other in order to raise his own stake. And the clans he pretends to be aiding aren't exactly filled with noble do-gooders. One of them is run by a fierce, domineering woman who has colder blood than Lady Macbeth. Mifune is no more upstanding than the corrupt townspeople; he's simply better with a sword. But then he is threatened by a hired killer, a man with a brand-new weapon—a gun. The actor who plays this assassin bears an uncanny resemblance to the black-clad gunslinger played by Jack Palance in *Shane*. Mifune barely survives the clash; he ends up beaten and near death, but like a bedraggled Popeye who finally gets a fix of spinach, Mifune rises from the grime and finally wipes out his enemies. We cannot take great comfort from the hero's resurrection; the film has a vivid, nihilistic spirit. It inspired another perfectly amoral western, Sergio Leone's *A Fistful of Dollars,* in which Clint Eastwood's the Man with No Name became the spaghetti western equivalent of the cheeky samurai killer. Later directors Walter Hill and Quentin Tarantino also cited *Yojimbo* as an influence.[26]

Experienced directors like Kurosawa, Buñuel, and Bergman enriched the cinematic landscape of 1962. But some newer cinematic voices intensified the overseas explosion. The French New Wave was still in its first flush. Jean-Luc Godard and François Truffaut had both started as film critics, and their early movies illustrated their reverence for Hollywood genre pictures, along with a distinctly un-Hollywood appetite for experimentation and shock. In the summer of 1962 a rendezvous of film cultures took place when the New Wave met the remnants of Golden Age Hollywood in a historic series of interviews between Truffaut and iconic director Alfred Hitchcock. Their conversations were later published and became a landmark treatise for future generations of filmmakers.

Truffaut demonstrated his infatuation with classic Hollywood not just in those piercing interviews but in many of the films he chose to direct. His second feature film (following his autobiographical debut feature, *The 400 Blows*), *Shoot the Piano Player,* was based on an American crime novel by David Goodis about a saloon piano player who gets involved with a group of gangsters. The film opened in France in 1960 but did not hit American theaters until 1962, after Truffaut's follow-up film scored a hit with critics and art-house audiences. The director's third film, *Jules and Jim,* was a more purely European creation than *Shoot the Piano Player.* It was based on a novel by respected French author Henri-Pierre Roche and was set against a backdrop of European history, moving from early twentieth-century Paris to Germany in the years between the two world wars.

In an interview with French television soon after the release of *Shoot the Piano Player,* Truffaut described that film as his "homage to American movies."[27] He commented that *The 400 Blows* was "too French," with too little plot, so he sought a project with more narrative drive. But in the same interview, he also said that he hated gangsters and gangster movies, so he did everything he could to rethink and explode that genre. He demonstrated this revisionist approach first of all through the use of humor. In one scene a thug tells his cronies, "If I'm lying, may my mother keel over this instant." There is a quick cut to an iris shot of an old woman falling over and dying. The producer of the film wanted that throwaway scene deleted, but Truffaut insisted on retaining it, and the puckish aside remained one of the most memorable bits in the movie.

More crucial to embellishing the gangster genre was the mood of romantic tragedy that suffuses the film. As Suzanne Schiffman, Truffaut's longtime collaborator, said in one interview, "All François's films are love stories."[28] In a flashback sequence, we learn that the film's protagonist, Charlie (Charles Aznavour), was once a successful concert pianist who abandoned his career after the suicide of his wife. And her suicide was prompted by Charlie's rejection of her after she reveals that she slept with a music impresario in an effort to aid his career. Crushed by this tragic event, Charlie gives up his classical career and eventually ends up as a honky-tonk piano player in a low-class saloon. There he meets another woman, Lena (Marie Dubois), and ends up falling love with her, but his involvement with a pack of gangsters (pals of his brother) eventually leads to her death as well. The story of a man unintentionally responsible for the deaths of two women he loves recalls Hitchcock's romantic classic *Vertigo,* a movie favored by French critics and filmmakers before it ever achieved its current lofty status in America. The climactic sequence of Lena's death, a shooting in the snow outside the gangsters' hideaway, is one of the most haunting in Truffaut's oeuvre, enhanced by Raoul Coutard's stunning black-and-white photography and Georges Delerue's haunting musical score. The film ends with Charlie back at his honky-tonk piano, and a final close-up reveals a devastating sense of sadness and hopelessness in his eyes.

Aznavour had acted in a few films but was better known as a singer when Truffaut cast him. As Aznavour recalled in a 2005 interview, Truffaut chose him because "he wanted me to express the fragility and vulnerability of my songs." Truffaut also said that it was the climactic scene in the snow that made him want to make the movie. For Aznavour the movie established him as a formidable actor as well as a singer, and it gave him a new level of prominence. In fact, the actor recalled with amusement that when he performed a sold-out concert at Carnegie Hall after the movie's release in America, he was surprised that so many Americans were familiar with his musical career. But in speaking with audience members after the performance, he realized that it was not his reputation as a singer that drew the crowds. "They came only because of *Shoot the Piano Player*," the actor recalled.[29]

The romanticism of *Shoot the Piano Player* received even fuller and richer expression in Truffaut's next film, *Jules and Jim*. In 1961, as he was readying the film for production, Truffaut wrote to Helen Scott, a friend in New York, "Now, just about to start my third film, I'm suffering a real dreadful bout of nerves; it can be put down to a mixture of pride, vanity, ambition . . . what I would like for *Jules et Jim* is the most complete success imaginable."[30]

Most viewers agreed that he achieved his goal. The movie is in effect three love stories. Both Jules (Oskar Werner) and Jim (Henri Serre) are in love with the enigmatic Catherine (Jeanne Moreau). But the movie opens by celebrating the love between Jules and Jim before Catherine ever enters the picture. It would be wrong to call this a homoerotic love affair, but it is certainly more intense than most stories of male friendship enshrined in the movies. Jules and Jim meet in Paris in 1912, and they find that they share a love of literature and ideas, and their devotion to each other is transcendent. They find themselves on opposite sides of World War I, and their deepest prayer is that they do not end up killing each other on the battlefield. When they reconnect after the war, Jules has married Catherine, but he realizes that he cannot satisfy her, and he offers Catherine to Jim without any sense of jealousy or regret.

It was undoubtedly this casual attitude toward extramarital sex and an implied ménage à trois that earned the film a Condemned rating from the Legion of Decency. The Legion assailed the "story of an unconventional 'household-for-three' arrangement developed in context alien to Christian traditional natural morality."[31] Truffaut in effect answered this pious critique in a letter he wrote to poet Jean Mambrino: "Though it has a very salacious theme, it's a film I believe is profoundly moral, if on no other evidence than the frightful melancholy that emanates from it."[32]

Even the film's harshest critics could not deny the breathtaking assurance and imagination of Truffaut's direction. The film uses voice-over narration in one of the most effective examples of that technique in the history of movies. Rather than slow the film down, this narration only adds to the breakneck speed of Truffaut's approach. The director dares the viewer to keep up with the flow of words and images. The pacing of the early scenes detailing Jules and Jim's verbal sparring matches and casual love affairs before they meet Catherine remains exhilarating some six decades after the film's release. Yet the director knows when to slow down the action and linger on a sequence like the one in which Jules and Jim and Catherine, not yet lovers, travel to the seashore and explore remnants of what they whimsically call a

FIGURE 1.5 Jeanne Moreau wins the race against Henri Serre and Oskar Werner in *Jules and Jim*. (Screen shot)

lost civilization. Truffaut used an arsenal of cinematic techniques, including jump cuts, freeze frames, and dissolves, and he even altered the size of the image in certain scenes. All of this technical experimentation mirrors the audaciousness of the bohemian characters in the early years of the twentieth century.

Amid the critical acclaim for the film, Truffaut took special satisfaction from an endorsement he received from one of his heroes, director Jean Renoir, who had been a giant in French cinema for decades. In February 1962, Renoir wrote to the young director, "I wanted to tell you *Jules and Jim* seems to be the most accurate expression of contemporary French society that I've ever seen on-screen. . . . I thank you with all my heart!"[33]

Among the achievements of *Jules and Jim*, special mention should be made of the musical score by Georges Delerue, who scored eleven of Truffaut's films in all. The music varies between rousing passages that underscore the camaraderie of the characters to more somber, melancholy themes that express the dying of romantic love. In one of the film's most indelible scenes, Catherine sings a lyrical composition that highlights the notion of "life's whirlpool of days," exhilarating but inevitably transient. Delerue went on to have an extraordinary career all over the world, scoring many important Hollywood films (*Julia*, *A Little Romance*, *Platoon*). As a matter of fact, French composers were among Europe's greatest gifts to cinema during the early 1960s. Two other remarkable French composers emerged in 1962. Michel Legrand, who scored Jacques Demy's *Lola* and Agnes Varda's *Cleo from 5 to 7*, went on to an acclaimed career in Hollywood (*The Thomas Crown Affair*, *Summer of '42*, *Yentl*). The best picture of 1962, *Lawrence of Arabia*, and the year's Oscar-winning best foreign film, *Sundays and Cybele*, were both scored by another magnificent French composer, Maurice Jarre.

FIGURE 1.6 François Truffaut and Jeanne Moreau on the set of *Jules and Jim*. (Photofest)

Despite Truffaut's technical achievements and fine performances by Werner and Serre, the most enduring element of *Jules and Jim* is the character of Catherine, as embodied by Jeanne Moreau. The actress had already made a splash in films by Louis Malle, Roger Vadim, and Michelangelo Antonioni, but it was her iconic characterization in *Jules and Jim* that established her as one of the great screen sirens of all time.

Truffaut had wanted to work with Moreau since seeing her in her very first movies. In 1957, when he was still writing film criticism, he called Moreau "the greatest sweetheart in French cinema." But he hoped to highlight some of the star's talents that other directors had overlooked. Commenting on *La Notte,* he said, "Antonioni had exploited the 'Bette Davis' side of Jeanne Moreau—the sullen face; she never laughed. I wanted to lift her features up; she has a surprising laugh."[34]

Not conventionally beautiful in the Hollywood style, but deeply sensual and always conveying sharp intelligence, Moreau embodied the audience's vision of the brainy, sophisticated European woman. She achieves this status despite the fact that Catherine is far from an entirely sympathetic character. From her early appearances, we can see that she is selfish and destructive. She cheats in a comical foot race with the two heroes, and when she cannot answer their learned dismissal of a play they have all seen, she protests by jumping into the Seine and forcing the two men to plunge in to rescue her. Later on she impulsively woos and discards a number of men in addition to her husband and his best friend, and at the very end of the film, in a macabre echo of that jump into the Seine, she kills herself and Jim by driving their car off a pier and into a lake. Is Catherine therefore a male nightmare of a neurotic independent woman? Jim criticizes her at one point by saying, "You wanted to invent love, but pioneers must be unselfish," and Catherine is anything but an unselfish paragon.

One might think that female viewers would reject the negative elements in the characterization of Catherine, but in fact, she proved to be more disturbing to male critics. Stanley Kauffmann, for example, labeled her a "psychopath." Pauline Kael did not entirely disagree; as she wrote, "Catherine is, of course, a little crazy." But Kael went on to applaud the richness of Moreau's characterization: "She has, despite her need to intrude and to dominate, the gift for life."[35] Even though this film was created by men and does contain suspicion of a strong-willed, selfish, independent woman, few feminists have ever assailed the film's portrayal. Perhaps that is because they appreciate the sublime complexity of the characterization and performance, which cannot ever be reduced to a neat example in gender studies.

In fact, one of the achievements of the European films of 1962 was the depth of the female characterizations, something that Hollywood movies of that era only occasionally matched. *La Notte*, *Through a Glass Darkly*, *Boccaccio '70*, *Viridiana*, and *Shoot the Piano Player* all present sharply drawn female characters who challenge American audiences. And the greatest of these characterizations is Moreau's Catherine, the destructive but absolutely mesmerizing free spirit.

One French movie of 1962 was even directed by a woman. Agnes Varda's *Cleo from 5 to 7* chronicles two hours in the life of a female singer (Corinne Marchand) as she awaits the results of a potentially devastating biopsy. As Kael wrote, it was "one of the few films directed by a woman in which the viewer can sense a difference."[36] Varda had started out making documentary films, and some of the best scenes in *Cleo* are long tracking shots that simply capture the lives of people on the streets of Paris, eating, flirting, brawling as the heroine tries to forget the health issue weighing on her. "Today everything amazes me," she says at one point, and the film uses fresh cinematic techniques to capture her sense of wonder. In recent years a number of female filmmakers have recognized Varda's pioneering achievements. Director Ava DuVernay (*Selma*, *When They See Us*) is one who has testified to the impact of Varda's work, including *Cleo from 5 to 7*.

Varda's husband, Jacques Demy, made his directorial debut in 1962 with a fable called *Lola*, about a cabaret singer whose life intersects with that of several men over the course of just a couple of days. The film helped to propel the career of leading actress Anouk Aimee, who always demonstrated skill at delineating distinctive, nonstereotypical female characters. She had a neat role in Fellini's *La Dolce Vita* and an even better role as Marcello Mastroianni's wife in *8 1/2*, and a few years later, she scored one of the biggest art-house successes of the decade in Claude Lelouch's *A Man and a Woman*.

Surprisingly, none of these exciting French films figured in the foreign-language Oscar race in 1962. It was up to the French film industry to select the movie that would be France's official entry for the Academy Awards. These industry decision makers overlooked innovative works by Truffaut, Varda, and Demy and selected another film by a brand-new director, Serge Bourguignon. Their judgment proved to be shrewd, since Bourguignon's *Sundays and Cybele,* about a shell-shocked soldier from the French Indo-China conflict and his tragically misunderstood relationship with an orphaned girl, ended up winning the Oscar in the foreign-language category. Hardy Kruger played the debilitated soldier, and his familiarity to American audiences through his supporting part in the summer hit *Hatari!* contributed to the film's popularity. The bold strategy of a New York world premiere engagement paid off handsomely; the film became an art-house hit.

In recognition of increasing box office potential, discussions about premiering more foreign-language films in the United States took place. But they were soon pushed aside by a New York City newspaper strike in early December 1962 that lasted more than three months—and forced the cancellation of the annual New York Film Critics Circle Awards, the only time in its history. A backlog of films ensued, as nervous producers and distributors decided not to open their specialized-audience movies without the benefit of reviews or print advertising. United Artists/Lopert learned that the hard way, as its acquisition *Electra*, according to *The Hollywood Reporter,* "wrapped up the niftiest NY notices since *La Dolce Vita*, but no newspapers are available for printing them."[37] The momentum surrounding the *Sundays and Cybele* experiment was lost, and similar efforts were not seriously attempted again.

Aside from experimenting with film structure (*Last Year at Marienbad*) and content (*Divorce Italian Style, Sundays and Cybele*), these foreign films of 1962 also had a cultural impact that was not so immediately apparent. Support for censorship continued to deteriorate, and by 1967 the Legion of Decency and the Production Code had collapsed. By endorsing these mature foreign films, via their nominations and awards, top Hollywood players were sending an implicit message—that it was time for censorship to be either vastly revised or eliminated altogether.

Of course not everyone in the Hollywood community embraced the international infiltration. Conservative syndicated columnist Hedda Hopper admonished filmmakers for "European depravity" creeping into Hollywood films. Actor Stephen Boyd (*Ben-Hur*) publicly regretted making an Italian film, *Imperial Venus,* which he said flaunted sex in a "disgusting" manner. Producer-director Morton DaCosta (*Auntie Mame, The Music Man*) touted Hollywood cinema as "still the very best films being made, and nuts to *Last Year at Marienbad.*" Oscar-winning director William Wyler was also bewildered by the popularity of *Marienbad* and other foreign films that he felt "glorify confusion." And acclaimed actor Montgomery Clift spurned international film festivals, stating, "The trouble with festival movies is too much Ingmar and not enough Ingrid." These members of Hollywood's old guard tenaciously resisted the winds of change, even if their conservative biases seemed increasingly irrelevant.[38]

2 · NEW AMERICAN AUTEURS

While critics were extolling the work of foreign auteurs like Truffaut, Antonioni, Resnais, and Kurosawa, a new wave of American directors was also altering the cinematic landscape of 1962. Several of these directors emerged from the fertile field of live television in the 1950s, an early golden age for the small screen, when dramatic series like *Playhouse 90* provided a stimulating creative environment for filmmakers on the rise. By 1962 many of these acclaimed series had already run their course; and ambitious directors wanted to make their mark in feature films in addition to the less prestigious medium of television. Hollywood legend Bette Davis, who would be back on the big screen later in the year, dismissed television as "a great way to ruin your career," at least for established actors, in a February 1962 interview.[1] That bias toward television as an inferior medium would be reversed in the twenty-first century, when a second television golden age was proclaimed and feature filmmaking became more formulaic and sterile.

Among those TV-trained directors of the era, perhaps the one with the greatest natural talent for filmmaking was John Frankenheimer. When he was still in his twenties, he was directing well-received TV dramas like *The Comedian* with Mickey Rooney, *A Town Has Turned to Dust* with Rod Steiger and William Shatner, and *The Turn of the Screw* with Ingrid Bergman. He made his feature debut in 1957 with *The Young Stranger,* but the movie bombed, and Frankenheimer returned to television.

By the early 1960s, however, *Playhouse 90* had come to an end, and Frankenheimer was determined to graduate to feature filmmaking. Astonishingly, he had three movies released in 1962, something that would be unthinkable today. When the studio system was at its peak, top directors often made at least one movie a year. Producers and studio executives were far more decisive then, and with many more movies being made by studios than is the case today, directors had more opportunity to refine their craft. Of course in the heyday of the studio system back in 1939, major studios like MGM and Twentieth Century-Fox released more than 300 movies a year. The number had fallen by 1962, but even that year, MGM released 28 movies and Fox released 25, about double the number that each studio releases today.

In March 1962 Frankenheimer released *All Fall Down,* which was based on a novel by James Leo Herlihy (who later wrote *Midnight Cowboy*), with a script by Pulitzer Prize–winning playwright William Inge (*Picnic, Bus Stop*), who had just won an Oscar for his original screenplay for 1961's *Splendor in the Grass.* John Houseman (*The Bad and the Beautiful, Julius Caesar, Lust for Life*), who started out working with Orson Welles in the Mercury Theatre, produced the film. Houseman was interested in movies "that represent serious contemplations of our society," and he further noted in *Show* magazine, "I think we'll get the audience back when we return to pictures that reflect American life."[2]

All Fall Down starred Eva Marie Saint and Karl Malden (who had worked together on *On the Waterfront*), Angela Lansbury, Brandon De Wilde, and exciting screen newcomer Warren Beatty in only his third feature film. The film is essentially an intense family drama centering on the relationship of two brothers—the irresponsible Berry-Berry (Beatty) and younger brother Clint (De Wilde), who idolizes him. They both have to contend with an ineffectual father and an overbearing mother, who clearly worships the charismatic Berry-Berry.

Frankenheimer actively sought the directing job on this prestige project. He had worked with Houseman on a television drama, and the young director cultivated their friendship, even renting a house near Houseman in Malibu. According to Frankenheimer, Houseman "had just started a three-picture contract with MGM and he told me that one of the properties was a novel by James Leo Herlihy called *All Fall Down,* which, incidentally, I had read and loved, and another was Irwin Shaw's *Two Weeks in Another Town.* He offered me the choice of filming one of them."[3] Frankenheimer wisely selected the Herlihy novel, since *Two Weeks in Another Town,* eventually directed by Vincente Minnelli and also released in 1962, turned out to be one of the year's notable fiascoes.

With all the talent on board, expectations were high for *All Fall Down,* but the film failed to ignite the box office, perhaps because it was simply too downbeat to seduce the public. And it was admittedly an imperfect film. The first third focuses on Berry-Berry's life as a criminal and stud, seducing and abandoning a series of women before he finally returns home to Cleveland for

Christmas. These scenes allowed Frankenheimer a chance to shoot on location in Florida and achieve some visually striking moments, but the lurid scenes—probably intended as bait in the film's marketing campaign—seem flashy and sensational rather than illuminating. They highlight Beatty's sex appeal but come off as shallow and exploitative.

The film finds its heart in the humorous and telling family scenes back in Cleveland. *New Republic* critic Stanley Kauffmann took note of the disparity between the two worlds of the film. "When the film leaves the Willart home to explore Berry-Berry's life, it loses its texture and forsakes truth for fake realism," Kauffmann wrote. "The scenes in the Florida jail, in strip-joints and bars, with avid lonesome women, are full of movie hand-me-downs: sweat, dark glasses, cruelly frank lighting, sordidness drooled over and treasured."

On the other hand, Kauffmann wrote, "All the scenes in the Willart home are done with fluency and a truth that is more than veracity of detail, that projects contradictions of character and the piteous inability to communicate within the four walls of one home." Kauffmann praised the performances and said that Lansbury in particular "paints a brilliant tragicomic portrait of a mother who does all the right things—with disastrous results."

In a sense the film reflects the Freudian dogma of the era, where an overprotective mother is responsible for the destructive behavior of her favorite son. But Lansbury finds so many pithy and poignant details that we never feel we are watching a mere case study. Her blindness to the effect her smothering love has on the magnetic Berry-Berry represents one of the most acute psychological portraits of the era. Many other moments in the film are memorable. The love scenes between Beatty and Saint, caught by Frankenheimer with almost no dialogue, demonstrate his intuitive flair for filmmaking.

The box office failure of *All Fall Down* did not have a chance to taint Frankenheimer's career because he already had another film in the can—a powerful plea for prison reform, *Birdman of Alcatraz*, which starred Burt Lancaster, Frankenheimer's most frequent cinematic collaborator. (They made a total of five movies together.) And right after completing *All Fall Down*, Frankenheimer began work on another movie that would turn out to be the high point of his career.

Lansbury recalled that while they were working together on *All Fall Down*, Frankenheimer told her he had another part for her that he thought might spark her interest. In a way it was an outrageous casting idea and might never have come to pass if Frankenheimer had not been so enthralled by Lansbury's talent while they were making *All Fall Down*. The part he had in mind was another role of a domineering mother, though in this case a more malevolent matriarch than the well-meaning, misguided Annabel of *All Fall Down*. Perhaps the fact that Lansbury made a convincing mother to Warren Beatty (only eleven years her junior) made the director believe that she could be credible as mother to Laurence Harvey, who was only three years younger than she was. Additionally, Lansbury's deft performance in the Spencer Tracy—Katharine Hepburn drama *State of the Union* (1948), where she effortlessly portrayed a strong-willed political operative (even though she was only twenty-three at the time), could have inspired Frankenheimer.

"I'll never forget when John Frankenheimer sent me the book," Lansbury reported in an interview in 2018. "He said to me, 'I want you to read this book and tell me what you feel about this character, Mrs. Iselin.' I read it, and I was absolutely transfixed. I thought this is an incredible part. . . . It's probably the role I'm most proud of."[4]

The project that teamed these two artists was a far more daring and unconventional piece than *All Fall Down,* which fit neatly into the tradition of realistic drama of the 1950s and 1960s. *The Manchurian Candidate,* taken from Richard Condon's novel, was a far more outlandish political thriller and fantasy, laced with black comedy that was enhanced by screenwriter George Axelrod, best known for his comic plays and screenplays (including *The Seven-Year Itch* and *Breakfast at Tiffany's*). It was a bold piece that dealt with the subject of political assassination, an almost unthinkable premise in 1962. Yet the studio honchos at United Artists were nervous enough about presenting a story that speculated on a plot to assassinate a presidential candidate that they initially balked at financing the film. However, Frank Sinatra—a producer as well as star of the film—was friendly with the Kennedy family, and he spoke with JFK about the project. President Kennedy was a fan of the book, and his endorsement helped to soothe the studio's fears. Kennedy did have one question for Sinatra: "Who's going to play the mother?"[5]

Frankenheimer already had that question answered, and he assembled the rest of the cast, with Janet Leigh as Sinatra's love interest, and seasoned actors like James Gregory (in the role of Lansbury's dimwitted husband) who had worked with the director in television. Frankenheimer put his background to use in scenes that incorporated television cameras as a part of the action. One of the most brilliant of these set pieces is a Washington press conference, in which Senator Iselin (Gregory) rails about the number of card-carrying Communists in the Defense Department, as the action is caught by a number of TV cameras immersed in the chaos. In this choice scene Lansbury as Iselin's manipulative wife does not have a single line of dialogue, but the framing of

FIGURE 2.1 The brainwashing scene from *The Manchurian Candidate*. (Screen shot)

the shots, with her in the foreground, makes it clear that she is the mastermind of this politically disruptive confrontation.

Frankenheimer's cinematic flair is notable in several other sequences, especially in the startling dream scenes that demonstrate the brainwashing of Raymond Shaw (Harvey), Bennett Marco (Sinatra), and other members of their platoon during the Korean War. Marco's dream begins at a garden party, where a number of well-heeled ladies are lecturing about the joys of hydrangeas. Gradually their soft faces mutate into the stern visages of officials of the Soviet and Chinese Communist governments who are conducting a grim experiment on the captured American soldiers. Their goal is to turn Raymond Shaw into a cold, remorseless assassin by making him feel that an act of murder is just as routine as an afternoon garden party. The brilliant editing keeps shifting the faces, with clever matchups between the overweight ladies and the bearish commissars. The scene builds to a powerful climax, as Raymond strangles one of his fellow soldiers while the others yawn in boredom—until Marco wakes up screaming in terror. Production designer Richard Sylbert (*Who's Afraid of Virginia Woolf?, Chinatown, Dick Tracy*) and Frankenheimer sought detailed accuracy in these sequences. Sylbert contacted researcher Lillian Michelson, who remembers providing extensive background on brainwashing techniques, which were then so efficaciously depicted by the filmmakers.[6]

There is a linking sequence a little later in the film, when a black soldier in the platoon also experiences the same unrelenting nightmare. But in his dream, the women at the garden party are all black, a nifty, unexpected touch that conveys the filmmakers' sensitivity on racial issues. In another unconventional touch, the psychiatrist trying to unravel Marco's dreams is an African American, and no mention is made of his racial identity.

In remarkably prophetic comments, Frankenheimer said that the brainwashing plot appealed to him because of disturbing trends in American society. As he explained in an interview a few years before his death, "I think our society is brainwashed by television commercials, by advertising, by politicians, by a censored press.... More and more I think that our society is becoming manipulated and controlled."[7] Needless to say, those comments take on added relevance in the aftermath of the 2016 election.

Beyond that, Condon's novel meant to riff on the insanity of Cold War politics, and the film reinforced his sharp satirical vision. Frankenheimer described what appealed to him most about the project: "This country was just recovering from the McCarthy era and nothing had ever been filmed about it. I wanted to do a picture that showed how ludicrous the whole McCarthy Far Right syndrome was and how dangerous the Far Left syndrome is. It really dealt with the whole idea of fanaticism, the Far Right and the Far Left being exactly the same thing."[8]

That is the diabolical symmetry of the plot. The Communist agents who are plotting the takeover of America are impersonating fervent, jingoistic anti-Communists. In a sense the film is saying, a pox on both your houses. And it conveyed its message so effectively that it was savagely attacked by both right-wing and left-wing pundits. After screening the film, the American Legion urged the House Committee on Un-American Activities or the Senate Internal Securities Sub-Committee "to conduct a hearing at the earliest time possible covering the motion picture industry." The American Legion chided the film for "a successful attempt to create a hostile image of patriotism in the minds of the audience." The Legion also contended that an investigation was needed to "determine once again to what extent this vital information medium (motion pictures) has been recaptured by agents of the Communist conspiracy."[9]

Learning of the attack, Axelrod replied dryly, "As good, solid comedy material is hard to come by these days, I would be most interested in learning if the movie rights to this hilarious, if somewhat ungrammatical, document are available."[10] At the same time, however, the *People's World,* a Communist newspaper, denounced the film as "the most vicious attempt yet made by the industry to cash in on Soviet-American tensions. The film is poison, all the more lethal because it is presented with ingenuity and genuine suspense."[11]

All of these critics missed the wicked humor that represented the film's most daring element. The right-wing senator is constantly framed against portraits of Lincoln, and in the costume party that is one of the film's set pieces, he dresses as Lincoln, while Lansbury as his hard-driving wife impersonates Little Bo Peep. Some of the wry touches can even produce gasps. When Raymond shoots his father-in-law, a liberal senator, the bullet penetrates a carton of milk that the man is holding. Instead of blood, milk seems to spill from the breast of the liberal. Yet this eerily humorous moment is followed by the most shocking image in the film, when Raymond coldly murders his wife as she tries to intervene to save her father.

The skilled mix of humor and terror is what set the film apart from other political thrillers, and these darkly witty touches were not even attempted in the misbegotten remake perpetrated by director Jonathan Demme four decades later. Filmmakers in an earlier era would not have dreamt of inserting wild humor into a thriller about political assassination. And they would not have dared to try it in later years either. For the tragic irony is that a year after the movie opened, President Kennedy was assassinated, and after that, a terrible wave of assassinations made the film seem frighteningly prescient—and a little too disturbing to bear. A few years after its release, *The Manchurian Candidate* was essentially unavailable theatrically until finally being rereleased to rave reviews in 1987. The Library of Congress later deemed the film worthy of preservation, including it in the National Film Registry in 1994.

Upon the film's original release on October 24, 1962, United Artists mounted a vigorous marketing campaign, urging viewers to see it from the beginning. The ad copy exclaimed, "If you come in five minutes after this picture begins, you won't know what it's all about!" In a timely touch, UA also informed exhibitors that the studio would sponsor midterm election returns the first week of November on the ABC network with sixty-second TV spots for the film, an uncommon investment in that period.[12]

Bosley Crowther, in his otherwise mixed *New York Times* review, praised certain aspects of the picture, stating that "the film is so artfully contrived, the plot so interestingly started, the dialogue so racy and sharp, and John Frankenheimer's direction so exciting in the style of Orson Welles when he was making *Citizen Kane* and other pictures that the fascination of it is strong." Some of Crowther's peers were even more enthusiastic about the film as a whole. The public responded appropriately, and the film finished as one of the top grossing pictures of the year.

Even critics who were troubled by the deliberately outrageous brainwashing plot appreciated Angela Lansbury's performance. The National Board of

FIGURE 2.2 Menacing mother Angela Lansbury looms over Laurence Harvey in *The Manchurian Candidate.* (Screen shot)

Review and the Hollywood Foreign Press named her the year's best support-ing actress in an era when there were fewer groups handing out film prizes. Consequently, she emerged the favorite to win an Academy Award on her third try (after two previous nominations for *Gaslight,* her film debut in 1944, and *The Picture of Dorian Gray* in 1945). But the Oscar went to Patty Duke, and Lansbury found bigger stardom on Broadway and television for the rest of her lengthy career.

One part of the film's legacy is that Lansbury's Mrs. Iselin was named one of the fifty great villains in the American Film Institute's survey of cinematic miscreants. Great villains are always charismatic as well as frightening. Shake-speare's depictions of Richard III or Lady Macbeth proved the point centu-ries ago, and audiences have continued to be drawn to criminal masterminds. Lansbury later reminisced that she was attracted to the role because it offered such "a well-written villain." Lansbury was so convincing in the role that she purposely avoided similar parts, apprehensive of being typecast. She recalled in a 2014 interview (about finding success in musical theater after *The Man-churian Candidate*), "You can't live down a part like that. I decided, forget it. I'm going to sing now."[13]

The climactic scene in *The Manchurian Candidate,* in which Lansbury coaches her son to carry out the assassination designed to sweep her and her husband into the White House, was described by one critic as an "aria of evil," and Lansbury delivers it with such breathtaking panache that some mesmer-ized viewers might find themselves secretly rooting for her plot to succeed. She ends her diabolical pep talk by kissing her son passionately on the lips, another of the film's sly and startling touches.

The assassination scene itself, one of the masterly suspense sequences of the era, demonstrates Frankenheimer's ingenuity and that of production designer Sylbert. The film company shot for four days in Madison Square Garden, but the bulk of the sequence was shot at another auditorium in Los Angeles and on a Hollywood sound stage. "Sylbert is so clever you are never really aware of it," Frankenheimer said of the melding of different locations.[14] The editing by Ferris Webster also helped to conceal the cinematic trickery. The director's extensive experience in transcending the limitations of television sets also aided him in bringing off this cinematic tour de force.

Frankenheimer was not the only director bred in television to oversee major films in 1962. He started as an assistant to Sidney Lumet, a veteran of live TV who directed two films in 1962: adaptations of Arthur Miller's *A View from the Bridge* and Eugene O'Neill's *Long Day's Journey into Night*. Blake Edwards created the *Peter Gunn* TV series in the 1950s, and he also had two films released in 1962: the thriller *Experiment in Terror* and the drama about alcoholism, *Days of Wine and Roses*. George Roy Hill, whose TV credits included the first version of Abby Mann's *Judgment at Nuremberg*, made his feature debut in 1962 with an adaptation of Tennessee Williams's stage comedy *Period of Adjustment*, an early Jane Fonda vehicle. Ralph Nelson, a theater actor who made the transition to directing, began working steadily in television from its infancy in the late 1940s right up to his 1962 film debut, an adaptation of Rod Serling's teleplay, *Requiem for a Heavyweight*. Frank Perry, whose directorial debut, *David and Lisa,* brought him an Oscar nomination in 1962, had a background in television documentaries.

But there were other rising American directors at work that year who served very different apprenticeships. Stanley Kubrick had started as an acclaimed still photographer for *Life* and other magazines, and he made low-budget experimental films (*Fear and Desire* and *Killer's Kiss*) in order to learn the craft of filmmaking. He was a quick study. His tense 1956 caper film, *The Killing,* and his 1958 antiwar film, *Paths of Glory,* put him on the map as a director to watch. And when Kirk Douglas got into conflicts with director Anthony Mann while shooting *Spartacus,* Douglas fired Mann and hired Kubrick to take over the film. That Roman epic was a box office hit, and Kubrick had a chance to tackle one of the most controversial projects of the decade, a movie version of Vladimir Nabokov's explosive best-selling novel, *Lolita*. Despite widespread praise for the author's dazzling literary style, the controversy surrounding *Lolita* never really died down, and the story remains incendiary today, in an era even more sensitive to charges of sexual abuse of children and adolescents.

James B. Harris, Kubrick's producing partner on *The Killing* and *Paths of Glory* as well as *Lolita,* recalls that he expected to be able to buy the rights to Nabokov's novel for the same $10,000 that he had paid for those earlier books. "I contacted Putnam, offered them $10,000, and thought we would close the deal instantly," Harris reports. "The gentleman on the other end of the phone said, 'I think we're so far apart that I'm going to turn you over to the Hollywood agent that represents Nabokov, Mr. Irving Lazar, known as Swifty Lazar.'"[15] Lazar confessed to Harris that he had been unable to sell the book to any of the major studios but still demanded $150,000 for the film rights. He suggested that he would accept just $75,000 for a one-year option so that Harris could then walk away from the project if he was unable to secure financing. Harris paid the retainer and then went to work.

He quickly discovered that indeed no studio would back the project, so he decided to seek independent financing. He turned to a classmate from his prep school in New York. "In my senior class," Harris recalls, "were David Wolper, Steve Ross [who later ran Time Warner corporation], George Kaufman [later the owner of Kaufman Astoria Studios], and Kenneth Hyman. Kenny and I were cocaptains of the soccer team in high school."[16] By the time Harris entered the film business, Hyman and his father, Eliot Hyman, were running a company that would later become Seven Arts, and they were excited by the prospect of backing *Lolita.* They immediately offered $1 million, and another $750,000 came from British financiers.

The filmmakers decided to approach Nabokov about writing the screenplay. Harris went to meet the author at a party at the Waldorf Astoria Hotel in New York. The producer recalls, "I was introduced to Nabokov: 'This is Mr. James Harris, who just bought your book.' Nabokov said, 'I hope you enjoy reading it.' He thought I had bought it in a bookstore. 'No no,' my friend said, 'he bought the film rights.'"[17] Harris asked if Nabokov would consider writing the screenplay. At first Nabokov declined, but he rethought it later and accepted the assignment. He turned in a 400-page draft. "I could hardly lift it," Harris laughs. So he and Kubrick did a massive rewrite. Their final script (credited to Nabokov alone) represented a remarkable interpretation of what was widely thought to be an unfilmable novel, especially in light of the censorship restrictions at the time (under the scrutiny of the Production Code Administration and the Legion of Decency). The frank eroticism of the novel could not really be translated in 1962, but the film did an outstanding job of capturing the author's irreverent humor and vivid characterizations. Nabokov later called the film "absolutely first-rate."[18]

Even with major modifications, Harris knew that it would be a challenge to get the film approved by the Production Code office. So he hired Martin Quigley as consultant. Quigley had helped to formulate the restrictive Production Code back in the 1930s. Thirty years later, times had changed, and so had Quigley, but he still had close contacts with the Hollywood censorship office, then administered by Geoffrey Shurlock. Harris felt that Quigley could be a useful liaison with the Production Code office, and Quigley helped to negotiate some compromises between the filmmakers and the censors. One choice scene early in the film takes place at a high school dance where Lolita's mother, Charlotte, approaches avant-garde playwright Clare Quilty and reminds him that they had met once before when he was in town visiting his uncle, a local dentist. Quilty barely remembers Charlotte, but he definitely remembers her "lovely" daughter, Lolita. "Wednesday she's going to have a cavity filled by your Uncle Ivar," Charlotte explains. The line obviously had sexual innuendoes that Kubrick and Harris did not want to lose. It was Quigley who recommended that if the filmmakers had Charlotte point to her cheek while delivering the line, it could seem perfectly innocent and yet still work as a wicked double entendre.[19]

Casting of the film's four principal roles was perfectly on target. Some critics carped that newcomer Sue Lyon was too old to play Nabokov's nymphet heroine, but she was actually only fourteen at the time of filming. If she seemed somewhat older, that was in keeping with Nabokov's concept of the nymphet as a tantalizing hybrid of child and woman. Lyon certainly caught the brattiness of the American teenager, along with her sexual seductiveness. Kubrick helped her to bring off astonishingly varied moods. At times she is whiny and petulant, and at other moments she exudes worldly sophistication. As the besotted Humbert Humbert, James Mason perfectly captured the lecherousness, unctuousness, hypocrisy, and utter lovestruck vulnerability of a professor in thrall to a sexual compulsion he can neither control nor tame. Alternately shifty and urbane, creepy and contrite, Mason honors the complexity of the character etched by Nabokov. Shelley Winters gave one of her sharpest performances as the culturally pretentious Charlotte Haze, Lolita's mother and fierce rival for Humbert's affections.

Casting of these roles initially hit some roadblocks. Mason was the first choice of Kubrick and Harris to play Humbert Humbert. Mason was enthusiastic, but he was committed to a play on Broadway and had to decline the film of *Lolita.* Then Kubrick turned to one of the stars of *Spartacus,* Laurence Olivier, who was tickled by the prospect but reconsidered the offer after his agents informed him that portraying a child molester would be career suicide for the distinguished Shakespearean actor. Then the filmmakers approached David Niven, who had won an Oscar when he veered from his customary polished image and played a man convicted of a sex crime in *Separate Tables*. Niven himself was enthusiastic about *Lolita,* but his agent had the same reservations as Olivier's representatives. Harris remembers being called in for a meeting by the head of William Morris, Abe Lastfogel: "He said to us, 'Boys'—Stanley and I were considered boys at that time—'David is one of the stars of Four Star Playhouse on television. We have sponsors, and they will never tolerate the idea of one of their actors playing a pedophile.'"[20]

Another possible choice was actor Errol Flynn, who was then near the end of his career. Flynn had actually played a variation on Humbert in real life, having been involved in a notorious statutory rape case in 1943. In 1959 the fifty-year-old former swashbuckling star was dating a fifteen-year-old aspiring actress, Beverly Aadland, and Aadland's mother was actually pushing for her daughter to play Lolita, suggesting a package deal with Flynn. But when Harris met Flynn, he felt the onetime matinee idol now looked much too dissipated to make a sympathetic screen incarnation of this controversial character. So the filmmakers were stymied until Harris received a surprise phone call from James Mason, who inquired if the part was still available; his play had been canceled, and he was ready to work on *Lolita*.

Sue Lyon was one of many young actresses who came in to audition for the title character. Initially she did not make a strong impression on the filmmakers. But Kubrick and his wife happened to see her in an episode of *The Loretta Young Show* on TV, and Kubrick was so impressed with her performance that he called her back and eventually gave her the plum role.

But Kubrick's most brilliant casting coup was choosing Peter Sellers to play Quilty, the villain of the piece who steals Lolita away from Humbert. Sellers was a rising star of British film (*The Mouse That Roared, I'm All Right Jack*), but he had yet to reach American movie stardom. Yet his flair for impersonation made him an inspired choice to play Quilty, a master of disguises who torments Humbert in many different incarnations through the course of the story.

In adapting the novel, Kubrick shrewdly chose to veer from the text and introduce Quilty at the very beginning of the film, in a scene when Humbert comes to a decaying mansion to find the man who destroyed his chance at happiness by kidnapping and corrupting Lolita. When Quilty emerges from underneath a slipcover on a chair, Humbert asks, "Are you Quilty?" "No, I'm Spartacus," Quilty replies, a neat little Kubrickian in-joke. As the scene

FIGURE 2.3 James Mason watches Sue Lyon and her hula hoop in *Lolita*. (Screen shot)

progresses, Quilty suggests they play Ping-Pong while Humbert questions him about his sexual history, and the brilliantly written and performed pas de deux sets the madcap, macabre tone of the entire film. When it then goes into flashback to recount the meeting of Humbert and Lolita, the film has already established a mood of anxiety and apprehension that it will sustain throughout. In his review of the movie, the *Saturday Review*'s Hollis Alpert wrote of the opening scene, "There hasn't been a scene of equal imaginativeness in movies since, perhaps, *Citizen Kane*." Nabokov himself declared that Kubrick's opening scene was "a masterpiece."[21]

Sellers has only half a dozen scenes in the course of the film, but each of them stands out as a comic set piece. In the scene in which Humbert first seduces Lolita (or is seduced by her), Quilty appears as a policeman staying at the hotel and prying into the curious relationship of Humbert and his "daughter." And perhaps Sellers's most bravura turn comes when Quilty pretends to be a German school psychologist who visits the Humbert home and inveigles the nervous, guilt-ridden child molester into allowing his "daughter" to appear in the local school play. At first Kubrick and Sellers planned to have Quilty impersonate a female psychologist, as indicated in the novel, and Sellers had rehearsed the scene in drag. But at the last minute, they decided this might seem too farcical. So they rethought the character and found a new disguise for Quilty as the stern Dr. Zempf. These duets between Sellers and Mason—one teasing and tormenting while the other struggles to keep his balance—represent screen acting at its best.

While the scenes of comic discomfort are the most bracing in the movie, Kubrick also finds a genuinely tragic dimension in the doomed affair of Humbert and Lolita. For we gradually come to realize that what Humbert feels for Lolita is not simply lust but profound love, and here Mason's performance achieves moments of searing pathos and genuine agony. A climactic hospital scene in which Humbert learns that Lolita has disappeared demonstrates Kubrick's visual brilliance, and Mason's performance highlights the desolation that Humbert feels. In his later films Kubrick became a somewhat icy technician more concerned with his visual compositions than with nuances of human behavior. *Lolita* remains his most moving and humane achievement. The one area where the film fails is in its evocation of middle America, perhaps because it was actually shot in England (thanks to British cofinancing) and could not quite approximate the look and feel of suburban Americana.

But in its combination of humor and pathos, it was a strikingly original movie, undervalued by many critics at the time. Pauline Kael, a new voice on the scene, appreciated it best and took her fellow critics to task for their uncomprehending reviews. She asserted boldly, "It's the first new American comedy since those great days in the forties when Preston Sturges recreated comedy with verbal slapstick. *Lolita* is black slapstick, and at times it's so far out that you gasp as you laugh. An inspired Peter Sellers creates a new comic pattern—a crazy quilt of psychological, sociological commentary so 'hip' it's surrealist."[22] Critic and historian Arthur Schlesinger Jr., who also served as a special assistant to President Kennedy at this time, agreed with Kael's evaluation. Writing in *Show* magazine, Schlesinger called *Lolita* "wildly funny and wildly poignant. It is willful, cynical and repellent. It is beautiful and it is depraved. . . . Kubrick renders farce and satire and comedy and pathos and melodrama and psychopathology with equal skill."

Kael was also one of the few critics at the time to respond to the black comedy of *The Manchurian Candidate*. Others considered the movie merely irresponsible—or a trifle bewildering. Although the Academy of Motion Picture Arts and Sciences would recognize both films, the more conservative Academy voters very well may have been among those bewildered. The two films collected only three nominations between them—Ferris Webster's film editing accompanying Angela Lansbury's acting nod for *Manchurian,* and Vladimir Nabokov's screenplay nomination for *Lolita*.

Both Kubrick and Harris were content to let Nabokov take sole writing credit. It was far more important to them to get the film produced and released than to haggle over screenplay billing. This strategy allowed Nabokov's name to sell the movie as an authentic, prestige item to the public, who made it a box office hit. The question posed in the ads—"How could they ever make a movie of *Lolita*?"—was answered resoundingly by record-breaking opening week engagements in New York, Los Angeles, Washington, San Francisco, Philadelphia, Dallas, and other cities.

It could be that one reason the films of 1962 loom even larger today than they did at the time is that we've amassed a greater appreciation of the sophisticated, genre-bursting storytelling that audiences—and critics—of the early 1960s were a little too naive to grasp. *The Manchurian Candidate* engaged audiences as a suspense thriller, and *Lolita* attracted attention because of its bold sexual theme, but it would take several more years for their innovative approach to comic storytelling to be more fully appreciated and endorsed. But there was no doubt even at the time that some intriguing new American directors were changing the face of the medium.

Another new face in 1962 was a director who also came from television, but a very different side of television than the prestige dramas of *Playhouse 90*. Sam Peckinpah directed western series like *Gunsmoke* and *The Rifleman* in the 1950s, and no one thought of those oaters as a fertile spawning ground for budding auteurs. Yet he was an interesting personality who in a way bridged older and newer models for directors. He had joined the Marines at the end of World War II, and in the 1950s he was one of the first aspiring directors to attend film school at the University of Southern California. His contacts there helped him to land his TV gigs. Peckinpah made his feature directorial debut in 1961 with *The Deadly Companions,* a western starring Maureen O'Hara and Brian Keith that attracted very little attention. But in 1962 *Ride the High Country* heralded the arrival of another major new talent.

Peckinpah liked the script by N. B. Stone Jr., though he rewrote most of the dialogue. The central character of Steve Judd (Joel McCrea), a former western marshal trying to retain his integrity at the dawn of the twentieth century, reminded Peckinpah of his own father, a distinguished judge, and he viewed the story as a kind of elegy for the heroes of an earlier era. In an interview at that time, the director stated, "In simple terms it was about salvation and loneliness . . . the loneliness of that breed of almost legendary Western peace officers who were left behind when the country they tamed grew up. It had a theme, and I believe *Time* magazine said it very well: 'That goodness is not a gift but a quest.'"[23] In its themes the movie resembled another 1962 western, John Ford's *The Man Who Shot Liberty Valance,* but it exhibited an edgier, more modern sensibility, along with daring sexual themes that Ford would probably not have known how to handle.

Peckinpah was not averse to the irreverent humor that also enlivened the movies by Frankenheimer and Kubrick. In the movie's opening scene Steve Judd rides into a western town as the townspeople cheer. He doffs his cowboy hat in gratitude, not realizing that the townspeople have no idea who he is; they are cheering not for him but for a chintzy Wild West show organized by a former partner, Gil Westrum (Randolph Scott in his final performance). Although Judd is the hero of the piece, he is not without a touch of vanity; we see this again a little later when he demands privacy to read a contract from the banker who hires him, and we realize that he does not want his employer to know that he needs a pair of spectacles to decipher the fine print in the contract.

The humor grows even darker in the sequence in which Judd, Westrum, and a young protégé escort a sheltered farm girl to the mining town where she is scheduled to marry a prospector she barely knows. What she does not realize is that her fiancé plans the wedding in the town brothel with leering whores as bridesmaids and a wedding night celebration that includes the groom's four brothers as bedmates for the bride. This sequence is a bold one for 1962, a mixture of macabre farce and genuinely discomfiting drama.

Judd and his companions rescue the terrified bride-to-be, touchingly portrayed by Mariette Hartley. They take her back to her father, a religious fanatic who is another of the movie's vivid characters. The miners pursue Judd and Westrum, and the climactic gun battle gives another hint of the director's burgeoning talent. Peckinpah acknowledged the influence of the film's editor, Frank Santillo, who cut the gunfight with quick, almost subliminal cuts that the director later used with even more breathtaking artistry in *The Wild Bunch* and *Straw Dogs*. The death of Judd lends a truly elegiac tone to the conclusion, and the movie's final shot, of Judd falling directly toward us as the camera pans to the vastness of mountains and sky, gives grandeur to this story of the end of an era.

For newcomer Mariette Hartley, making the film turned out to be a highlight of her career. She was astonished by the emotion that the final scene stirred in costar Randolph Scott. "I looked at Randy, and I saw these tears coming down his face," Hartley recalls.[24]

Her agent had set up her first interview with Peckinpah in his office at MGM. "He was very flirtatious," Hartley remembers. "After I read, he said, 'I think I'm in love with you.' I didn't need that because my husband at the time was very jealous." A week after that first meeting, Peckinpah called her back for a screen test. "I wore Deborah Kerr's wig from *Quo Vadis*," she laughs. "And they kept building up my chest because that's what Sam wanted. He didn't give

FIGURE 2.4 Mariette Hartley in *Ride the High Country*. (Photofest)

me a lot of direction. From what I've been told, he worked the way John Ford worked. He hired people he thought were right for the part, and after that, he didn't feel they needed much direction."[25]

Hartley does recall some tensions with the studio that set the director on edge. Originally Peckinpah hoped to shoot the entire picture on location in the High Sierras near Mammoth, but the studio ordered the company back to Los Angeles to film the mining camp scenes. "Sam was furious," Hartley says. "The first time I ever saw him get really drunk was on the bus ride back to Los Angeles."[26]

That was not the end of the director's troubles with the studio. Remarkably, *Ride the High Country*—which rode into the National Film Registry in 1997—almost failed to make it into theaters. When MGM president Joseph Vogel viewed the finished film, he declared, "This is the worst film that's ever been perpetrated on the American public."[27] Vogel decided to dump it. The studios often cast off movies they considered unworthy of an expensive advertising campaign by shoving them into neighborhood theaters as part of a double feature. When *Ride the High Country* opened in May 1962, it was on the bottom half of a double bill that included a chintzy European-made epic, *The Tartars,* starring two faded movie stars seeking tax relief overseas, Orson Welles and Victor Mature.

To Vogel's surprise, however, critics discovered *Ride the High Country* and gave it rave reviews. The *New York Herald Tribune,* for example, called it "a consummate work of art." And critics remembered the film at year's end. It headed *Newsweek*'s ten-best list and the Paris Council of Film Critics' ranking of the best films of 1962. The day after it opened, theater managers had to get up on ladders and reverse the billing of the two movies. Reviewers could not turn *Ride the High Country* into a box office hit after this misguided release pattern, but they did wisely recognize a major new directing talent at work. And it could be that the downbeat ending would have kept Peckinpah's film from box office glory even with stronger studio support. It's worth noting that all of these movies by brilliant young directors are unmistakably tragic stories presented without compromise.

Of course there were also more uplifting films made in 1962, and one of the most memorable came from another young director who had worked in television but honed his craft in a very different medium. Arthur Penn contributed to several television series in the 1950s, and he directed one feature, *The Left Handed Gun,* an offbeat Freudian western written by Gore Vidal and starring Paul Newman as Billy the Kid. But that movie never caught on, and Penn decided to try his hand in the theater. He had worked with playwright William Gibson on television, and when Gibson wrote *Two for the Seesaw*, a two-character play about a stuffy Midwestern businessman who has an affair with a Greenwich Village beatnik, Penn directed the play and cast Henry Fonda and a young refugee from Hollywood, Anne Bancroft, in the leads.

That play was a hit, and for their next collaboration, Gibson and Penn reworked a story that they had first told on television, about the young Helen Keller and Annie Sullivan, the teacher who taught the blind and deaf girl to understand language. *The Miracle Worker* became a smash on Broadway, and Penn was hired to translate the story to film. At first United Artists wanted to cast bigger stars in the film; the studio offered a budget of $2 million if Penn hired Elizabeth Taylor or Audrey Hepburn to play the part of Sullivan. But Penn insisted on using the same two actresses who had played the roles on Broadway, Anne Bancroft and Patty Duke. The studio grudgingly agreed but slashed the budget to just $500,000. Penn's gamble paid off, since the movie scored at the box office and won unexpected Oscars for both actresses.

Penn's work in the theater and his interest in psychoanalysis made him an especially sensitive director of actors. As a matter of fact, both Penn and Gibson were married to therapists, and their wives' insights into the workings of the human psyche enriched the play and the film. In the movie version of *The Miracle Worker*, Penn included visually stylized flashback sequences meant to fill in some of Sullivan's background and motivation. But the most effective scenes focused on the conflict between the two main characters—the ferocious wild child Helen and the equally strong-willed teacher determined to tame her and bring her into the civilized world.

In a series of interviews completed shortly before her death, Duke recalled that when she first auditioned for the stage play with Anne Bancroft, "The audition consisted of us beating each other up. She smacked me, and I smacked her back. It wasn't until years later that I noticed an interesting thing in that she was a street kid from the Bronx, and I was a street kid from New York. Somehow, I think, those allegiances came into play. I was probably thinking, Bronx is not going to beat New York, I'm going to whoop your ass! . . . At any rate, we beat each other up and rolled on the floor. There were bruises just from that audition. Little did I know how many bruises there were going to be over the next two years!"[28]

In the film version these scenes are savagely physical battles, effectively filmed with handheld cameras that give the conflicts an immediacy they could not have matched onstage. Close-ups also enhance the impact of the two lead performances, as antagonism gradually gives way to understanding between

FIGURE 2.5 Anne Bancroft as Annie Sullivan and Patty Duke as Helen Keller in
The Miracle Worker. (Screen shot)

the girl and her teacher. In her last interviews, Duke revealed that during the
filming of the movie, she began to be sexually molested by her managers, John
and Ethel Ross. Although she was too ashamed to tell anyone at the time, she
admitted that it was more than surreal to be molested in the morning and then
report to the studio for shooting. But the work was somewhat therapeutic. As
she said, "Playing that role and being there with Annie and Arthur and everybody almost erased in my mind what had happened. Being able to compart-
mentalize helped me get through a lot of it."[29]

In any case, the results on-screen were searing. The climax of the film, in
which the fiercely determined Annie finally breaks through and gets Helen to
understand the meaning of the word "water," remains one of the most deeply
stirring scenes in any movie of the period. Because Penn filmed the conflict
between these two characters with unvarnished realism, the inspirational conclusion seems fully earned and completely unsentimental. Penn would earn
an Oscar nomination for best director, and Gibson was nominated for his
screenplay.

United Artists released *The Miracle Worker* in late May 1962, with a broader
release in July; MGM opened *Lolita* in June. They represent inspired adaptations of an acclaimed Broadway play and a provocative adult novel, respectively. By comparison, twenty-first-century summertime moviegoing means
basically commercial escapist fare, emphasizing family-friendly films, comic
book franchises, and sequels. A few low-budget independent films are the

only alternatives to this steady diet of lowbrow entertainment. But in 1962, the major studios offered a much richer variety of summer movies. Along with films aimed at general audiences (*Bon Voyage, Hatari!, Mr. Hobbs Takes a Vacation, The Music Man*), serious dramas and films with mature subjects were released routinely in the vacation months. In addition to *The Miracle Worker* and *Lolita,* they included *Hemingway's Adventures of a Young Man, Advise and Consent, Lonely Are the Brave, Five Finger Exercise, Hell Is for Heroes, The Counterfeit Traitor,* and *Birdman of Alcatraz.* The cinematic diet of contemporary moviegoers is pitifully undernourished by contrast.

These ascending auteurs had very different backgrounds and perspectives, but their startling achievements in 1962 testified to the emergence of an American new wave that rivaled the more highly publicized ferment in France and other European countries. Later in the decade, Penn's *Bonnie and Clyde,* Kubrick's *2001: A Space Odyssey,* and Peckinpah's *The Wild Bunch* stirred a lot of press coverage about the new maturity of American cinema. But these directors all had earlier breakthroughs in 1962 that were perhaps a little too far ahead of their time to be fully appreciated until years later. And it could be that during a somewhat more placid period in America, before all the upheavals of the late 1960s, artistic ferment was not quite ready to be noticed by critics or audiences. But these triumphs of 1962 set the stage for a coming revolution in American cinema.

3 · SURVIVORS

Con Men and Hollywood Honchos

Talented young directors from America and abroad helped to brighten the cinematic landscape of 1962. But what made the scene so vibrant was that these newcomers from theater and television found themselves working in an industry that also remained hospitable to many of Hollywood's old masters who were still thriving. Of the directors who helmed the important films of 1939, several had died or retired. Ernst Lubitsch, the director of *Ninotchka*, died in 1947. Victor Fleming, who was the credited director of both *Gone with the Wind* and *The Wizard of Oz,* died in 1949. Michael Curtiz, who made *The Private Lives of Elizabeth and Essex* in 1939, worked right up until his death in 1962. William Wellman, the director of *Beau Geste,* announced his retirement in 1962. Frank Capra, who directed *Mr. Smith Goes to Washington* in 1939, made a film in 1961, *Pocketful of Miracles,* but he was not happy with the experience and retired from directing after completing that film.

Nevertheless, several prominent filmmakers were still behind the cameras, as the last of the studio era masters and craftsmen faced the twilight of their careers. John Ford (*Stagecoach*), Howard Hawks (*Only Angels Have Wings*), George Cukor (*The Women*), Leo McCarey (*Love Affair*), and William Wyler (*Wuthering Heights*) were all still working in the early 1960s. Some of these directors had started in the silent or early sound era, so they provided a link to the very earliest cinematic achievements. It must have been stimulating for talented new directors like Frankenheimer and Kubrick to be working alongside these award-winning veterans. Shortly after the release of *Ride the High Country,* Sam Peckinpah met John Ford on the steps of the Thalberg Building at MGM and expressed his admiration for the old master's films. There is no record of whether Ford returned the compliment.[1]

Of course these directors and many of the stars they helped to nurture were working in a very different industry. The decline of the studio system, along with the public's changing moviegoing habits, found only a select group of the stars and other players from Hollywood's so-called golden year 1939 fortunate to be making movies by 1962. A number of the screen immortals from that year—Humphrey Bogart, Tyrone Power, Errol Flynn, Clark Gable, and Gary Cooper—had recently died. Significantly, the surviving leading men and male newcomers from 1939 had an easier time securing roles than their female counterparts, who faced sexist, ageist prejudices that were common in the era and that, unfortunately, are still in play in the twenty-first century.

The shift toward male-oriented movies began during World War II, and as theatrical attendance declined after the war, the trend became more pronounced. Whereas women had been the majority of the audience since the 1920s, the audience demographic gravitated younger and male in the 1950s. The studios increasingly invested in genres with a masculine emphasis: westerns, war films, adventures, and film noir, which flourished in the late 1940s and 1950s. The wide-screen era of the 1950s brought male-focused epics and spectacles, a trend culminating in 1962 with three of the five best picture Oscar nominees (*Lawrence of Arabia*, *The Longest Day*, *Mutiny on the Bounty*) completely dominated by men. But during the 1960s, one time-honored genre, the western, would lose some of its appeal.

John Wayne, known primarily as a cowboy actor in 1939, had become one of Hollywood's biggest stars by the 1950s. In 1962 he ranked number four at the box office in the annual Quigley exhibitor poll of the top ten moneymaking stars, the customary barometer of that day, and was widely visible throughout the year. With twenty-five poll appearances, spanning 1949–1974, he was the all-time champion.[2] In 1962 Wayne starred in two films by legendary directors of the old Hollywood guard, Howard Hawks and John Ford, and was part of the huge international cast of the World War II opus *The Longest Day* and the all-star western epic *How the West Was Won*. Hawks's *Hatari!*, an African-set adventure, was an enormous summer hit, while Ford's penultimate western, *The Man Who Shot Liberty Valance*, in which Wayne costarred with another major star from 1939, James Stewart, was no slouch at the box office either.

By this time in his career Wayne had become a cultural icon, symbolizing the conservative all-American cowboy-soldier hero, both on and off the screen. This was somewhat ironic, since he had never served in the military. Despite this image, Wayne had no qualms about supporting overseas production to the detriment of American jobs, venting in the *Hollywood Reporter* about the high cost of making movies domestically because of union labor expenses. Wayne also bristled at the thought of government interference with free enterprise as a solution to runaway production, stating, "Trying to legislate where a film should or should not be made is pure nonsense."[3] *Hatari!* was shot entirely in Africa for authenticity.

In *Hatari!* (Swahili for "danger"), Wayne stars as a big-game hunter in Tanganyika, present-day Tanzania, leading a small band of international colleagues to capture wild animals for zoos and circuses. The film plays as a group-confronting-peril ensemble piece, with a heavy dose of testosterone, similar to some of Hawks's best-known works (*Only Angels Have Wings, Red River, The Thing from Another World, Rio Bravo*). Additionally, the film's love affair between characters played by fifty-five-year-old Wayne and his Italian costar, twenty-eight-year-old Elsa Martinelli, exhibits the routine practice of casting much younger actresses as the romantic interest of older male stars. That was nothing new in Hollywood, as exemplified by the romance between forty-four-year-old Humphrey Bogart and nineteen-year-old Lauren Bacall in Hawks's *To Have and Have Not* in 1944, but this casting imbalance had become even more exaggerated as the actors aged. The studio bosses and some filmmakers showed little interest in attempting to make movies with mature actors and actresses as romantic costars.

While *Hatari!* is not vintage Hawks, its release coincided with the director's veneration by a new generation of film critics and cineastes. In 1962 critic Andrew Sarris wrote his famed essay, "Notes on the Auteur Theory." In this influential manifesto, Sarris gave the highest praise to strong-willed directors like Alfred Hitchcock and John Ford, who stamped their movies with an unmistakable personal vision. He ranked Hawks alongside them in the first tier as one of the fourteen greatest directors in film history.[4] Auteur critic Peter Bogdanovich, who would become an acclaimed director himself with *The Last Picture Show* in 1971, was an ardent Hawks admirer and called *Hatari!* a "rollicking African romance."[5] Another Hawks admirer, François Truffaut, in his seminal treatise on Alfred Hitchcock, compared the two directors and their approach to filmmaking—Hawks as an exhibitionist, Hitchcock as a voyeur. Following Truffaut's lead, the influential French magazine *Cahiers du Cinema,* ranked *Hatari!* third in its list of 1962's top ten films.

New critic Pauline Kael, who countered Sarris's auteur premise in a celebrated war of words in the scholarly journal *Film Quarterly,* was more disdainful of Hawks's movie, calling it a "bore." In her essay "Circles and Squares: Joys and Sarris" (1963), Kael seemed to have more fun eviscerating Sarris and his adherents than she had in viewing *Hatari!* or other auteur-acclaimed movies she disliked from 1962, such as Robert Aldrich's *What Ever Happened to Baby Jane?* and Otto Preminger's *Advise and Consent.* She showed her exasperation with Sarris, especially his premise of "interior meaning," which, according to him, "is extrapolated from the tension between a director's personality and his material." Kael asserted bitingly, "'Interior meaning' seems to be what those in the know know. It's a mystique—and a mistake. The auteur critics never tell us by what divining rods they have discovered the élan of a [Vincente] Minnelli or a Nicholas Ray or a Leo McCarey. They're not critics; they're inside dopesters. There must be another circle that Sarris forgot to get to—the one where the secrets are kept."[6]

Wherever moviegoers might fall on this critical divide, what remains clear is that Hawks bridged the two eras of classic Hollywood and a newer mode of filmmaking, as evidenced in *Hatari!*'s extensive improvisations. Hawks later said, "A script is important as a basis, but it doesn't have to be followed exactly."[7] That was particularly true of the action-hunt sequences, with their jagged energy and sense of real danger captured by Russell Harlan's color cinematography in the pre-CGI era. As noted in a favorable review in the *New York Times,* "These sequences are authentically sound-and-fury-filled and strikingly reveal the beauty, speed and ferocity of the animals." Hawks asserted, "There were no doubles or tricks on that picture, they really did it. And that's one of the reasons why it was popular. The audience saw them doing it."[8]

Auteur critic Stuart Byron, a longtime contributor to the *Village Voice* and other publications, identified another element that represented a new direction in Hawks's work. The director had always incorporated strong female characters in his movies, but they were rarely professional women. In *Hatari!,* Byron wrote, "[Elsa] Martinelli earns her living as a photographer, and thus, unlike almost any other Hawks heroine, does a job a man could do (indeed, the men at the compound are expecting a male photographer before she appears)."[9]

Hawks also opted for something other than a conventional symphonic score. Third-choice composer Henry Mancini came onto the project and delivered the alternative goods, after Hawks veterans Dimitri Tiomkin and Hoagy Carmichael did not work out. Tiomkin represented the 1930s film music masters who evoked the European romantic tradition. Mancini, who had emerged in the 1950s in the postwar generation of composers, presciently rerecorded his film music for soundtrack sale purposes. In light of the giant success of his soundtrack for the *Peter Gunn* television series, and the chart-topping album of his Oscar- and Grammy-winning *Breakfast at Tiffany's* score earlier in the year, Paramount, the studio behind *Tiffany's* and *Hatari!,* recommended Mancini to Hawks. The director's search for a different sound was amply rewarded when Mancini's soundtrack became a top album best seller, highlighted by the instrumental hit tune "Baby Elephant Walk."

Hatari! is now best remembered for Mancini's innovative music. Mancini melded pop tunes and jazz variations in his musical approach; he reimagined "the language of film scoring" as he captured the public's ear. His underscore to the film's opening, a chase sequence during an animal hunt, illustrates the effect. Utilizing authentic African instruments that Hawks provided, Mancini's percussive main theme transcends conventional scoring. This title music has a surprising, solemn quality that emphasizes the primitive majesty of the animals, favoring the hunted over the hunters.[10] In its review *Variety* praised the colorful score as the film's best asset, for bringing "both character and humor to the picture—for example, an inspired bit of boogie to accompany an elephant's bath. Mancini's melodies are contagious and they are haunting." In 1962 Mancini also deftly scored the suspense thriller *Experiment in Terror,* the James Stewart comedy *Mr. Hobbs Takes a Vacation,* and the alcoholism drama *Days of Wine and Roses,* a remarkable body of work for a single year.

If Hawks showed a willingness to work with younger collaborators, John Ford chose to stick with familiar players. Nevertheless, Ford's autumnal western, *The Man Who Shot Liberty Valance,* took some chances with the formulas of the genre. The film opened in April with John Wayne sharing the screen for the first time with fellow screen legend James Stewart. This triumvirate of venerable talent had strong marquee appeal and leveraged the film to box office success, despite mixed reviews and a general overexposure of westerns in popular culture. Paramount, the distributor, again profited from the link between popular music and box office sales, as it had with *Hatari!* The title song from *The Man Who Shot Liberty Valance* by up-and-coming songwriters Burt Bacharach and Hal David, recorded by teen favorite Gene Pitney, reached number four on the pop charts in June, which was ironic because the song was never heard in the movie.

Wayne and Ford had collaborated on some of the most acclaimed, influential westerns in movie history, principally *Stagecoach* (1939), *She Wore a Yellow Ribbon* (1949), and *The Searchers* (1956), which had essentially mythologized the West. Stewart was also no stranger to sagebrush stories, having spent a good deal of the 1950s in saddles and spurs in a series of celebrated westerns directed by Anthony Mann. He had just worked with Ford the previous year in another, lesser oater, *Two Rode Together.*

FIGURE 3.1 Director John Ford (far right) with actors James Stewart, John Wayne, and Vera Miles on the set of *The Man Who Shot Liberty Valance.* (Photofest)

In *The Man Who Shot Liberty Valance,* Stewart plays Ransom "Ranse" Stoddard, a U.S. senator who returns to the small town of Shinbone around the turn of the twentieth century for the funeral of Wayne's character, Tom Doniphon, who had been a rival for the hand of his wife, Hallie, played gracefully by Vera Miles. A persistent newspaper editor presses Stewart for the significance of this trek back to the town, where his shootout as a young lawyer with the infamous outlaw Liberty Valance (Lee Marvin) propelled him to political success in this unidentified prestatehood territory some thirty years earlier. Stewart's recollection then constitutes the heart of the film, in which Ford and his writers re-create a compressed history of the West in a metaphorical tale of unvarnished simplicity.

Shooting in black and white, and using studio interiors that did not disguise their artifice, Ford and company deliberately spun a yarn of archetypes and myths. Ford had been perpetuating the legend of the West throughout his career, and the artificial sets and some of the characterizations fit into that mythmaking. For instance, Stewart is clearly too old to play his character as a young lawyer. Andy Devine as a comical, cowardly sheriff and Edmond O'Brien as a drunken newspaperman paint in broad strokes that come close to caricature. On the other hand, Lee Marvin's riveting turn as the snarling, savage outlaw helped propel him to major stardom. He would be Oscar's best actor for 1965's parody western, *Cat Ballou.* Veteran film critic Kenneth Turan of the *Los Angeles Times* defended the film's spare, lean approach in a twenty-first century assessment; he praised Ford for "using the most classical means at his disposal to tell his image-busting story. Pared down with a vengeance and told with a simplicity that feels almost like ritual, . . . *Liberty Valance* unfolds seamlessly, with not a frame wasted or out of place."[11]

Wayne as a stalwart rancher who tutors the greenhorn easterner Stewart in the ways of the West, Woody Strode as Wayne's loyal black ranch hand, Jeannette Nolan and John Qualen as the Swedish immigrants who run the town eatery, and Miles as their kindhearted employee all represent the voices of decency and civilization supporting Stewart's crusade for education, law, and statehood. Ford also calmly, matter-of-factly reflects the civil rights era in a brief scene in which Wayne insists that Strode be given a drink by a reluctant bartender. Roger Ebert later applauded the cowboy acting legend: "Wayne as usual provides the calm center, never trying for an effect."[12] At this stage of his career, Wayne had become so reliable that he was often taken for granted, but in *Liberty Valance* he gives an assured performance of reserved authority as well as a hint of unexpected melancholy.

Prodded by the editor to whom he recounts the story, Stoddard finally reveals the truth about the gunfight: it was Tom who actually shot Liberty Valance, although Ranse got the credit. This draws the editor's aphorism, "This is the West, sir. When the legend becomes fact, print the legend." And he declines to publish the true story. Ford's earlier westerns had almost invariably enshrined the myths of the West, spinning tales of righteous men vanquishing evildoers to preserve civilization. In *Liberty Valance* the director showed a new self-awareness and even a sense of irony about the lies that were told to propagate an idealized version of American history. The famous, oft-quoted declaration of the editor—"Print the legend"—acknowledges some of the complexities underlying all the tales about the winning of the West. This double-edged manifesto is reinforced by the elegiac tone of the film, as the western frontier is finally closed at film's end, yielding to eastern interests.

The end of the frontier is also conveyed through a bittersweet undertone that persists in the final scene, when Ranse and Hallie are leaving the town by train and he asks her who placed the cactus flowers on Tom's coffin. When Hallie indicates that she had left the flowers, a lingering mood of regret is evident, suggesting that her forsaken love for Tom was a sacrifice, one of the themes of the movie and ultimately of the West. And Ranses's reaction to Hallie's confession suggests some cracks in their marriage that a typical western rarely acknowledged. The movie's sardonic last line only adds to the mood of unease. Thus, the winning of the West as told in *The Man Who Shot Liberty Valance* is hardly idealized, as Ford appears to be revising his previous romanticization. This time, mixed emotions prevail. Ford would make only one more western, the appropriately titled *Cheyenne Autumn* two years later, but his legacy is fulfilled in that *The Man Who Shot Liberty Valance* is now rightfully regarded as a seminal film in the western canon, selected for preservation by the National Film Registry in 2007.

Another definitive expression of the West's mythology in popular entertainment would wait until February 1963 for the domestic release of *How the West Was Won,* with both Ford and Wayne contributing. The Cinerama roadshow epic boasted an all-star cast, three prominent directors (Henry Hathaway, George Marshall, and Ford helming the Civil War segment featuring Wayne), and later inclusion in the National Film Registry. It also marked the end of an era, as the last feature shot and projected in the three-camera process that was Cinerama's trademark. Although originally planned to hit the trail in American theaters by the end of the year, *How the West Was Won* had an international launch first with London and Paris premiere engagements in November 1962. This stateside postponement was designed by MGM so that the western extravaganza would not compete for box office and awards with *Mutiny on the Bounty,* the studio's costly seafaring epic that had been delayed and was finally about to be released..

The inclusion of three 1962 oaters (*Ride the High Country, The Man Who Shot Liberty Valance, How the West Was Won*) in the National Film Registry signified a kind of artistic benchmark for the western genre. Not before or since has a single year produced as many NFR-designated cowboy movies. Yet by this time the western was already in decline in the United States, both culturally and commercially. Only 15 were made by the studios that year, down from 130 in 1950.[13] Aside from their appropriation in Italian "spaghetti" westerns and revisionist sagas in the 1960s and 1970s, cowboys would never quite recapture the imagination of the American public in the ensuing decades.

Although *Hatari!* and *The Man Who Shot Liberty Valance* made some headway at the box office, it was *The Longest Day,* the star-studded re-creation of D-Day, that most forcefully captured the public's attention. It was the personal project of one of the studio potentates of 1939, Darryl F. Zanuck, who had resigned as head of production at Twentieth Century-Fox in 1956 to become an independent producer. After five years of meager commercial success, he finally saw an opportunity to return to the industry's top ranks with a movie of author Cornelius Ryan's best-selling account of the Normandy invasion, hiring Ryan to adapt his book for the screen, with assistance by prominent novelists Romain Gary and James Jones. The virtually all-male, all-star cast included Wayne, Henry Fonda, Robert Mitchum, Sean Connery, Richard Burton, Robert Wagner, Rod Steiger, Curt Jurgens, Robert Ryan, and Jeffrey Hunter.

Zanuck clearly had ambitions beyond just this one movie. Emboldened by the financial misfortunes of Twentieth Century-Fox brought about in part by *Cleopatra,* the biggest money sinkhole in movie history up to that time, Zanuck wrested control of the studio from his successor, Spyros Skouras, in June 1962 and brought his twenty-seven-year-old son, Richard, along to oversee production. The senior Zanuck had evidently reevaluated his own jaundiced but not entirely inaccurate view of the studio system at the time. In 1961 he had written to an old colleague, screenwriter Philip Dunne, about how the boss of the studio by that time was little more than the "slave of the agents and actors with their own corporations and insane competition from independent producers and promoters."[14] Obviously, Zanuck preferred to be the taskmaster.

Zanuck filmed *The Longest Day* in black and white to simulate a documentary style, and employed three directors: Ken Annakin, Andrew Marton, and Bernhard Wicki. He allegedly took over the director's reins himself for the British and American interiors, reasserting his old leadership swagger. That extended to giving the only female speaking part in the film to his mistress at the time, French model-actress Irina Demick. The overall macho approach is evident in the film's point of view, emphasizing the high testosterone level of victorious men in war.

Robert Mitchum, as Brigadier General Cota, stirringly rallies his command to take Omaha Beach under heavy fire after they are pinned down, their backs to the sea. Peter Lawford as British commander Lord Lavort eschews the "sob stuff" in a speech inspiring his troops, and no-nonsense John Wayne as Lieutenant Colonel Vandervoof orders his soldiers to "engage the enemy . . . send them to hell!" Zanuck publicly thanked Mitchum for being the first major star to accept a cameo role, which prompted other high-profile actors to, according to Zanuck, "rush to get into the act."[15] Former World War II colonel (later brigadier general) Frank McCarthy, a successful film producer in his own right for *Patton* (1970), served as a military adviser to the production. Unbeknownst to the film company, McCarthy was gay, so the overtly masculine spirit of the film has an intriguing edge.[16]

When *The Longest Day* was released in October as a limited roadshow engagement, the victors of the war, the Greatest Generation and their families, turned out in huge numbers, lured by the prospect of "42 International Stars!" trumpeted in the advertising materials. World War II was either the subject or the background for a dozen major releases that year. This World War II genre had thrived since the war years with a trove of notable films, including *Casablanca, The Best Years of Our Lives, Battleground, From Here to Eternity,* and *The Bridge on the River Kwai.* Since the generation that had won the war against fascism was now prospering and raising families, it was no wonder that Hollywood would cater to their hunger for stories about that conflict. World War II movies would be prominent throughout the 1960s and would be revisited continuously into the twenty-first century.[17]

The public turned this movie dramatization of the D-Day victory into a studio-saving smash hit, and the conservative National Board of Review named *The Longest Day* its top film of the year. It would become the box office champion of 1962.[18] Zanuck's production remained the definitive film account of D-Day for more than thirty-five years, until rivaled by *Saving Private Ryan* (1998), Steven Spielberg's more graphically violent take on the invasion.

Zanuck was back on top with a vengeance, reemerging as a master fox in the Hollywood henhouse. Early in 1963 he rebooted production at Fox and told the Hollywood Film Council exactly what it wanted to hear on combating runaway production: "I repeat, there is no economic saving in making pictures abroad."[19] Of course he did make one exception—location shooting—mentioning *The Longest Day* in passing, which he had filmed entirely overseas. He would command the studio for the rest of the decade, overseeing the creation of some of the studio's greatest hits, including *The Sound of Music, Planet of the Apes,* and *Patton.* But after elephantine movie missteps like *Doctor Doolittle, Star,* and *Tora! Tora! Tora!,* the last of Hollywood's Golden Age honchos would be forced into retirement in 1971.

Another of 1939's quintessential leading men, Henry Fonda, who appeared briefly in *The Longest Day,* starred in veteran director Otto Preminger's political drama *Advise and Consent,* noteworthy for its controversial content and the final screen performance of Charles Laughton, who died in 1962. But it was Robert Preston, a young Paramount contract player in 1939 (*Beau Geste, Union Pacific*), who had the greatest role of his career when he reprised his stage triumph in the film version of Meredith Willson's Broadway smash *The Music Man.*

The commercial and artistic masterstroke *West Side Story,* Oscar's best picture and the top-grossing film of 1961, earning most of its total gross playing throughout 1962, helped reignite the studios' burgeoning interest in the musical genre. Willson's creation had been the most popular hit of the 1957–1958 Broadway season, snagging the Tony Award from the critically anointed *West*

Side Story. Now the success of those two cinematic adaptations paved the way for the greatest run of movie musicals, both at the box office and with Academy Award accolades, since their acme in the postwar years. *Bye Bye Birdie, Mary Poppins, My Fair Lady, The Sound of Music, Funny Girl, Oliver!, Fiddler on the Roof,* and *Cabaret* led the parade of hits over the next decade

Warner Bros. had helped to pioneer the movie musical genre, creating some of the most memorable song-and-dance vehicles of the 1930s with hits like *42nd Street, Footlight Parade,* and *Gold Diggers of 1933.* But the entertainment staple since the dawn of the sound era had lost its cachet and slipped in popularity by the late 1950s. Jack L. Warner, the cofounder of the studio, had deleted all the songs from the 1961 screen version of the Broadway show *Fanny.* With the looming success of *West Side Story,* however, Warner abruptly changed his tune and prepped the movie adaptations of both *Gypsy* and *The Music Man.*

After buying the rights to *The Music Man,* Warner planned to replace Preston as "Professor" Harold Hill, the charming con man who attempts to fleece the citizens of the fictional River City, Iowa, but is beguiled by them instead. True to the customary studio practice of replacing Broadway actors with genuine movie stars, Warner wanted Frank Sinatra or Bing Crosby for the film's lead. Willson wisely held out for Preston, who had started his career in Hollywood before finding star-making success on the stage, and a reluctant Warner acquiesced. He then entrusted the film to the original Broadway director, Morton DaCosta, which was hardly a risk since DaCosta had helmed the huge hit screen adaptation of *Auntie Mame* four years earlier.

As both the film's producer and director, DaCosta ensured that the vitality of the stage show was transferred to the screen, hiring best-selling author Marion Hargrove to craft a faithful screenplay from Meredith Willson and Frank Lacey's stage book. DaCosta employed the same stylized approach, with soundstage sets and blackouts, he had utilized for the screen version of *Auntie Mame,* eschewing realism for joyful theatricality, enhanced by the warm color palette of cinematographer Robert Burks (*Rear Window, Vertigo, North by Northwest*). This approach allowed some reviewers who felt the movie was too stagebound to sing the few sour notes *The Music Man* received. Yet Willson was so impressed by the fidelity of the film version that he wrote a congratulatory trade ad letter to Warner. He exclaimed, "I know a writer or two who didn't recognize his child after it became a movie. . . . God (if the Supreme Court will pardon the expression) bless you."[20]

Willson, who began his career as a film composer at the start of the sound era before scoring big time on Broadway, probably anticipated an increase in royalties from the film version. The show's original Broadway cast album had been a huge best seller, and the movie soundtrack also proved a top chart success. Additionally, when the Beatles covered the show's lovely ballad, "Till There Was You," on one of their early albums, their phenomenal popularity boosted Willson's music to its broadest audience.

The film's cast included Shirley Jones and seven-year-old television actor and future Oscar-winning director Ron Howard. They were buoyantly supported by Hermione Gingold, Paul Ford, Buddy Hackett, Pert Kelton et al., as the stage musical was amplified on the big screen to winning effect, led by Preston's pitch-perfect performance. Critic Pauline Kael aptly observed, "The star, Robert Preston, has a few minutes of fast patter—conmanship set to music—that constitute one of the high points in the history of American musicals."[21] Preston's spirited rendition of the signature "Ya Got Trouble" and the rousing "76 Trombones," among other numbers, propelled him to movie stardom after laboring for years in the B ranks. Without a champion like Willson, many other legendary Broadway actors never had a chance to preserve their most famous performances on the screen. Preston delivered a vivid screen demonstration of show business bravura.

The Music Man opened in summer to capitalize on anticipated family business. Braced by the omnipresent threat of the era's Cold War, the nostalgic public flocked to see this celebration of early twentieth-century small-town Americana, with critical reception equally enthusiastic. It was the second-highest-rated film of the year in *Film Daily*'s annual poll of motion picture critics, trailing only *The Manchurian Candidate*. The cheerful musical represented a reassuring escape from a dangerous world and, as some relieved scribes pointed out, a feel-good alternative to all the adult, downbeat dramas so prevalent that year.

The Academy rewarded all that wholesomeness with a best picture nod among six nominations and one win for thirty-year Warner Bros. studio veteran Ray Heindorf in the category Scoring of Music–Adaptation. Even without an innovative director like Vincente Minnelli or Stanley Donen at the helm, *The Music Man* still stands out in the movie musical genre. Along with *Meet Me in St. Louis* and *Yankee Doodle Dandy*, both of which had uplifted audiences during World War II, it remains an unabashed celluloid tribute to the American spirit, a perennial broadcast event on the Fourth of July. In 2005, the movie was inducted into the National Film Registry for preservation in the Library of Congress, verifying its status as a faithful screen adaptation of a landmark stage musical.

Among those actors considered for the role of Harold Hill was one of Hollywood's most enduring stars, Cary Grant. He found due compensation when

FIGURE 3.2 Robert Preston in the title role of *The Music Man*. (Photofest)

he was voted the number three box office attraction of the year, largely on the strength of costarring in *That Touch of Mink,* one of the year's top-grossing pictures. The movie also typifies the leverage that independent stars like Grant now had with the studios, as his own company Granley coproduced the film with Universal, ensuring the savvy actor and businessman a lion's share of the profits. Grant seemed somewhat uncomfortable in the film, perhaps because his leading lady, Doris Day, was two decades his junior. Grant (age fifty-eight) had also been a former costar and paramour of Sophia Loren

FIGURE 3.3 Doris Day and Cary Grant with New York Yankees Roger Maris, Mickey Mantle, and Yogi Berra in *That Touch of Mink*. (Photofest)

(age twenty-seven), but he ultimately grew dismayed at the prospect of being paired with younger female costars who were often half his age. He seemed more concerned about appearing lecherous than most other older actors were, and he was the only one among his peers who chose to retire while still a major box office draw, in 1966.

That age gap between Grant and Day made no impression on Bosley Crowther, who favorably reviewed *That Touch of Mink.* Instead, he called out the "heartless" Day character, a working girl wooed by wealthy businessman Grant for a sexual escapade. Crowther found a link between *Mink* and *Lolita,* arguing that both films "make elaborately sadistic sport of the familiar disposition of women—or, rather females—to be cruel toward men." Crowther's male chauvinism was fully expressed in a *New York Times* article on June 24, 1962, "Girls Will Be Girls—Female Perversity Rife in Two New Films," in which he compared the two movies. In his view Lolita was "haughty," a "ruthless heartbreaker," and a "vicious little tease." Then he added, "Miss Day, in her way, is quite as nasty to the utterly beguiling Mr. Grant when he offers everything a man can offer—except the honor of being his wife."

Crowther was offended that both Sue Lyon's Lolita and Day's character toyed with their men, holding out their sexual favors, while he credited the male characters with "honesty" for their impulses. He proclaimed earnestly, "The girls are the devious ones." Crowther may have been reacting to Helen Gurley Brown's nonfiction best seller, *Sex and the Single Girl,* an advisory manifesto for the aggressive independent woman, which caused a sensation when it hit bookstores in May 1962. His ageist bias and misogyny were further demonstrated in his critique of several actresses' work throughout the year, particularly his dismissal of older stars like Rosalind Russell, Barbara Stanwyck, Dorothy Lamour, Joan Crawford, and Bette Davis.

Those hostile attitudes were in full evidence in his review of another summer comedy, *The Road to Hong Kong.* Show business luminaries Bing Crosby and Bob Hope, who had successful individual careers in 1939 before they teamed with their hit series of road comedies in the 1940s and 1950s, reunited for this seventh and final outing. This pallid installment (even the often cheerleading *Hollywood Reporter* found "roadblocks and detours" among the sporadic comic bits) ended the most successful franchise in film history up to that time.

With Crosby and Hope soon eclipsed as top marquee attractions, a character in a British movie adapted from the spy novels of author Ian Fleming replaced them as franchise kingpins. The symmetry of that transition occurred in October 1962, when the first movie about the exploits of an espionage agent, played by relative newcomer Sean Connery, premiered in England. *Dr. No,* the film that launched the 007 franchise, would not open in the United States until May 1963, allowing American moviegoers to experience one of the most famous introductory lines in movie history, "Bond. James Bond."

Meanwhile, 1930s and 1940s star Dorothy Lamour, the prior leading lady of the *Road* series, hadn't filmed in ten years when a cameo in *The Road to Hong Kong* led to a brief revival of her faded movie career. Her appearance, mostly an afterthought, was a glaring example of Hollywood's ageist casting practices. Joan Collins, a much younger actress, had the costar role that once would have gone to Lamour. As Lamour recalled, the production was in trouble when she got a call from Bob Hope. She acknowledged the large amount of money they paid for her brief appearance, but being passed over for the female lead still stung years later. She recollected, "And it hurt to have Bing infer that I was too old to be the leading lady, although he was more than ten years my senior."[22]

Crowther's take on the creaky vehicle demonstrated that sexist and ageist bias was not limited to Hollywood's power brokers. He welcomed back Hope and Crosby, saying, "But the old boys still come through nicely in another turn

FIGURE 3.4 Bosley Crowther, film critic for the *New York Times* (1940–1967). (Photofest)

in the old 'Road" act." However, he was especially ungracious toward Lamour, pointing out, "She, too, is a bit long in the tooth and a trifle too thick around the middle for anymore than one quick shot in a sarong, . . . with her old no-talent bumbling to make the sentimental journey complete."

Crowther, one of the powerful cultural tastemakers of that era, is a paradoxical figure. He used his platform as principal film critic of the *New York Times* to fight against film censorship and call for more social responsibility from Hollywood. He also championed international cinema, and that advocacy was a key factor in the popularization of foreign films in America.[23] Yet he displayed a misogynist streak that was inopportune. As the leading critic of the era, Crowther certainly contributed to the career challenges that faced so many of the actresses who were fighting for their professional lives in 1962.

4 · GRANDE DAMES AND A BOX OFFICE QUEEN

Of the top ten U.S. box office stars in the 1962 Quigley exhibitors poll, only three were women. Doris Day, who began her career as a big band singer in the 1940s and emerged as an audience and exhibitor favorite as "the girl next door" in the 1950s, was number one. Screen beauty Elizabeth Taylor also ranked highly, having finished on top in 1961. Sandra Dee, who rose to stardom in the late 1950s as an ingenue in teen flicks (*Gidget*) and lavish women's melodramas (*Imitation of Life, A Summer Place*), finished ninth, her next-to-last appearance. In 1962 she shared the screen with her husband, Bobby Darin, in the romantic comedy trifle *If a Man Answers*.

This comparatively deficient showing by actresses in the poll reflected the reality of fewer roles for women in Hollywood since the end of World War II. Although female stars had ruled the box office in the 1930s (the years of Mae West, Joan Crawford, and Shirley Temple), they slipped into minority status in the poll in 1939. Their stature was further diminished in the 1950s. After the studios jettisoned original musicals in the late 1950s (shifting to Broadway adaptations after a slowdown in popularity for musicals overall), producers and distributors also retrenched on other traditional female genres such as melodramas and biopics, while westerns and war movies flourished. In 1957, all of the top ten stars were male. Many of the leading ladies of the postwar era who had films in release in 1962 (Lana Turner, Jane Wyman, Susan Hayward, Maureen O'Hara, Eleanor Parker, Deborah Kerr, and Kim Novak) fell victim to this male-focused megatrend. With a few exceptions, quality roles would elude them in the 1960s; their movie careers were essentially over by the end of the decade.

With the dwindling opportunities for actresses in the twilight of the studio era, 1962 marks a short-lived resurgence and capstone for leading female roles and strong female characters in such films as *Lolita, Sweet Bird of Youth, The Manchurian Candidate, All Fall Down, Long Day's Journey into Night, Days of Wine and Roses,* and *Two for the Seesaw.* There were even a few female-centric films (*Gypsy, Light in the Piazza, The Miracle Worker, What Ever Happened to Baby Jane?*), a genre still scarce in twenty-first-century Hollywood. The studios could not take sole credit for this creative outburst, as some of these films were independent productions, distributed but not financed by the major companies.

It was over this landscape that Doris Day reigned as box office queen. She had accomplished that feat with two giant hit comedies during the year. *Lover Come Back* with Rock Hudson opened nationwide in February 1962 after an Oscar-qualifying release in 1961; Day also dominated the summer smash *That Touch of Mink,* costarring Cary Grant, a key survivor of Hollywood's Golden Age. Her coronation had already been assured by the time of the Christmas release of *Jumbo,* her return to movie musicals in a polished adaptation of showman Billy Rose's 1935 theatrical spectacular.

Billy Rose's Jumbo had been greenlit by MGM to cater to the family trade, and this plan was bolstered by Day's desire to sing again in a big-screen musical. Golden Age icon Busby Berkeley, best known for his elaborate, geometrically choreographed musical numbers from the 1930s, made inventive contributions to the circus sequences and to the film overall. *Jumbo* became his movie swan song after a three-decade career. But the film might have worked better ten years earlier when originally planned, during the heyday of the MGM musical. *Jumbo* failed to return its high cost, and the first-rate work of Day, who was at the top of her game vocally, went undervalued. Yet the film verified the cinematic versatility of 1962, when veterans like Berkeley, costars Jimmy Durante and Martha Raye, and the great songwriting team of Richard Rodgers and Lorenz Hart had a chance to demonstrate their enduring talents.

In a way, Day was the victim of her own success; box office expectations had been set much higher as a result of her smash hit romantic comedies with Rock Hudson, *Pillow Talk* (1959) and *Lover Come Back.* Day's grasping husband and manager, coproducer Martin Melcher, was in control of her career, and *Jumbo's* relatively underperforming box office jeopardized his ill-gotten share of Day's lucre. Consequently, she never made another musical. She missed out on *The Sound of Music* (1965), which became the all-time box office champion up to that point, when Melcher decided not to pursue that project. Richard Rodgers had considered her a "foregone conclusion" to be cast in the leading role, but the film's director, Robert Wise, favored the eventual star, Julie Andrews.

Melcher sabotaged his wife in several other instances as well. Day hoped to improve the quality of music for her movies by hiring a top-flight composer like Henry Mancini, but she was thwarted by Melcher, who would not pay Mancini's fee. Later Melcher failed to show Day the script for *The Graduate*, after director Mike Nichols had been captivated by the icon-smashing possibility of casting America's sweetheart as the adulterous Mrs. Robinson. She had already demonstrated skill as a dramatic actress in the 1955 screen biopic of 1920s torch singer Ruth Etting, *Love Me or Love Me*, opposite James Cagney, so Nichols's instincts were well placed. In her autobiography, Day acknowledged that Mrs. Robinson was "an effective part," but said "it offended my sense of values."[1] Day turned age forty in 1962. Despite her accomplishments in roles as a proto-feminist working woman, by this period in her career she had been frozen in the public's mind as a symbol of American purity. As one producer put it, "It is difficult for foreigners to understand that Doris Day's virginity is one of America's revered institutions."[2] But that rigidity in choosing screen roles as a coy heroine would ultimately undermine her box office success. By the mid-1960s Day was saddled with a series of wanly scripted comedies that she later lambasted as "trite."[3] Unfortunately, they took their toll, effectively killing her movie career by decade's end.

If the number one movie star of the period (Day finished first in 1960 and 1962–1964, and ultimately became the top female box office draw of the twentieth century) was inhibited from a wider selection of roles by economic concerns, then older female stars were in an even more precarious position. As far as the studios and exhibitors were concerned, male-oriented and family-friendly films ruled the box office, Day's success notwithstanding.

Rosalind Russell, one of the memorable ensemble players in 1939's *The Women*, defied this dismaying trend. She had one of the best roles of her illustrious career in the film version of the Broadway musical *Gypsy*, based on the life of burlesque queen Gypsy Rose Lee and her mother, Rose, the ultimate stage mother. The two lead roles, strikingly portrayed by Natalie Wood and Russell, make the movie one of the few female-centered stories of the era. However, the cautious studio gave Karl Malden, fine in the now slightly built-up part of their manager Herbie, equal billing for a role that was essentially supporting.

Natalie Wood, the former child actress (*Miracle on 34th Street*) and teen-age star (*Rebel Without a Cause*), was at the peak of her career in 1962. Earlier in the year she had been Oscar nominated as best actress for *Splendor in the*

Grass (1961) and was costarring in best picture winner *West Side Story* when she was cast to play the queen of the striptease. Robert Wagner, Wood's husband at the time, suggested to Warner that he cast Judy Garland in the role of Rose, but Warner vetoed that choice.[4] Purportedly, Wood and Russell did not get along during filming, but that tension between them ultimately worked well for the film.[5] Although Wood received mixed reviews, her marquee appeal solidified the film's box office take.

Despite her acting renown and box office success in *Auntie Mame,* Russell had to contend with grousing on several fronts when she was announced for the part of Rose, displacing Broadway legend Ethel Merman, who had originated the role. Jack Warner was taking no chances with Merman, who had made only a handful of movies and never proved much of a film actress.[6] Unlike his experience with the casting of *The Music Man,* this time Warner prevailed. *Gypsy* joined a long list of Broadway shows, which for economic or aesthetic reasons had their female leads supplanted in their screen transfers. *South Pacific, West Side Story, My Fair Lady, The Sound of Music, Camelot, Hello Dolly!, Cabaret,* and *Mame* were just a few of the others.

Warner had both a fine actress *and* a genuine movie star in Russell. What he did not have was a top-flight singer, but Russell's vocal limitations were masked by dubbing and voice blending with Broadway performer Lisa Kirk. This tactic irked the purists, who further grumbled about negligible alterations to the story and the elimination of one song in the second half. They conveniently ignored that the film, as adapted by Leonard Spigelgass and helmed by veteran director Mervyn LeRoy (coproducer of *The Wizard of Oz*), remains a faithful, vibrant celluloid version of one of the greatest musicals ever staged. The memorable score by Jule Styne and Stephen Sondheim, skillfully adapted by Frank Perkins, clearly strengthened the film.

Despite Russell's inability to do all of the singing, her thirty years of acting experience in many different genres paid off in her searing performance. Russell pulls no punches in her uncompromising portrayal of the stage mother as egocentric monster. The highlight of the film (the first-act finale in the Broadway show) is the scene at a Midwestern train station, where Rose learns that her more talented daughter, June (Ann Jillian), has abandoned their vaudeville act and run off to get married. This devastates her, and the forlorn expression on Russell's face carries unmistakable emotional impact. But Rose refuses to stay defeated for long. She turns her attention to her older, less talented daughter, Louise (Wood), and declares that she will now pour all her energy into making Louise a star, whether Louise wants it or not. Her daughter is appalled at the prospect, but Rose pays no attention and belts out the most

FIGURE 4.1 Natalie Wood and Rosalind Russell in *Gypsy*. (Photofest)

famous number from the show, "Everything's Coming Up Roses." When heard out of context, on the radio where the song became a pop hit, or in Merman's recorded version from the Broadway original, the song can sound like an unabashed anthem of optimism and hope. But Russell delivers it as more of a savage manifesto of maternal domination and control; she will turn her daughter into a headliner even if she has to destroy her in the process. As Russell performs it, the song inspires chills rather than cheerful uplift.

Although Russell goes all the way with the darker implications of the story, there are other colors to her performance. A scene in which she pretends to be ravished by her landlord in order to avoid being evicted demonstrates the comic chops that Russell had perfected in several decades of screen comedy, and her energy can be charismatic as well as frightening. We certainly understand Rose's hold over all the people who encounter her, even if her single-minded ambition ultimately drives most of them away. In the scene where she describes all the people who abandoned her, beginning with her own mother, Russell helps to highlight the sense of loss underlying Rose's lust for success.

In spite of the carping from certain circles, including the creators of the Broadway show, a few critics endorsed Russell's bold approach to the role. Veteran film critic Joe Baltake (*Philadelphia Daily News, Sacramento Bee*) later noted that Russell, "whose line readings are flawless, . . . fleshed out the character of Rose as no one else ever has."[7] Members of the Legion of Decency, wearing their censor robes, responded to all the perceived naughtiness by burdening the movie with a B rating as "morally objectionable in part for all." They took a dim view of the unmarried relationship between Rose and Herbie and the "gaudy attempt to rationalize and glamorize a morally questionable occupation." The Legion hoped its admonitory rating would inhibit business, but the public paid no attention. *Gypsy* soared at the box office, opening with "boffo" engagements at New York's 6,200-seat Radio City Music Hall in November and Hollywood's vintage movie palace the Pantages in December, on its way to becoming one of the year's top ten hits. The public didn't seem to miss "The Merm."

Meanwhile, screen legend Katharine Hepburn had not filmed for three years before returning assuredly in the critically lauded indie *Long Day's Journey into Night*. Golden Age leading lady Olivia de Havilland (*Gone with the Wind, The Snake Pit, The Heiress*) had been off the screen for three years when she starred in the touching, underseen mother-daughter drama *Light in the Piazza,* written by Julius J. Epstein (*Casablanca*), adapting the Elizabeth Spencer novel. Produced by the venerated MGM musical kingpin Arthur Freed (*Meet Me in St. Louis, An American in Paris, Singin' in the Rain, Gigi*), who brought all his studio professionalism to bear, it proved to be his final film. *Piazza* would achieve greater prominence when it was adapted as a successful Broadway musical four decades later.

With appropriate roles few and far between, the situation of another of the great female stars of the studio era symbolizes the collective plight of women in Hollywood as they dealt with the passage of time. Barbara Stanwyck, perhaps the best untrained actress in Hollywood history, had not been in a movie for five years when she resurfaced in *Walk on the Wild Side,* a curious mix of sensationalism and sentiment. It was loosely based on the 1930s-set Nelson Algren novel about a Texan (played by Laurence Harvey, costar of *The Manchurian Candidate*) seeking his lost love (Capucine), finally tracking her to a bordello in New Orleans.

Director Edward Dmytryk (*Murder My Sweet, Crossfire, The Caine Mutiny*), no stranger to controversial subjects, gained notoriety as one of the blacklisted Hollywood Ten in 1947; his hard-edged style is recognized as a key foundation of film noir. He revisits that visual approach in the black-and-white *Walk on the Wild Side,* abetted by cinematographer Joseph MacDonald (*My Darling Clementine, Niagara, The Young Lions*) and lifted by Elmer Bernstein's jazz-inflected score.

Columbia, the film's distributor, mounted an aggressive campaign to lure the crowds with the racy tagline "a side of life you never expected to see on the screen!" and the cautionary label "This Is an Adult Picture; Parents Should Exercise Discretion in Permitting the Immature to See It." That advisory note was part of an agreement to avoid condemnation by the Legion of Decency. In the industry trades, the studio took out glossy ads promoting younger actresses Capucine, who was romantically linked to the film's producer, Charles K. Feldman, and Jane Fonda (in only her second film), leaving both Stanwyck and costar Anne Baxter out in the cold. Ironically, it was the fifty-five-year-old Stanwyck who would satisfy the thrill seekers, as she provided acting fireworks when the brothel scenes, which enticed the public in the first place but had been bowdlerized by the Production Code, fizzled. The advertising caption "a new kind of love story" took on added meaning as a result of her gutsy performance.

Stanwyck took fifth billing but has a formidable presence as Jo, described in the movie's promotional material as the "perverse and possessive madame," who is enamored with Hallie, the chief attraction of her "doll house," played by Capucine. Stanwyck's sexuality had been whispered about in Hollywood circles for years, so her portrayal of a repressed lesbian, however veiled, is remarkable on more than one level. As homosexuality on the screen was just beginning to emerge from the Hollywood shadows, an actress of her stature taking a role tinged with lavender is significant in film history.

The film's highlight, Jo's confessional scene declaring the love she has for Hallie, expressed implicitly and indirectly to her crippled husband, is both revealing and riveting, as if Stanwyck finally had an opportunity to express her own hidden feelings.[8] The dexterous range of emotions she conveys in a scene that lasts only a few minutes is a salient example of fine screen acting. Stanwyck had not had a scene of such bold frankness since the pre-Code era thirty years earlier. The Code had been modified in 1961, and for the first time permitted the intimation but not the overt depiction of homosexuality. Screenwriter Edmund North took advantage of the newly permissible subject matter and inserted the lesbian leaning of the madam where it did not exist in the novel.

Stanwyck seized the moment. Her adroit turn makes Jo the most interesting character in the movie, and the resourceful actress dominates every scene in which she appears, rendering this lurid melodrama eminently watchable. The film got mixed to negative reviews, as most critics saved their kudos for the cast, particularly for Stanwyck, who received her best notices in a decade. The *Los Angeles Herald Examiner* typified the critics who singled out

FIGURE 4.2 Barbara Stanwyck as the lesbian madam with her henchmen in *Walk on the Wild Side.* (Photofest)

her unorthodox role: "Barbara Stanwyck, as the brassy Lesbian, gives a penetrating portrayal." Another reviewer's wry appraisal illustrates the effectiveness of her performance: "Barbara Stanwyck, . . . who isn't seen too often these days, helps herself to several scenes as if there were no one else within the focus of the cameras."[9]

One dissenter was a curmudgeonly Bosley Crowther, showing an ageist bias by calling Stanwyck "something out of mothballs." Another naysayer was columnist Hedda Hopper, who railed against the movie. "Stories such as 'Walk' . . . don't belong on the screen. Hollywood is borrowing the decadence of centuries of European depravity and weaving a rope to hang itself," she warned in her syndicated review. After initially doing brisk business due to the salacious subject matter, the film ultimately did not make enough of an impact to revitalize Stanwyck's stagnant movie career.

Stanwyck and Fred MacMurray, the lethal lovers of Billy Wilder's *Double Indemnity* in 1944, were now at the opposite ends of the bankable star spectrum as far as the studios were concerned. She had been the highest-paid woman in the United States at the time she made that film noir classic, and was more highly regarded than her costar, claiming well-deserved accolades for her depiction of the cold-blooded femme fatale. Now MacMurray was enjoying the greatest commercial run of his career with Walt Disney, one of the surviving moguls from 1939 still active in 1962. Disney had fashioned a string of featherweight family films for him in the early 1960s that mined box office gold, and the trend continued when their 1962 summer offering, *Bon Voyage*, struck further pay dirt. Meanwhile, Stanwyck was struggling to keep her movie career afloat. Although her talent and professionalism had remained undiminished by the passing years, her main problem for the studio moneymen was that she had committed an unpardonable offense: growing older.

On the other hand, her *Double Indemnity* costar and his aging fellow actors had no such troubles. MacMurray, John Wayne, Henry Fonda, James Stewart, Cary Grant, and William Holden (whose career Stanwyck had rescued in 1939's *Golden Boy*, intervening with the producers when they were about to fire him), continued to thrive into the 1960s. Stanwyck could have used a decent, age-appropriate part opposite any of these actors, but those roles rarely materialized.

A look at the postwar career paths of Stanwyck and one of her legendary leading men of that era, Clark Gable, sheds some light on her predicament amid the sexist and ageist inclinations of Hollywood. The two Golden Age stars (both had started in the 1920s) were paired romantically in 1950 in a forgettable racing-car drama, *To Please a Lady*. For the rest of the decade Gable held on with rugged adventures, war stories, and westerns opposite some of the period's biggest female stars (Ava Gardner, Grace Kelly, Susan Hayward). Stanwyck had a few prominent roles (*The Furies, Clash by Night*) in the early 1950s, then had to settle for a series of lesser oaters and minor melodramas as the decade wore on. Gable, before his untimely death at age fifty-nine in 1960, finished his career partnered with the most popular (and much younger) actresses of the era: Doris Day (*Teacher's Pet*), Sophia Loren (*It Happened in Naples*), and Marilyn Monroe (*The Misfits*). Meanwhile, Stanwyck resorted to television in the late 1950s, returning to the big screen for the provocative part in *Walk on the Wild Side*. After supporting Elvis Presley in 1964's *Roustabout,* she soon called it quits to moviemaking, or, more accurately, the studios quit on her. She would return to television for the rest of her career, in intermittent, award-winning performances (*The Big Valley, The Thorn Birds*). Shortchanged moviegoers could only speculate about what they were missing at their local theaters.

Like Stanwyck, two other Golden Age survivors would be forced to take an unconventional path back to the big screen. Bette Davis and Joan Crawford, both approaching their midfifties, were long past their glory days as royalty at their former studios, Warner Bros. and MGM, respectively. They were also hard-pressed to find suitable film roles. Davis had been seen the prior year in *Pocketful of Miracles,* but that film was mainly a vehicle for Glenn Ford, and it was not particularly well received. Moreover, Davis had suffered through a decade-long career drought after deftly playing a has-been Hollywood actress in the inadvertently prophetic *The Star* in 1952, with fewer films and increasingly irrelevant roles.

In September 1962 Davis even resorted to placing a situation wanted ad in the trade paper *Variety,* listing "Thirty years experience as an actress in motion pictures. . . . Mobile still and more affable than rumor would have it. Wants steady employment in Hollywood (Has had Broadway)." Whether a stunt (as Davis claimed) or a legitimate solicitation of work, the subsequent publicity put her back in the spotlight, just in time for the release of a new movie.

Crawford had somewhat better luck in the 1950s; after squaring off against Bette Davis in the 1952 best actress contest, nominated for the noir melodrama *Sudden Fear,* she was cast as the female lead in *From Here to Eternity* (1953). However, her insistence on protecting her glamorous image bested her aesthetic judgment when she departed the film after deciding she didn't like the way she photographed, abandoning the role that was then so memorably inhabited by Deborah Kerr.[10] Crawford recovered partially from that misstep by starring in a number of popular women's melodramas, *Female on the Beach, Queen Bee,* and *Autumn Leaves* among them, but none of those films reached the artistic or commercial heights of *From Here to Eternity.* At any rate, her successful run was over by the time she made *The Best of Everything* in 1959, and she had not filmed since.

The fact that Davis was 1939's top adult female box office draw, just behind child star Shirley Temple, underlined her vexing career circumstances in 1962. Neither she nor Crawford had been tied to a studio since Crawford left Warner Bros. in 1952, where she had been in residence after departing MGM in 1943. Davis had vacated Warner Bros. in 1949 after eighteen years, so their simultaneous tenures there in the 1940s fueled rumors that they were rivals both on- and off-screen, particularly after Crawford won the 1945 best actress Oscar for *Mildred Pierce,* a role allegedly rejected by Davis. Their paths had crossed only once before on-screen, in cameo roles in 1944's *Hollywood Canteen,* but they had not shared scenes. The widely speculated feud between them helped excite the press when they were cast for the first time together as the leads in a new film project.

That film was an adaptation of a novel about two sisters, a former vaudeville child star and a crippled ex–movie actress, locked in a bitter psychological battle while living in run-down Hollywood obscurity. Robert Aldrich, the macho filmmaker who helmed the film noir classic *Kiss Me Deadly,* along with Clifford Odets's downbeat view of Hollywood, *The Big Knife,* Crawford's vehicle *Autumn Leaves,* and later *The Dirty Dozen,* bought the movie rights for $61,000, electing to produce and direct. Screenwriter Lukas Heller, who worked several times with Aldrich throughout his career, adapted the Henry Farrell suspense novel. Heller crafted a solid screenplay, expanding the source material into a dramatic narrative. The low-budget movie resulting from their collaboration, *What Ever Happened to Baby Jane?,* would make motion picture history.

Aldrich was forced to seek financing with the independent production company Seven Arts after being turned down by every studio in Hollywood and the withdrawal of his original financial partner, Joseph E. Levine. The pecuniary moguls had no faith in the box office appeal of either Davis or Crawford, a callous legacy for the aging stars who had made considerable coin for them in their prime. When press interest escalated during the shoot, which Aldrich had cannily opened to journalists, Jack Warner, the actresses' old studio boss and now sole head of Warner Bros., agreed to distribute the film. Some members of the press and many of the stars' loyal fans perceived parallels between the careers of the two movie legends and their characters in the film, and were hoping for a celluloid showdown. They would not be disappointed.

Publicly both stars downplayed the rivalry that the press seemed eager to foment. Just before shooting started, Hedda Hopper arranged a dinner at her home for the two movie queens, whom she diplomatically called "stars of equal magnitude." Crawford assured her that there would be no discord. As she told Hopper, "Very few story properties for stars like this come along. Of course everyone expects us to clash but I'll be a so-and-so if I'm going to fight."[11]

Warner's seeming munificence in distributing the movie after rejecting the project initially was not entirely for old times' sake. Rather, he saw it as a calculated gamble, since he would still collect a hefty distribution fee without assuming the greater capitalization risk. Davis recalled the studio heads' reluctance: "Nobody could see the 'electricity' of putting 'those two old broads' in the same picture."[12] The "old broads" appellation displeased Crawford, and she asked Davis to refrain from using it. If the apprehensive studio chiefs no longer had confidence in older actresses' ability to sell tickets, then Aldrich, Davis, and Crawford would have to rely on the film's tantalizing subject matter and the stars' aging fan base.

Although the film was budgeted at bargain-basement rates under $1 million, Aldrich did not shortchange production values entirely, cutting costs where he could but preserving overall quality. For director of photography he astutely hired studio veteran Ernest Haller. While at Warner Bros., Haller had worked with Crawford and Davis several times, notably on *Jezebel, Dark Victory,* and *Mildred Pierce,* among others. His familiarity with the actresses proved propitious during the efficient, six-week shoot that commenced on July 23. Haller's use of sharp, deep focus heightens the suspense in several key scenes, especially within the gloomy interiors of the sisters' once grand Hollywood house. The close-ups of Crawford as the crippled Blanche Hudson, enduring mental and physical torment at the hands of her increasingly deranged sister, Jane, are particularly harrowing.

Those scenes contain some of the movie's most memorable moments, with Jane serving her hapless sister her own twisted version of "surprise" pet and rodent cuisine. After one incident, Haller films from overhead, with the camera peering down on the now hysterical Blanche circling furiously in her wheelchair, trapped in the imaginary cage erected by the demented Jane. Haller's black-and-white photography and adroit lighting also accent the grotesque cosmetic look Davis achieved by applying her own makeup, a chalky mask she recalled from *Mr. Skeffington,* her 1944 success that was also shot by him. Frank DeVol's music also makes a major contribution, expertly shifting the mood from light to menacing throughout the movie.

Aldrich and his craftsmen, led by Haller, achieve a mise-en-scène of lavish decay partially by deglamorizing Crawford's heretofore carefully protected image. Crawford's reluctant surrender to this approach demonstrates her eagerness to maintain her star status. On the other hand, Davis never had qualms about the way she looked on-screen. Her top priority was creating character, and she pushed that propensity right to the edge as the adult Baby Jane Hudson. Since she had nothing to lose career-wise, her instincts were on target.

Aldrich elicited strong, vivid performances from both actresses and from Victor Buono, a twenty-five-year-old rotund actor making his screen debut, cast as Jane's musical director when she is delusional about returning to show business. After enduring desultory parts in the previous decade, Davis fully inhabits the showy role of Jane, holding the advantage over the wheelchair- and bed-bound Crawford. But this is not a one-note, undisciplined performance. Whether wallowing in alcoholic self-pity, disdainfully dismissing their nosy neighbor (Anna Lee), or gazing contemptuously on both Blanche and their anxious housekeeper, Elvira (deftly played by Maidie Norman), Davis achieves many striking effects. Her delineation of Jane's mental regression into childhood by film's end is particularly affecting, as she dances on the beach for puzzled onlookers, reliving (in her mind) her child star glory. There is

FIGURE 4.3 Director Robert Aldrich with costars Joan Crawford and Bette Davis on the set of *What Ever Happened to Baby Jane?* (Photofest)

genuine pathos underneath the grotesquerie. Richard Schickel, longtime film critic of *Time,* later cited Davis's "cracked grandeur, and there's not an actor in the picture who can stand up to her ferocious attack."[13]

For her part, Crawford shrewdly underplays, a perfect complement to Davis's tour de force. Never considered a great actress, or for that matter a subtle one, Crawford had risen to stardom in Hollywood's Golden Age principally through sheer determination. In the 1930s, the period of her greatest popularity, F. Scott Fitzgerald, while working on a script for her, wrote, "She can't change her emotions in the middle of a scene without going through a sort of Jekyll and Hyde contortion of the face, so . . . one must cut away and then back."[14] Now confronted with Davis, a superlative actress in full steam, Crawford summoned her survival skills reaching back to the silent era and gave one of the outstanding performances of her career.

Aldrich also culled a memorable moment from ten-year-old child actress Gina Gillespie, who fifty-five years later recalled, in an exclusive author interview, "Bette Davis had requested me to play her as a child [in the film's vaudeville prologue set in 1917]. But when Robert Aldrich saw me, he said I looked like Joan Crawford—he was correct." Aldrich switched roles on her so she now had the secondary part of the younger Blanche Hudson. She was consigned to watching from the wings of the theater as Baby Jane (Julie Allred) and their doting father (Dave Willock) performed the film's mawkish theme song, "I've Written a Letter to Daddy." Aldrich cuts to Gillespie intermittently during Baby Jane's act, as Blanche silently registers her resentment at being pushed to the sidelines. Their mother (Ann Barton) tries to comfort Blanche, predicting that she will be successful someday. Their mother pleads, "Try to be kinder to your sister and your father than they are to you now." A glowering Blanche responds, "I won't forget. You bet I won't forget!"

Gillespie made the most of her brief role. She related her disappointment at losing the part of Baby Jane. "I was upset," she said. "I channeled all of that anger into that scene."[15] After working in television from the age of four, Gillespie chose a different career path and left show business when she was a teenager. However, her fleeting few minutes on-screen in *Baby Jane* make an impression; some viewers have even suggested that Blanche's parting remark in the prologue foreshadows the film's surprise ending.

Marketing the film as a suspense shocker in hopes of a repeat of *Psycho* box office—with ads, trailer, and poster art using the lurid tagline "Sister, sister, oh so fair, why is there blood all over your hair?" and the image of a doll's broken head—the advertising campaign cautioned the fans of the two stars that "this is quite unlike anything they've ever done." And there was an advisory note in the advertising: "When the tension begins to build, try to remember it's just a movie." Yes, it's just a movie, but what to make of its enduring impact?

What Ever Happened to Baby Jane? has since gained a reputation as a "camp classic." Camp as a sensibility was defined by philosopher and writer Susan Sontag in her essay "Notes on Camp" (1964), in which she distilled camp to its essence, the "love of the unnatural; of artifice and exaggeration . . . of the 'off,' of things-being-what-they-are-not." Sontag went on to define camp as "only that which has the proper mixture of the exaggerated, the fantastic, the passionate, and the naïve." She contended that camp was not necessarily bad art, but art worth admiring and studying. And those who appreciated camp (mostly sophisticated urban cliques) and who shared the sensibility "are not laughing at the thing they label as 'camp.' They're enjoying it."[16]

Interestingly, Sontag did not cite *Baby Jane* among her cinematic examples of pure camp, which included Busby Berkeley movies and *The Maltese Falcon,* though she cited Davis, Barbara Stanwyck, and Tallulah Bankhead as camp movie stars, "great stylists of temperament and mannerisms." Curiously, she did not mention Crawford, who escaped Sontag's purview despite her embellished turns in the 1950s in such films as *Torch Song,*

Johnny Guitar, and *Queen Bee,* performances that attracted camp enthusiasts in later years.

Undoubtedly, subsequent parodies and countless drag impersonators through the years helped garner *Baby Jane* its populist camp designation. The emotive acting styles of Davis and Crawford and their screen-filling, expressive eyes contribute to this judgment. The great movie stars of the Golden Age acted persuasively with their eyes, and it is their faces, enhanced by skillful close-ups, that linger in the collective movie memory. *Newsweek* commented that in the role Crawford's eyes "blaze out soulfulness." And those "Bette Davis eyes," celebrated and further immortalized in song two decades later, are on full, florid display here.

Even with its exaggerated moments, *What Ever Happened to Baby Jane?* is an expert mix of black comedy and suspense. Roger Ebert splits the difference in the camp debate, asserting that at some point during Jane's descent into madness the film "stops becoming a 'camp classic' . . . and starts becoming the real thing, a psychological horror story."[17] It also represents a distinctive film version of Grand Guignol, the French theatrical showplace of naturalistic horror that highlighted madness and murder in the Gothic tradition. Coincidentally, that Parisian theater closed in 1962, leaving *Baby Jane* and the films it spawned— in a subgenre dubbed Grande Dame Guignol (or, to the most acerbic commentators, "hagsploitation")—to carry on the tradition. Prime examples, which had varying degrees of success, include *Hush . . . Hush, Sweet Charlotte* with Davis and Olivia de Havilland, *Strait-Jacket* with Crawford, *Lady in a Cage* with de Havilland, *Die! Die! My Darling* with Tallulah Bankhead, *What Ever Happened to Aunt Alice?* with Geraldine Page and Ruth Gordon, and *What's the Matter with Helen?* with Debbie Reynolds and Shelley Winters. Even Barbara Stanwyck tried her hand in the genre with *The Night Walker* from horrormeister William Castle, but the film disappointed and finished her movie career. Grande Dame Guignol ran its course by the early 1970s.

Of course, that specific trend would never have exploded if *Baby Jane* had not been a massive box office hit. The film received mixed positive reviews, with perceptive critics lauding the powerful acting of the two stars. Among the film's admirers were auteurist critics both here and abroad, touting the work of director Aldrich. Andrew Sarris later indicated that Aldrich became a financially viable producer-director "largely on the lucky gamble involving the chemical combustibility of Bette Davis and Joan Crawford."[18] Sam Lesner in the *Chicago Daily News* saw more than luck, noting, "The film is a field day for Bette Davis, Joan Crawford, and director Robert Aldrich, who saw in Henry Farrell's novel . . . the outlines of a modern Greek tragedy. Yet it is great fun, too, because this is pure cinema drama set in a real house of horrors." Arthur Knight in *Saturday Review* praised all the talent, stating, "Scenes that, in lesser hands, would verge on the ludicrous simply crackle with tension—or they are filled with unbearable pathos."

On the other hand, critic and historian Arthur Schlesinger Jr. was so dismayed by the film (he openly admitted he left a press screening halfway through) that he wrote in his review for *Show*, "Bette Davis has been a distinguished actress, and it is hard to understand why either she or Miss Crawford should demean themselves by appearing in trash." Bosley Crowther was also among the detractors, calling the two stars "formidable freaks" who "wear grotesque costumes, make up to look like witches and chew the scenery to shreds." Ironically, Crowther's employer, the *New York Times*, would later include *Baby Jane* in its "Guide to the Best 1,000 Movies Ever Made," replete with his negative review.

Schlesinger and Crowther may have overstated the case for the prosecution, while they also failed to appreciate the career problems confronting the aging female stars. But they made a valid point in observing the gulf between Aldrich's "freak show" and the memorable, high-class projects these actresses had once graced. In her heyday, Davis had been accustomed to great roles in such literate films as *Jezebel*, *The Private Lives of Elizabeth and Essex*, W. Somerset Maugham's *Of Human Bondage* and *The Letter*, Lillian Hellman's *The Little Foxes*, and *All About Eve*, written by Joseph L. Mankiewicz. Crawford had once claimed strong parts in important movies like *Grand Hotel*, *The Women*, and the career-revitalizing *Mildred Pierce*, her finest hour on the screen.

By 1962 Crawford was reduced to playing a victimized cripple and Davis a demented hag in a low-budget shocker—an unmistakable comedown from their past glory days. However, the veteran stars were allowed one more unexpected commercial success. Following rousing sneak previews in mid-October, the *Hollywood Reporter*'s Mike Connelly predicted, "Davis . . . can brush her teeth with champagne after *Baby Jane* makes the world her domain." The movie opened in 400 theaters nationwide on November 6 (an unusually high number in those days of limited release and gradual rollouts) and touched a responsive nerve in the audience.

The nine-day Cuban missile crisis had just played out in late October, with nuclear war against the Soviet Union averted, and the nation could release pent-up anxiety by watching a movie fright fest that had the imprimatur of Hollywood Golden Age class in Davis and Crawford. The stars' fans came out in droves, and the audience expanded exponentially, as the film became an overnight show business sensation. The $48,000 it made in the initial week at the

3,900-seat Chicago Theatre, where the average ticket price was a mere $1.40, indicates its blockbuster appeal. It made back its cost in just eleven days, then energized the November box office, winding up as one of the year's top-grossing pictures after only two months in release.

The film's impact on popular culture was immediate. Warner Bros. had commissioned *New Yorker* magazine cartoonist Charles Addams to create an illustration for the film's pressbook in his comically macabre style, depicting his Addams family characters horrified at Baby Jane's treatment of her sister, Blanche. This imagery seeped into the popular consciousness and helped sell the film worldwide. In May 1963 the prestigious Cannes Film Festival officially invited *Baby Jane* to screen with only two other American entries, joining *To Kill a Mockingbird* and Alfred Hitchcock's *The Birds* among the international fare in the south of France.

At awards time, everyone loved a comeback success, especially an unforeseen one. *Baby Jane's* surprising total of five Academy Award nominations testifies to its impact, with well-deserved acknowledgment for Ernest Haller among the nominations. An Oscar win for sixty-three-year-old costume designer Norma Koch (*Hush . . . Hush, Sweet Charlotte, Lady Sings the Blues*) reinforced the regard of the Hollywood community; that category afforded Academy voters a perfect opportunity to honor the film in that fiercely competitive year. At the ceremony Koch appropriately thanked "all the Baby Janes wherever you are."

Bette Davis's nod for best actress, her tenth, turned out to be the last on-screen peak of her movie career. It was her final nomination. The other Oscar nods were for sound (a ravenous Blanche devouring chocolates after being starved by Jane is one noteworthy example) and newcomer Victor Buono as best supporting actor. Some incredulous members of the press speculated that Davis's nomination was some sort of inside Tinseltown joke. For example, the *Los Angeles Times* sneered, calling the recognition for Davis's Baby Jane "a macabre gag."

In spite of the few scoffers, the movie industry and her legion of fans hailed Davis's comeback, and she was widely considered the sentimental favorite to win a third Oscar. But her eventual loss and Crawford's alleged campaigning for that result are now part of Hollywood lore. Despite being overlooked for a nomination, Crawford found another way to steal the spotlight. After volunteering to accept for any absentee best actress winner, she did just that at the ceremony when Anne Bancroft's victory roiled Davis, who watched from the wings as a seemingly exultant Crawford accepted the award for best actress of 1962. Backstage afterward, Crawford was copiously photographed with an

FIGURE 4.4 Academy Award winners Gregory Peck, Patty Duke, Ed Begley, and interloper Joan Crawford on Oscar night. (Photofest)

Oscar that did not belong to her, and smilingly told the press, "I don't want to give it up."[19] (She finally gave it up a week later, personally delivering the statuette to Bancroft, who was appearing on Broadway.)

In its own way, *Baby Jane* serves as an indictment of Hollywood, not unlike Billy Wilder's mordant film noir classic, *Sunset Boulevard* (1950), which it resembles in tone and content as a dark view of the movie capital. Both films share a similar setting of dilapidated houses from a bygone Hollywood era. *Sunset Boulevard*'s Norma Desmond, the forgotten movie queen of the silent era (played by silent star Gloria Swanson), is desperate for a "return" to the silver screen in midcentury Hollywood, and descends into madness and murder. The delusional Desmond has a stygian soul sister in Baby Jane Hudson. And Blanche Hudson, who harbors a corrosive secret (embodying a key noir theme of a haunted past), finds there is no happy ending for her either. While *Baby Jane* does not reach the artistic heights of Wilder's masterpiece, and the keepers of the noir vault have not identified it as a full-fledged film noir, it has a permanent address adjacent to the same dark neighborhood.

Sunset Boulevard afforded the aging Swanson a prime leading role and opportunity for a movie comeback of her own, which she was unable to fulfill after her singular triumph as Norma Desmond. In 1962, *What Ever Happened to Baby Jane?* offered further damning commentary on studio hiring practices of the time. However, the film's box office and Academy recognition were vindication for Davis and Crawford taking such unorthodox and risky roles in the first place. More important, *Baby Jane* resuscitated their moribund movie careers.

A grateful Davis told Hedda Hopper that her phone kept ringing with new offers and ruminated, "You remain the same person as always, but, as we might abhor it, money talks."[20] To television talk-show host Jack Paar on the *Tonight Show* Davis expressed relief that after the prior ten years of box office duds, "at least I'll be on the books as a potential moneymaker, and believe me, that's a new career for me." For posterity, Davis's characterization of Baby Jane Hudson ranks among the American Film Institute's fifty best movie villains in history. And the film continues to fascinate more than half a century after it opened, with Ryan Murphy's popular, somewhat fictionalized 2017 television series *Feud,* about the rivalry between Davis and Crawford (starring Susan Sarandon and Jessica Lange), reviving interest in the 1962 movie.

Unfortunately, Crawford, who had previously demonstrated a peculiar talent for career self-sabotage, inopportunely quit the next Aldrich-Davis collaboration, the 1964 hit *Hush . . . Hush, Sweet Charlotte.* Virtually all her subsequent films were unworthy B pictures (*Strait-Jacket, I Saw What You Did, Berserk*) as she failed to take advantage of her recharged career momentum. Crawford ended her long film career in the sci-fi horror cheapie *Trog* (1970) and died a virtual recluse in 1977.

For the indefatigable Bette Davis, however, *Baby Jane* provided her with renewed popularity and esteem that she capitalized on to remain in the limelight for almost three decades, garnering accolades and remaining a vivid presence on screen, stage, and television up until her death in 1989. While on a publicity tour for the film's opening in 1962, appearing at New York City movie theaters before appreciative and enthusiastic crowds, an energized Davis was interviewed by film journalist and critic Vincent Canby. Davis took the opportunity to acknowledge the dearth of women's roles in the 1960s, in contrast to the situation during her heyday, when the star system flourished. Canby reported that in the end, however, Davis was a reminder that "the star system may be dead, but stars aren't."[21]

Tragically, Hollywood found its most luminous star permanently dimmed in August 1962 when Marilyn Monroe's sudden death at the age of thirty-six rocked the movie industry and saddened fans worldwide. Monroe had been fired in June from George Cukor's presciently titled and unfinished *Something's*

Got to Give after delaying production with her erratic behavior. The emerging New Hollywood could no longer indulge its eccentric stars, not even the last great creation of the old studio and star system. Monroe had been the highest-ranked female box office draw three times in the mid-1950s but yielded that spot to Elizabeth Taylor and Doris Day by the start of the 1960s, when she dropped out of the poll. However, Monroe would soon be immortalized as a cultural and screen icon, while her passing symbolized both the decline of female stars in the Hollywood firmament and the demise of the classical studio era. Fortunately, thanks to the creative vision of some veteran filmmakers as well as some brand-new voices, the cinema of 1962 remained as vital as ever.

5 · CALLING DR. FREUD

Marilyn Monroe, the greatest star of the 1950s and early 1960s, was known not only for her sensual image and her temperamental behavior on the set. She was also, like many actors of the era, a passionate devotee of psychoanalysis who spent years sampling the wares of a series of fashionable doctors. In 1960 John Huston, who had directed her in one of her best early films, *The Asphalt Jungle,* and in her latest picture (which would turn out to be her last), *The Misfits,* offered her a key role in his ambitious tribute to the founder of psychoanalysis, Sigmund Freud. Marilyn was intrigued by the opportunity to tackle such a challenging dramatic role, but she ultimately turned it down, partly at the urging of her current analyst, Ralph Greenson, a close friend of Anna Freud, who was vehemently opposed to the idea of a Hollywood picture about her sainted father's life. In a letter to Huston dated November 5, 1960, just after *The Misfits* finished shooting, Marilyn declined the role. "I have it on good authority that the Freud family does not approve of anyone making a picture on the life of Freud," she wrote, then added that she could not be involved in the project, in part because of "my personal regard for his work."[1]

Monroe's devotion to psychoanalysis was far from unique. In that era, many of the top stars and directors did their time on the couch; it was almost an obligatory rite of passage in Hollywood. But if this obsession with Freud's talking cure had its trendy and even foolish side, it was also a sign of the film community's serious commitment to exploring the hidden depths of character. Sidney Lumet, who directed two of 1962's ambitious films (*A View from the Bridge* and *Long Day's Journey into Night*), once commented about the difference between films of that era and more recent movies. "I think that lack of analytic awareness has a great deal to do with the kinds of movies we see now that are totally geared to the present and the momentary feelings and sensations," Lumet said. "In modern moviemaking there is no pre-life to the characters. They exist only for the time of the picture itself, and they're not burdened by anything in the past."[2] In other words, fast and furious action pictures have come to trump piercing psychological dramas.

Writers and directors of 1962, by contrast, probed thoughtfully into the inner lives of their characters and the many ways in which they were haunted by the family dynamics that shaped them. Sometimes the Freudian underpinnings of these films were simplistic, but their depth of characterization puts most present-day movies to shame.

Several of the films of that year were explicitly about psychiatry, and the most ambitious of these undertakings was Huston's production of *Freud*. Huston first became interested in psychoanalysis back in the 1940s, when he directed the World War II documentary *Let There Be Light,* an exploration of the techniques used to relieve the torment of shell-shocked soldiers, who would now be described as suffering from PTSD. Huston worked on that project with producer Julian Blaustein and screenwriter Charles Kaufman, who later teamed up with him to make *Freud.* Blaustein eventually left the project, but Kaufman coauthored the Oscar-nominated screenplay for the 1962 biographical film.

Huston described his passionate interest in the movie as "an eighteen-year-old obsession based on the firm conviction that very few of man's great adventures, not even his travels beyond the earth's horizon, can dwarf Freud's journey into the uncharted depths of the human soul."[3] *Freud* begins with narration, spoken by Huston himself, about three great thinkers who challenged what he called human "vanity." The first of these sages was Copernicus, who refuted the idea that all other planets revolved around the earth. The second was Charles Darwin, who declared that humans were not distinct from other animal species. And the third was Freud, who demonstrated that people often acted not out of conscious design but as a result of dark, unconscious impulses that they could neither comprehend nor fully control.

Copernicus's discoveries are by now settled science, but controversies continue to swirl around the theories of Darwin and Freud (at least in a few circles), partly because the latter two thinkers challenged the teachings of religion. They may no longer be derided as heretics or blasphemers, as they were during their lives, but some of their theories are still debated. In the case of Freud, some questioning of his ideas is legitimate, but the basic thesis of Huston's movie—that we are all subject to fears and desires beyond the sway of reason—is no longer controversial.

Huston, who had won two Academy Awards for 1948's *Treasure of the Sierra Madre,* was one of the most respected American directors when he set about preparing *Freud.* To write the screenplay, drawn from Kaufman's outline, the director hired the French existentialist sage Jean-Paul Sartre. But Sartre's script turned out to be 1,500 pages long, so Kaufman was rehired to pare it down to a manageable size. Kaufman eventually shared screen credit with the film's producer, Wolfgang Reinhardt. The film focuses on just one brief period in Freud's life, when he begins to formulate his shocking theories on childhood sexuality.

Most of his discoveries come from his examination of one patient, a disturbed woman named Cecily, the role once envisioned for Monroe but which was played by the gifted young British actress Susannah York. (After Monroe declined, Elizabeth Taylor, Kim Novak, and Brigitte Bardot were all considered by the studio for the role. Shelley Winters and Susan Kohner had written directly to Huston requesting the part. Kohner got a consolation prize—the rather stock role of Freud's supportive wife.) The character is a composite based on a number of women whom Freud treated early in his career. He first follows the approach of his mentor, Dr. Joseph Breuer (Larry Parks), in using hypnosis to probe Cecily's memories, but then he develops his famous "talking cure," in which he guides her while she is still awake to delve into her fantasies and dreams. In one of these stylized flashbacks, artfully filmed by Huston and cinematographer Douglas Slocombe (*The Lavender Hill Mob, Julia, Raiders of the Lost Ark*), she reports being molested by her father. Freud is startled by the confession, but in digging deeper, he decides that the rape never occurred but was a fantasy growing out of Cecily's desire for her father. And this leads him to the revelation that even children can have sexual fantasies involving their parents, a theory that shocks and appalls his Viennese colleagues.

In 1962 audiences were inclined to take Freud's discoveries at face value, but a reevaluation by later psychiatrists, including many women, suggests that Freud may have been correct in his first formulation that a number of his female patients were sexually abused by their fathers or other adults in their lives. This does not disprove the idea that children might harbor sexual fantasies involving their parents, but it is now believed that Freud and his contemporaries underestimated the amount of sexual abuse that went on behind the closed doors of many respectable nineteenth-century homes.

Despite these simplifications, the film is well directed and well acted by a talented cast, down to the smallest roles. One of the young actors in the film, newcomer David McCallum, who also had a part in *Billy Budd* in 1962, gave a vivid performance as a tormented young man involved in an intense oedipal

FIGURE 5.1 Montgomery Clift as Sigmund Freud and Susannah York as his patient in *Freud.* (Photofest)

triangle involving his father and mother. One of the striking dream sequences in the film shows McCallum dragging Montgomery Clift's Freud into the abyss of his own unconscious. McCallum recalls the agonies of filming that scene:

> Huston started with one grip and then wound up putting four grips on one end of the rope and pulling from the other end. Monty's arm began to bleed and swell, and this went on and on. I walked off the set. I said, "I will have nothing more to do with this." I went to my dressing room and shut the door. Production stopped.

Larry Parks came to me and said, "You can't hold up production like this." I said, "I'm not going to stand there and watch Huston kill [Clift]." Larry persuaded me to go back. I went up to John and said, "John, why are you doing this?" Huston put his arm around me—he was much taller than me—and said, "It's good for him, David. It's good for him." Much later on, toward the end of Monty's life, somebody asked Monty who he would like to direct him, and he said John right away. That sort of sadomasochistic relationship between John Huston and Monty Clift was quite extraordinary and a real eye-opener to me at the time.[4]

Huston kept tabs on his star throughout the production. McCallum recalls having dinner with Clift at a time when the actor was on a break "to escape Huston's clutches," as McCallum puts it. "Huston tracked him down while he was at dinner with me at a London restaurant," McCallum says. "The waiter put a telephone on the table and said, 'You have a call, Mr. Clift.' Monty picked up the phone and I could hear Huston's distinctive voice, 'Hello, Monty.'"[5]

Susan Kohner, who worked with Clift for a longer period over the course of the European shoot, had a chance to observe the challenges that plagued the actor. "He was not in very good shape, either physically or mentally," Kohner reports. "He was a sad figure—vulnerable and fragile but trying to hold it all together. He had a lot of dialogue, and he had trouble remembering. We were all hoping he would not fall apart. I think he knew he had a friend in me."[6] In fact, Clift visited Kohner in New York after the film was completed. She recalls having tea with Clift and with Walter Huston's widow, who was John's stepmother.

Kohner had known John Huston since she was a child. Her father, Paul Kohner, was Huston's agent. "He was Uncle John to me," Kohner says. "He always treated me as an adult. I was on the set of *The Red Badge of Courage,* and it was exciting to meet Audie Murphy." (Kohner made her first screen appearance in *To Hell and Back,* the movie version of Murphy's World War II memoir, in which Murphy played himself. In 1959 Kohner earned an Academy Award nomination for her performance in Douglas Sirk's *Imitation of Life.*) Over the years the actress gained plenty of firsthand knowledge of the director. "Of course I knew about all John's lady friends," Kohner laughs. "He was a charmer. I remember he had a monkey as a pet. He was a bit crazy but a fascinating individual. It was lovely for me to work with him on the movie."[7]

Despite the problems on the set, Huston drew a sympathetic performance from Clift, as he had also done on *The Misfits* a year earlier. Although the script included some now questionable ideas about female sexuality, it had other moments that were genuinely incisive. Some of the best scenes detail Freud's ambivalent relationship with his own father and his buried memories of a childhood journey when he slept in a bed with his mother and was jealous when his father drew his mother away from him. One of Freud's greatest strengths as a psychologist was his willingness to scrutinize his own memories and fantasies with unflinching honesty, and the film does an admirable job of capturing this side of Freud's journey to understanding.

Huston (like Howard Hawks with *Hatari!*) wanted an unconventional score for his expressionistic film, and he gave the assignment to a composer new to movies, Jerry Goldsmith, after admiring his contributions to two television series, *The Twilight Zone* and *Thriller*. Goldsmith, who scored another noteworthy 1962 movie, *Lonely Are the Brave,* gave Huston exactly what he was looking for—a daring, mostly string-based atonal score. As the composer noted, strings were "the perfect expression of the human psyche."[8] Goldsmith received the first of eighteen career nominations (including *Planet of the Apes, Chinatown,* and *The Omen*) for this breakthrough work, which was a startling departure from traditional Hollywood symphonics. His music had an unexpected afterlife. When he scored Ridley Scott's sci-fi horror classic *Alien* in 1979, Goldsmith discovered that Scott had edited the film using the score for *Freud* on a temporary music track, and the composer was discomfited when Scott used several of those cues in the finished film, replacing portions of his new score.

Although today's critics probably consider *Freud* to be one of Huston's lesser efforts, when compared with *The Maltese Falcon* or *The Treasure of the Sierra Madre* or even *The African Queen,* reviewers in 1962 were quite ecstatic about this ambitious undertaking. *The New York Times'* Bosley Crowther pronounced the movie "as daring and dramatic as the probing of a dark, mysterious crime," and he sang the praises of Huston's direction: "so graphic, so expressive of the rhythms and moods of troubled individuals, so illustrative in its use of cinema's styles, that it drags the viewer into the picture with the disturbance of a patient on the couch." Philip K. Scheuer of the *Los Angeles Times* was equally bewitched, and his prose was almost as tremulous. "Not all the traumatic experiences in the enthralling, remarkable motion picture called *Freud* are confined to the screen," Scheuer wrote. "Each viewer may well have the sensation that he is undergoing one himself—that he is finding out things about himself which are closer than his skin." The prickly Legion of Decency recognized Huston's artistic achievement but, like some of the doctor's nineteenth-century critics, felt that the film left the impression that Freud was only concerned with "pansexualism" in formulating his theories. So the watchdog group gave the movie a "Separate Classification" for adults.

Psychiatrists appeared as major characters in other films of 1962, though these characters did not have quite the stature of Sigmund Freud. Perhaps the most lavish of these psychiatric dramas was *Tender Is the Night*. In 1946 David O. Selznick, the producer of *Gone with the Wind* and always known for his interest in bringing classic literature to the screen, had bought the rights to F. Scott Fitzgerald's novel about a psychoanalyst whose life is destroyed after he marries a beautiful and wealthy but deeply troubled patient. Partly because of the downbeat nature of Fitzgerald's story and partly because of Selznick's reputation for reckless spending, it took him more than a dozen years to scrounge together the necessary financing to make the film. But by the time filming began in 1961, Selznick had been forced to relinquish the reins as producer. Twentieth Century-Fox considered him an impossible perfectionist. Throughout his career, Selznick harassed other producers and directors relentlessly. He was particularly vehement when it came to the appearance of his second wife, actress Jennifer Jones. When Vincente Minnelli directed Jones in *Madame Bovary* in 1949, Selznick sent him a memo on the subject of his wife's eyebrows: "It would be sheer folly to tamper with them to the slightest extent. I will appreciate it if you will leave them strictly alone, and will assume this to be so unless I hear from you further."[9]

Dismayed by this kind of mania for control, Fox replaced Selznick as producer of *Tender Is the Night* and hired Henry Weinstein, a newcomer from Broadway (who would later work on Marilyn Monroe's unfinished last project, *Something's Got to Give*). But Jennifer Jones remained cast in the leading role of the neurotic Nicole Warren. And Selznick watched over every detail of her performance even if he had to do it from off the set. While the company was filming in Europe, Selznick had long-distance conversations with his wife almost every day after watching the rushes flown to Fox studios in Los Angeles. Jones also had a Selznick surrogate on the set—acting coach Paula Strasberg, who played the same role with Marilyn Monroe. Costar Joan Fontaine (who played Nicole's protective older sister) later wrote in her autobiography, "Talented, charming Jennifer was the most insecure actress I ever worked with."[10]

Finding an actor to play Nicole's analyst, Dr. Dick Diver, proved to be difficult. Christopher Plummer was originally cast but walked off the picture. William Holden and Richard Burton turned down the role, so Selznick finally turned to a newer actor from Broadway, Jason Robards Jr. He had recently played a Fitzgerald-like novelist in Budd Schulberg's play *The Disenchanted*, so he seemed like a logical enough choice. Some of the other casting was less felicitous. Twentieth Century-Fox was in financial trouble at the time, and one of the ways it cut costs was to use as many of its contract players as possible in all of its films. That is how miscast performers like Tom Ewell and Jill St. John ended up in *Tender Is the Night*. Robards remembered crusty director Henry King telling him, "We have a lot of lousy actors on this picture. And we should get all this Scott Fitzgerald shit out of the script."[11]

Henry King (*Tol'able David, The Song of Bernadette, The Gunfighter*) had been making movies since the silent era and was one of the thirty-six original founders of the Academy of Motion Picture Arts and Sciences in 1927. *Tender Is the Night* would be his final film. Bosley Crowther later confirmed King's judgment of the supporting players in his review of the film. As Crowther wrote, the character of the Hollywood starlet "is played with gross incompetence by squeaky Jill St. John." Robards felt that one of his costars, veteran actress Fontaine, stood out because of her professionalism. "She was with me every step of the way," Robards later recalled.[12]

His collaboration with Jones was less satisfying, partly because of Selznick's interference and partly because Jones was somewhat too old to play the younger Nicole. When Selznick first bought the project in 1946, she was the right age, but by 1961, she was already in her forties and strained to portray the troubled young woman in the film's flashback scenes. The script by Ivan Moffat (*Giant*) remained quite faithful to Fitzgerald's novel. The film begins in the 1920s, when Nicole and Dick Diver are living in luxury on the French Riviera (thanks to Nicole's family fortune), then flashes back to their meeting in a Swiss sanitarium a decade earlier, where he helps to root out the causes of her schizophrenic behavior, primarily her incestuous relationship with her father. As Dr. Diver helps to relieve her symptoms, he begins to fall in love with her. Although his mentor (sensitively played by veteran actor Paul Lukas) tries to warn him of the dangers of romance with a patient, Dick marries Nicole and eventually gives up his practice to care for her and then gradually surrenders to her life of privilege. The film is unusual for portraying the psychiatrist as a flawed character rather than a paragon of wisdom like Montgomery Clift's Freud. The melancholy conclusion, in which Nicole finally leaves the broken and alcoholic Dick for another man, does retain some of the emotional impact of the novel, thanks in part to the haunting musical theme by Sammy Fain.

Other films of 1962 presented a more exalted picture of the psychiatric healer. *Pressure Point*, a low-budget picture produced by Stanley Kramer, cast Sidney Poitier as a dedicated psychiatrist trying to uncover the reasons for the violent antisocial behavior of a young racist played by Bobby Darin. Poitier confirmed his dignified screen presence a year before winning the first-ever Oscar given to a black actor for 1963's *Lilies of the Field*.

In *Pressure Point* baroque flashbacks and dream sequences help to fill in the background of Darin's character, who seems to suffer from the same oedipal traumas that afflicted many other characters in films of the period. He has a harshly critical father and a weak, demanding mother, a family dynamic that was often used to serve up simplistic explanations for aberrant behavior. The film's idealization of the psychiatrist played by Poitier was also very much in keeping with the reverence for analysis that Hollywood filmmakers favored in 1962.

A more believably human psychiatrist appeared in *David and Lisa,* one of the first independently financed features ever to score a major box office success. As the *Saturday Evening Post* reported shortly after the film's release, "*David and Lisa* is the most successful example to date of a new kind of American film, the low-budget picture shot outside the Hollywood Factory System."[13] The film was based on a book—a fictionalized case study—written by a psychiatrist, Dr. Theodore Rubin. It told the story of two young people who fall in love in a sanitarium. It marked the feature debut of two gifted filmmakers, screenwriter Eleanor Perry and director Frank Perry, both of whom won Oscar nominations for their work on the low-budget film.

Although screenwriting was one of the few fields open to women in that period, Eleanor Perry was the only woman to earn a writing nomination in 1962. She was born in Cleveland, where she worked as a playwright for the Cleveland Playhouse and other local theaters. She divorced her first husband and moved to New York, but as she later said, the theater began to lose its appeal. Instead, she was inspired by films of the French New Wave like *The 400 Blows* and *Breathless,* and she turned her attention to screenwriting.[14] Eleanor already had grown children when she married Frank Perry, a man who was sixteen years her junior—quite an unusual arrangement in that era. They teamed up with producer Paul Heller, a former scenic designer who had worked with Frank Perry on a television show, and set out to raise the money on their own.

The budget eventually came to a minuscule $137,000. Heller and the Perrys called on friends and relatives to cough up a few hundred dollars here and a few hundred more there, and cobbled together a limited partnership with thirty-four contributors. (The most notable among them was lyricist E. Y. Harburg, who wrote "Over the Rainbow.") In a documentary series about screenwriting filmed by Terry Sanders and Freida Lee Mock, Eleanor recalled that she tapped any possible source to provide the backing. She even got her son's girlfriend to chip in $300. One wealthy businessman provided a heftier share of the budget, but Eleanor remembered that her heart sank when the man told her that his wife had hated the script. But that was no deterrent to him. "I'll back anything my wife hates," he told Eleanor gleefully.[15]

To play the role of the compassionate psychiatrist, the filmmakers turned to Howard Da Silva, who had been blacklisted during the past decade but made an impressive return to the screen in *David and Lisa*. Of course the more crucial casting was of the two central characters. Keir Dullea had given a strong performance the previous year as a young criminal in *The Hoodlum Priest*. (He secured his most prominent role six years later when he won the lead in Stanley Kubrick's *2001: A Space Odyssey*.) Since he was supposed to be playing a teenager in *David and Lisa*, twenty-five-year-old Dullea feared that he might be too old for the part. But the Perrys felt he could get by with it because of David's intellectual precociousness. Newcomer Janet Margolin, on the other hand, was just eighteen, and she later said, "I got to use all my years of being a troubled, lonely, sensitive, high-strung, miserably shy girl."[16] She noted that Frank Perry did not want her to visit mental hospitals and try to imitate the patients. "He wanted us to draw everything out of ourselves," she reported. Dullea confirmed Margolin's recollection. Shortly after the film's release, he told the *New York Times*, "Frank Perry did not want an imitation of mental disorder. He put it this way: schizophrenia is just an exaggeration of normal quirks. We're all of a rainbow."[17]

In the script David is a brilliant boy with a pathological fear of being touched. In a couple of scenes with his family, we learn that the culprit is the usual bogeyman of Freudian movies of the era, an overbearing mother. Lisa's problems are less explicitly articulated. She is a schizophrenic who speaks only in rhymes, and she seems to share David's suspicion of others. But they are drawn to each other, and the film convincingly conveys the growing attraction between them. A number of scenes achieve genuine poignancy. When the patients visit the art museum in Philadelphia—the same museum that was later the site of Rocky Balboa's climactic training run—Lisa is haunted by a sculpture of a woman and crawls into the woman's lap. "At every showing, audiences cried during that scene," Eleanor later recalled.[18] But the emotional high point comes at the very end, when the frightened David overcomes his phobia and nervously asks Lisa, "Take my hand."

As Eleanor commented in an interview about the making of the film, "In these times of nihilism and the threat of the Bomb, something miraculous is going on between human beings. . . . That's what we're trying to say in this picture: there is a powerful healing quality in love and trust between human beings."[19]

FIGURE 5.2 Janet Margolin and Keir Dullea as the troubled teens in *David and Lisa*. (Screen shot)

The film's modest but unmistakable emotion appealed to audiences wherever it was shown. It had its premiere at the Venice Film Festival in late August and found a small indie distributor that opened the film in December, during the New York newspaper strike. Fortunately, magazine reviews—which played a stronger role in those days—helped to spread the word about the film's strengths. Referring to the neophyte filmmakers, *Time* magazine raved, "Amazingly, this gang of greenhorns has produced a minor masterpiece, easily the best U.S. movie released in 1962." Bolstered by the reviews, *David and Lisa* became a genuine word-of-mouth hit. It played at New York's Plaza Theatre for fifty-one weeks and caught on in art theaters around the country, buoyed by its two top Oscar nominations in the spring.

In addition, teenagers flocked to theaters playing the film; they were drawn to a story featuring lead characters in their own age-group, even though the realistic drama was far removed from their usual favorites, Elvis Presley vehicles and rock 'n' roll movies. They embraced a film that helped to popularize the allure of psychiatry, far more than the bigger-budget productions of *Freud* and *Tender Is the Night,* both of which were box office flops. In the film David's suspicion of the doctor played by Da Silva eventually gives way to admiration and gratitude. In one late-night conversation over chocolate cake and milk, David confesses that he is thinking of becoming a psychiatrist himself.

He was not the only one. The book's author, Dr. Theodore Rubin, said, "The movie had a considerable effect on getting people into the field of psychiatry, and on raising money for mental health. It showed disturbed people as human beings." The movie also increased sales of the book. As Rubin said, "It sold more and more copies over the years. It's been translated into several languages and has sold more than a couple of million copies. It began to be used in a lot of college classes. It has the advantage of being extremely short, so students love it for a book report."[20]

Although these movies centering on psychiatry testified to the influence of Freudian thinking on artists of the era, that influence probably showed more potently when it was more indirect. Many of the memorable films of 1962 explored the inner torment of complex characters, probing their unconscious motivations and conflicts. You could see this psychological influence in the year's Academy Award–winning best picture, *Lawrence of Arabia,* a new kind of screen epic—one that exposed the neurotic tendencies of its flamboyant, masochistic hero. Sam Peckinpah's 1962 western, *Ride the High Country,* introduces the heroine (played by Mariette Hartley) living on an isolated ranch with her widowed father, a religious fanatic. He resists her plans to marry, and she finally lashes out at him and accuses him of harboring repressed desires: "Every single man is the wrong kind of man—except you." Sibling rivalry was at the heart of *What Ever Happened to Baby Jane?,* and even the big-budget musical *Gypsy,* which was written by long-term analysand Arthur Laurents, probed the disappointments that led the ultimate stage mother, Rosalind Russell's Rose, to pour her own frustrated ambitions on to her daughters.

Although psychoanalysis was definitely a modish American pastime, international filmmakers also showed great interest in delving into the unconscious torments of complex characters. Ingmar Bergman was one of the foreign auteurs who demonstrated a psychoanalytic bent in many of his films. *Wild Strawberries* incorporated dreams and memories of the central character, a doctor taking stock of his life. Bergman confirmed his position in the international pantheon with *Wild Strawberries, The Virgin Spring,* and *Through a Glass Darkly.* The latter two films won Oscars for best foreign language film in 1960 and 1961.

Through a Glass Darkly, released in America in 1962, was different from many of Bergman's earlier movies, which had larger casts. *Through a Glass Darkly* was his first "chamber drama," with just four characters. At the time, this film and the two subsequent Bergman movies, *Winter Light* and *The Silence,* were discussed mainly in terms of their skeptical examinations of religious faith. In *Through a Glass Darkly* the central character, Karin (Harriet Andersson), is a schizophrenic who is waiting for God to appear to her. But all she sees is a large spider before doctors cart her back to the loony bin. Critics focused on Bergman's growing disillusionment with religion, but it is just as relevant to highlight the film's fascination with the psychoanalytic issues that animated *Freud* and *David and Lisa* in 1962.

Karin's mental instability is the central theme of the film, and we are encouraged to see her father's coldness as one trigger for her madness, though the arguments of nature versus nurture are complicated when we learn that Karin's mother also suffered from mental problems. Still, the role of parental neglect in Karin's decline cannot be overlooked. Bergman himself was the son of a minister, and he frequently admitted that his chafing against his stern father was one of the major influences of his life. In the film Gunnar Bjornstrand's David is a novelist who uses his daughter's instability as a source for his fiction. Whatever the reasons for her psychic wounds, Karin acts out by seducing her younger brother, Minus (Lars Passgard), a plot development drenched in the Freudian gospel of the era. We are told that Karin has lost her sexual desire for her husband (Max von Sydow), but her desires are inflamed by her brother. Although the incest scene is played in an indirect, nonsensationalized fashion, such a scene was strictly forbidden in Hollywood movies at the time, and it was cut in many American prints in deference to local censors.

Despite the superb acting and cinematography in *Through a Glass Darkly,* one reason that it does not hold up as well as some of Bergman's other films is that this intense family romance seems a bit simplistic when viewed through a contemporary lens. Nevertheless, the gradual disintegration of Karin is brilliantly rendered by Andersson in one of the finest performances in the Bergman canon. Brendan Gill, the *New Yorker's* critic at the time, wrote aptly, "Harriet Andersson gives a well-nigh perfect performance. Her mad scenes have a terrifying plausibility; she is doomed, and we know she is doomed, but, as in real life, we long for her to pull back from the brink in time." Her plight is every bit as poignant as that of the title characters in *David and Lisa.* Both of these films demonstrate the devotion to psychological scrutiny that characterized films of 1962.

Half a world away, master Indian director Satyajit Ray showed how far-reaching these psychological themes had become. Ray's 1962 film, *Devi (Goddess),* did not achieve the box office success of *Through a Glass Darkly.* Pauline

Kael, a Ray enthusiast, speculated on the different American reactions to these two directors in her review of *Devi*. "Ingmar Bergman, who was also a slow starter with American audiences, has definitely caught on," Kael wrote. "Why not Ray?" She suggested that Bergman's interest in religious questions captured the fancy of aspiring eggheads on the art house circuit. "Bergman is not a deep thinker," Kael declared, "but he is an artist who moves audiences deeply by calling up their buried fears and feelings. People come out of his movies with 'something to think about' or, at least, to talk about."[21]

As it happens, *Devi* also touches on the questions of religious faith that intrigued audiences for *Through a Glass Darkly*. In this case, however, the issues are somewhat different, since the film is set in the nineteenth century, on an aristocratic estate, when the master of the house becomes convinced that his seventeen-year-old daughter-in-law is the incarnation of the goddess Kali. Soon the neighboring community has become swept up in his religious frenzy, and beggars bring their children to the young woman asking her to heal them. More significantly, she starts to believe in her own magical powers, much to the dismay of her educated husband.

The film's sharp comments on superstition and religious zealotry have been examined in many different cultures and have often provoked controversy. But like *Through a Glass Darkly*, *Devi* is as much a psychological case study as a religious exploration. The early scenes subtly but clearly establish that the master of the house is attracted to his beautiful young daughter-in-law, especially when her husband goes off to university to complete his studies. During an intense dream he imagines her face merging with that of the goddess Kali, and he announces to the household that the stunning young woman is a contemporary incarnation of the goddess. Kael noted the "many Freudian undertones" in the film and suggested that "religion is the last outpost of the old man's sensuality, his return to childhood and 'Ma' love."[22] Freud himself argued that religious zeal often grew out of frustrated sexual desire, and if this argument is subtly tendered in *Devi*, we cannot help but notice the many jealousies in the household that are triggered when the family patriarch anoints his nubile young daughter-in-law as a goddess. The story ends in tragedy that grows out of the characters' psychological discord.

Ray had spent time in the West, so it is not surprising that he came in contact with the psychoanalytic thinking of the era. Young American directors John Frankenheimer and Arthur Penn spent time on the analyst's couch and brought their curiosity about troubled human behavior into many of their films. *All Fall Down*, *The Manchurian Candidate*, and *The Miracle Worker* all touched on family conflict and demonstrated sharp psychological insight. Psychoanalysis had an equally potent influence on director Sidney Lumet, who made two films in 1962 that were adapted from classic plays, Arthur Miller's *A View from the Bridge* and Eugene O'Neill's *Long Day's Journey into Night*. Both Miller and O'Neill had experience with psychoanalysis, and the Freudian gospel showed up in their work. *A View from the Bridge* is the story of a dockworker in love with his niece and increasingly jealous of the young man who courts her. The tragedy that ensues grows directly out of his buried, unconscious passion.

O'Neill had demonstrated his interest in Freudian psychology in several of his early plays. In *Strange Interlude* the characters broke the fourth wall to address the audience and reveal their innermost feelings. *Mourning Becomes Electra* was a modern-day reworking of the Electra myth centering on a young woman's unnatural love for her father. But *Long Day's Journey into Night* was the author's most personal and artful translation of his own family turmoil into drama. O'Neill had written the play years before it was actually produced; he considered it so nakedly personal that he did not want it performed, and it was only after his death that the playwright's widow gave permission to mount a production. Audiences were stunned by its insights into family conflicts. Unlike the literal-minded asides to the audience in *Strange Interlude*, *Long Day's Journey* represented a far more subtle expression of psychoanalytic theory. This searing drama illustrates the dark passions and guilty secrets hidden just beneath the surface of everyday life. In one of the great passages in the play, the older son, Jamie, who has appeared to be deeply solicitous toward his sickly younger brother, unleashes the hatred that he harbors, recalling his jealousy when he saw himself supplanted in his mother's affections. It is the oedipal drama removed from the textbook and transmuted into art. Jason Robards Jr., who had extensive experience in analysis, interpreted the role masterfully on both stage and screen.

Sidney Lumet was also enthralled with psychoanalysis and frequently examined family dynamics in the films that he directed. He admitted that *Long Day's Journey* touched deeply personal chords for him. In a documentary filmed before his death in 2011 and finally released in 2016, Lumet gave extensive interviews to the director, Nancy Buirski, and revealed many of the personal currents in his work. Several of his films—including *12 Angry Men*, *The Pawnbroker*, *The Sea Gull*, *Daniel*, *Running on Empty*, and his final feature, *Before the Devil Knows You're Dead*—focused on family relationships, and Lumet noted that family has always been the cornerstone of drama, going back to Greek tragedy. In the documentary, he spoke about some parallels between his own family history and the drama of *Long Day's Journey into Night*. The patriarch of

O'Neill's play is an actor known for his stinginess. Lumet's own father, Baruch Lumet, was a star of the Yiddish theater, and he brought young Sidney into acting, just as James Tyrone paves the way for his son Jamie. Sidney spoke about his father's obsession with money, his desperation on seeing empty theaters, and his rivalry with fellow Yiddish actors—themes that were at the heart of O'Neill's classic drama, even if the milieu was different.[23]

Partly because of his identification with the material, Lumet's interpretation of *Long Day's Journey into Night* remained one of the high points of the director's career. Pauline Kael, who was not always an admirer of Lumet's films, was a major champion of *Long Day's Journey*. As she wrote, "*Journey* is, at last, an American family classic: the usual embarrassments have been transcended and the family theme is raised to mythic heights."[24]

This autobiographical drama about O'Neill, his parents, and older brother is set in 1912, just before O'Neill was sent to a sanatorium to cure his tuberculosis. In the course of a single day the dynamics of a dysfunctional family are explored, with patriarch James Tyrone, a miserly alcoholic actor, his drug-addicted wife, Mary, alcoholic ne'er-do-well son, Jamie, and youngest son, Edmund, an aspiring poet (standing in for O'Neill).

Ely Landau, a successful television producer of the 1950s, made the O'Neill play his feature debut as a movie producer, partnering with Joseph E. Levine and his company, Embassy Pictures. Lumet had directed an acclaimed television production of O'Neill's *The Iceman Cometh* with Robards, so he was a natural choice to direct. All of the casting was inspired. Robards was the only holdover from the Broadway production, which had starred husband and wife Fredric March and Florence Eldridge, with Bradford Dillman as Edmund. For the movie version, Katharine Hepburn brought star power to the ensemble; she had been a major Hollywood actress for thirty years, though she had taken breaks from movies to return to the theater, in productions of Shakespeare and other classics. Hepburn considered *Long Day's Journey* the greatest drama written for the American stage, and she was eager to tackle the role of morphine-addicted Mary Tyrone.

Hepburn tried to convince her long-term partner, Spencer Tracy, to take the role of James Tyrone, but Tracy was wary of a nonstudio production and declined.[25] Esteemed British actor Ralph Richardson (*The Heiress, The Fallen Idol*) stepped into the role and acquitted himself admirably. The *New York Times* found his performance "controlled and magnificent." Dean Stockwell had started as a child actor in the 1940s, playing Gregory Peck's son in *Gentleman's Agreement* and the title character in the provocative fantasy film *The Boy with Green Hair*. When he matured, Stockwell sought out challenging roles like

the murderous mastermind in *Compulsion,* a fictionalized version of the notorious Leopold-and-Loeb case (in which he costarred with Bradford Dillman,
the original Edmund from the stage production of *Journey*). And Jason Robards
scored a triumph in what was only his fourth feature film. As Stanley Kauffmann wrote, Robards "repeats and deepens" his stage performance in the film
version of O'Neill's play.

Reactions to Hepburn's performance were mixed. The *New York Times*
called her performance "uneven," and Kauffmann praised her acting skill but
considered her "miscast." But Kael had no reservations whatsoever. As she
wrote, "The most beautiful comedienne of the thirties and forties has become
our greatest tragedienne; seeing her transitions in *Journey,* the way she can look
eighteen or eighty at will . . . one can understand why the appellation 'the
divine' has sometimes been awarded to certain actresses." And Kael went on
to rave, "For the other performers—Ralph Richardson, Jason Robards Jr., and
Dean Stockwell, for the director Sidney Lumet, and for the cinematographer
Boris Kaufman, perhaps even a critic can express simple gratitude."[26]

As Kael suggests, it is worth acknowledging the cinematic virtues of this
filmed play. Although the screenplay credit read, "Written by Eugene O'Neill,"
and his dialogue was transcribed almost intact, the film does not have the stag-
iness of many theatrical adaptations. Kaufman, an Oscar winner for *On the
Waterfront* and a frequent collaborator of Lumet's during the early part of the
director's career, contributed sharply etched black-and-white cinematography.
This mise-en-scène is further embellished by the art direction of Richard Sylbert, a rising talent who also designed *Walk on the Wild Side, The Connection,*
and *The Manchurian Candidate* in 1962. All of their efforts rescued the film from
the static quality of much filmed theater. Lumet uses telling close-ups to
heighten the drama in a very different way than audiences could have experienced it in the theater. In an early scene, for example, just after breakfast, a brief
but startling close-up shows Robards scrutinizing his mother suspiciously. A
later, brilliantly rendered scene at their lunch table begins with a shot of all four
characters, but then as the camera roams among them in silence, the scrutiny
of their faces and body language is astutely revealing.

Kael's tribute to the fluidity of Hepburn's performance is borne out by
the early scene in which Mary reminisces to her housekeeper about her first
meeting with James Tyrone, and the actress does indeed seem to shed thirty
years and return to her girlish self. Yet in later scenes in which she is in the
throes of morphine addiction, she dispenses with all vanity to appear shockingly ravaged. Hepburn would later say that the role in *Long Day's Journey*

FIGURE 5.3 The Tyrone family quartet: Jason Robards Jr., Ralph Richardson, Dean Stockwell, and Katharine Hepburn in *Long Day's Journey into Night.* (Screen shot)

was the best of her career, and she received her ninth Oscar nomination for her performance.

All of this craftsmanship was in service of a searing psychological drama. In some respects this film resembles the psychological chamber dramas of Ingmar Bergman, especially *Through a Glass Darkly,* also set at a family's summer home over the course of a single day. Coincidentally, the Swedes had been great supporters of O'Neill's works, and the Royal Dramatic Theatre in Stockholm had mounted the world premiere of *Long Day's Journey into Night* in February 1956. The 1962 film, like the play, illustrates how the past permeates the characters' present lives. Each of the four characters has at least one long monologue revealing his or her personal demons. For example, James Tyrone remembers his early triumphs as an actor as well as the painful compromises he made in his worship of the almighty dollar.

These pointed scenes of the male characters' memories take up much of the last part of the film, but it ends with Mary Tyrone, completely lost in a drug-induced stupor, coming downstairs with her wedding dress in tow. Her final monologue bursts the boundaries of realism, as she forgets where she is and returns to her convent days, reliving her hopes as a young aspiring nun. Mary surrenders to memories far more vivid than her present life. It is a scene that might have been acted out by one of Freud's patients under hypnosis. Her disorientation is mirrored by Lumet's directorial choices; the camera pulls farther and farther back as if retreating into distant memory. Then there is a startling cut to a close-up of Mary as her immersion in the past is shattered by her bittersweet recollection of the crucial turning point in her life: "Then I fell in love with James Tyrone, and I was so happy—for a time." The interplay of past and present, of memory and fantasy, has never been more tellingly rendered on film. O'Neill's piercing insight into human psychology, beautifully transcribed by Hepburn and Lumet, socks the drama home.

6 · ADAPTED FOR THE SCREEN

Prestige and Provocation

While *Long Day's Journey into Night* demonstrated psychological depth, it also illustrated a salient aspect of filmmaking in 1962: most movies produced were adaptations from other media. "Screen Originals Drop to 15%" blazed the *Hollywood Reporter* headline of January 22, 1962, trumpeting the facts of moviemaking in the era. The trade paper pointed out that "writing of original stories for the screen is about at its lowest ebb in the industry's history." Whether drawing from the stage, books, magazines, or television, Hollywood studios and filmmakers worldwide regularly turned to other sources for their storytelling muse. This continued a tradition that had been in effect since the advent of the sound era in the late 1920s. Those early sound hits—from the first "talking picture," *The Jazz Singer,* to *Cimarron* and *All Quiet on the West Front* and early horror classics *Frankenstein* and *Dracula*—were all adapted from plays and novels. This trend continued to dominate production, and many of the celebrated films of 1939 were adaptations (*Gone with the Wind, The Wizard of Oz, Wuthering Heights,* and *Stagecoach,* to name a few).

This trend was even more prevalent by the early 1960s. The studios had lost a sizable portion of their revenue through the forced divestment of their movie theater ownership and the entrenchment of television, leading to a severe decline in movie attendance in the postwar era. Thus the cachet of a previously produced property was attractive to the now penurious studios. A presold track record from best sellers, popular stage shows, and teleplays had an appeal to both movie audiences and studio accountants.

Many of the movies of 1962 were adapted from works by great writers like F. Scott Fitzgerald (*Tender Is the Night*), Vladimir Nabokov (*Lolita*), Herman

Melville (*Billy Budd*), Edgar Allan Poe (*The Premature Burial, Tales of Terror*), Ernest Hemingway (*Adventures of a Young Man*), as well as master playwrights Eugene O'Neill (*Long Day's Journey into Night*), Tennessee Williams (*Sweet Bird of Youth, Period of Adjustment*), and Arthur Miller (*A View from the Bridge*). Nowadays filmmakers rarely turn to literature or theater for inspiration; acclaimed novels and plays are seldom turned into movies. Of course there are still a few movies adapted from prestigious literary works, but the numbers are minuscule, and those that do manage to get produced struggle to find an audience. For example, Ian McEwan's provocative 2014 novel *The Children Act* was adapted for the screen and had its world premiere at the Toronto International Film Festival in 2017. Despite a superb performance by Emma Thompson and the presence of a gifted young British actor, Fionn Whitehead, the film did not reach theaters for a full year—and then only a tiny number of theaters. It was released mainly via streaming services and vanished quickly.

Although there are other examples of current adaptations, they seldom have literary merit and reach the screen only if they can be mass-marketed. Young adult novels are calculated into fantasy film franchises. Comic books become superhero spectaculars. Graphic novels and video games have replaced traditional text to stimulate filmmakers' imaginations. Movies emphasizing action and spectacle are supreme at the studios. Since the international market accounts for the vast majority of motion picture revenue in the twenty-first century (more than 70 percent), movies have been simplified for the broadest global audience. The visual and visceral experience is paramount.

It was an entirely different scenario in 1962. Broadway provided recent successes like *The Miracle Worker, Two for the Seesaw,* the London imports *Five Finger Exercise* and *A Taste of Honey,* along with the hit musicals *The Music Man* and *Gypsy.* Television was mined for serious dramas like *Days of Wine and Roses* and Rod Serling's *Requiem for a Heavyweight.* Popular and critically lauded fiction offered the greatest trove of filmable material. In addition to the acclaimed best seller *To Kill a Mockingbird,* many of the year's most durable films were based on novels: *The Manchurian Candidate, Jules and Jim, David and Lisa, Advise and Consent, Sundays and Cybele, Cape Fear, Shoot the Piano Player, Lonely Are the Brave,* and *What Ever Happened to Baby Jane?* Additionally, *The Man Who Shot Liberty Valance, The Loneliness of the Long Distance Runner,* and *Pressure Point* came from short stories. One of the pioneering independent films, *The Connection,* was adapted from a play. Nonfiction was the source for inspiring action adventures, biopics, and historical dramas like

The Longest Day, Mutiny on the Bounty, Birdman of Alcatraz, The Counterfeit Traitor, Merrill's Marauders, and *Lawrence of Arabia.*

The short supply of high-quality original scripts from the Hollywood studios was also a result of cost-cutting measures throughout the postwar period, which included the shedding of in-house writers. Because adaptations constituted the vast majority of film scripts, the Academy of Motion Picture Arts and Sciences was challenged to fill the original screenplay category for award recognition in 1962. The writers' branch nominated the enormously popular but threadbare comedy *That Touch of Mink,* following the lead of the Writers Guild, which named it "Best Written Comedy," a testament to the lack of competition (or imagination). There were a few worthier original scripts, such as N. B. Stone's *Ride the High Country,* which had been short-listed by its distributor, MGM. Unfortunately, the studio's botched release and the film's subsequent poor box office killed any chance at a nomination.

A more distinguished entry in the thin field was the biographical drama *Freud.* The writers' branch then quarried the international arena, a trend that had begun in the post–World War II years with the influx of foreign films. Foreign-language films dominated the category in 1962: the art house hits *Through a Glass Darkly, Last Year at Marienbad,* and the eventual winner, *Divorce Italian Style,* rounded out the nominees. By contrast, the adapted screenplay category was so overloaded that the final five nominees merely sampled the full range of remarkable movies from the year: *David and Lisa, Lawrence of Arabia, Lolita, The Miracle Worker,* and the winner, *To Kill a Mockingbird.*

The *Hollywood Reporter* further calculated that 70 percent of studio movies and well-financed independents were based on books and other story sources, with an additional 15 percent from plays. Renowned filmmaker Fritz Lang, who made one of the screen's landmark silent films, *Metropolis,* in 1927, and was one of the notable European émigrés to Hollywood in the 1930s, verified those statistics. In a 1962 article, Lang lamented the economic facts of life in the movie industry: "My whole life I have been fighting against the fact that many of the motion picture corporations and producers do not use scripts or stories that were written originally for the screen. They want best-selling books."[1] Lang made his final film, *The 1,000 Eyes of Dr. Mabuse,* an adaptation of a novel, in 1960.

Director Samuel Fuller (*Pickup on South Street, Shock Corridor, The Big Red One*) could testify to Lang's experience battling for original material. In 1962 Fuller helmed a film version of the exploits of American forces during the World War II Burma campaign, *Merrill's Marauders,* from Charlton Ogburn Jr.'s true account (a book). The movie starred the ill-fated Jeff Chandler in his final film role. (He died from surgical malpractice after completing the shoot.) Fuller was trying to get his original script for *The Big Red One* produced by Jack L. Warner, but the wily executive steered him into this adaptation first and economized by casting the film with television actors under contract at the studio. With *Marauders,* Fuller made a harrowing, realistic film about the horrors of war and succeeded perhaps too well, as Warner took the movie from him and tacked on an upbeat, conventional epilogue that infuriated the director. Fuller was not permitted to make *The Big Red One* until 1980. He was so disgruntled by the *Merrill's Marauders* experience that he vented to the *Hollywood Reporter* in 1963 about the deficiency of support for original works, lambasting Tinseltown for "above all, lack of guts. Why gamble on a virgin idea born [in] movieland when the studio will back you on an accredited winner?"[2]

Fuller and Lang might have been pleased that the percentage of original screenplays has grown significantly in recent years. The annual Writers Guild list of screenplays eligible for awards consideration now shows a larger number of original screenplays than adaptations. But one would be hard-pressed to argue that this shift has led to a boom in cinematic masterpieces. Looking back at the history of Hollywood, there is no doubt that some of the most memorable movies—including *Citizen Kane, Sunset Boulevard, Fargo,* and *Shakespeare in Love*—have been original scripts created by gifted writers. But an even larger number have been adapted from other media. This includes many Oscar-winning films, from *Gone with the Wind* and *Casablanca* to *L.A. Confidential* and *Brokeback Mountain.* And it includes quite a few films that won no awards but are now ranked among the greatest of all American movies, including *The Magnificent Ambersons, The Night of the Hunter, Vertigo,* and *Point Blank,* to name just a few. The reason that the number of original screenplays has multiplied is not because of a sudden artistic renaissance but because executives are fearful that literary and theatrical material may be too rarefied for fanboys and less literate international audiences, by far the most coveted demographic today. The quality of films has actually declined in part because of the rejection of adaptations, the mainstay of the film business in 1962.

One adaptation that year, *The Counterfeit Traitor,* an espionage thriller starring William Holden, was stewarded by veteran writer-director George Seaton (*A Day at the Races, Miracle on 34th Street, The Country Girl*) and proved solid at the box office. Filmed primarily in Europe, it was based on the nonfiction account of American-born Swedish oil executive Eric Erickson, played by

Holden, who spied for the Allies by declaring himself a Nazi sympathizer. This subterfuge enabled him to visit Germany dozens of times in the guise of helping to develop its synthetic oil industry. One of his contacts was a woman of position played by Lilli Palmer, who underscores the moral necessity of opposing the Nazis.

Seaton introduces a variation on the theme of the "banality of evil," a concept proposed by political theorist Hannah Arendt after observing the 1961 trial of Nazi war criminal Adolf Eichmann, who was hanged in Israel in June 1962, just after the release of Seaton's film in April. Arendt's book about Eichmann would be published a year later, but Seaton's approach anticipated Arendt's theory in chilling scenes of naturalistic horror punctuating a deceptively calm narrative among the picturesque European locations.

In key sequences, Palmer's character is wracked by guilt because information that she transmitted to the Allies resulted in the deaths of children in a bombing raid. She visits a church and unwittingly confesses her involvement to a Gestapo agent pretending to be a priest. Her later execution is depicted as a routine occurrence in the prison, witnessed by a horrified Holden, who has been detained for questioning. In another scene, one of Holden's German contacts has died, so he must retrieve incriminating evidence in the contact's house, but he is almost thwarted by the young son of the deceased, who blindly follows the indoctrination of the Nazi Youth movement. In these scenes and others, Seaton establishes a matter-of-fact tone to the proceedings, underlining the existence of evil among seemingly ordinary and everyday circumstances.

Of course not all evil in movies of that year was of the "banal" variety, and not all adaptations were taken from prestigious novels or nonfiction books. One of the vilest characters in film history appears in *Cape Fear*. That noir thriller, adapted by James R. Webb from the pulp novel *The Executioners* by John D. MacDonald, proved to be a challenge to the censors both at home and abroad. The movie gave Gregory Peck his second role that year as a southern lawyer, as his character Sam Bowden finds his family terrorized by an ex-con seeking revenge for his incarceration due to Bowden's testimony eight years earlier. Robert Mitchum memorably plays the psychopathic stalker, Max Cady, whose reptilian cunning drives the upstanding Bowden to bend the law. A desperate Bowden even acquiesces in the brutal beating of Cady by hired thugs. Bowden's ethical lapses in dealing with Cady stand in sharp contrast to Peck's depiction of the nobler Atticus Finch from *To Kill a Mockingbird*.

Director J. Lee Thompson (*The Guns of Navarone*), an admirer of Alfred Hitchcock, employs tropes from the master of suspense in character point of

view and camera angles (abetted by frequent Hitchcock collaborators, art director Robert Boyle and film editor George Tomasini). Thompson also hired composer Bernard Herrmann, another Hitchcock collaborator at that time. Herrmann's effectively unsettling score and the pervasive tone of moral ambiguity
represent distinctive noir elements, deepened by the outstanding black-and-
white photography of Sam Leavitt (*A Star Is Born, The Defiant Ones, Exodus*).

The film ran afoul of the Production Code Administration at script stage.
The censorship board objected to the use of the word "rape" from the novel,
particularly involving the threat to Bowden's wife (Polly Bergen) and young
daughter (Lori Martin), and expunged it from the script. Nevertheless, even
with the dialogue toned down, the sexual threat to both mother and daughter
remains frighteningly clear. As the daughter Thompson had wanted to cast
Hayley Mills, a young actress he had worked with previously (in 1959's *Tiger
Bay*), but she was too busy rising to stardom in Walt Disney movies. The PCA
also cautioned against the use of graphic violence, which is curtailed in the final
cut. Apparently even a modified version was too much for certain territories,
however, as Bergen complained to the press when the British censors hacked
away at the finished film for the UK release, leaving much of her role on the
cutting-room floor.[3]

Acclaimed filmmaker Martin Scorsese found no such restrictions when he
remade the movie in 1991, ratcheting up the viciousness. In one key scene in
the original, Mitchum beats bar pickup Barrie Chase behind closed doors,
while in the Scorsese version Robert De Niro assaults Illeana Douglas savagely
on-screen. Of course the passing years brought different sensitivities regarding what was considered viewable. In 1962 the Bowden family dog is poisoned
by Cady, a scene omitted entirely in the 1991 film. However, Herrmann's original score was so masterful in conveying Cady's malignity that Scorsese used it
again, with new orchestrations but essentially intact.

Partly due to the inhibitions of the times, the original film stands above the
remake, owing much to Mitchum's realistic, nuanced performance as opposed
to De Niro's overtly sadistic, exaggerated take on Cady. Bergen later recalled
the scene on the houseboat (where Bowden takes his family to hide from
Cady) in which Mitchum brutalizes her character. She described the episode
as the single most frightening moment of her career, since Mitchum's acting
was so convincing.[4] At an anniversary screening of the film in 2017, Barrie
Chase remembered Mitchum as deceptively focused, saying, "He was totally
prepared, and then threw it away as if it was improvised. He was always in that
character . . . there was this dichotomy of him being very attractive, and very

FIGURE 6.1 Robert Mitchum as one of the screen's great villains, Max Cady, in *Cape Fear.* (Screen shot)

menacing."[5] Incredibly, De Niro, otherwise a consummate actor, would score a best actor Oscar nomination for his over-the-top turn; no such luck in 1962 for Mitchum, who was not even mentioned as a serious contender. The American Film Institute would later rank Mitchum's characterization in the top thirty in its list of memorable screen villains, well-deserved recognition at last for his distinctive performance.

Post–World War II filmmaking took advantage of location shooting in the global arena largely for economic reasons. The sheer number of films shot overseas (55 percent of all films released in 1962), combined with the overall decrease in studio production, adversely impacted employment in the diminished Hollywood dream factories. One notorious example of peripatetic filmmaking that contributed to this labor distress was *Cleopatra,* Twentieth Century-Fox's mammoth historical adaptation starring Elizabeth Taylor, hopelessly over budget in Rome. That financial albatross contributed enormously to the temporary suspension of movie production at the Los Angeles studio in the summer of 1962. The epic's producer, veteran Walter Wanger (*Stagecoach, Scarlet Street, I Want to Live!*), had no patience for Hollywood bemoaning runaway production, stating, "The only thing that ran away was the audience." He pointed out that filmmaking "has always been an international business,"[6] as he named the foreign stars and talent that thrived in Hollywood during the Golden Age—for example, Ernst Lubitsch, Maurice Chevalier, and Marlene

Dietrich (not mentioning others like Greta Garbo, Billy Wilder, Charles Boyer, Fritz Lang, and Ingrid Bergman).

Cleopatra's historic cost overruns were due to Taylor's demands and other delays, adding up to a record-setting $44 million total budget, and threatening to bankrupt Twentieth Century-Fox. Taylor's unprecedented salary of $1.3 million (which doubled by the time the film's accounting was finished) underscored the trend of spiraling costs. Although studio insiders and the sycophantic press corps often portrayed Taylor as the villainess in the ongoing melodrama, she can also be viewed as a pioneer fighting for fair compensation for women, a battle that is still being waged in the twenty-first century. Marlon Brando had also secured a record salary for the new version of *Mutiny on the Bounty*, but his compensation did not draw nearly as much criticism as Taylor's payday.

Long before saturation media coverage of celebrities became commonplace, frequent news bulletins throughout the year kept curious millions worldwide titillated with the shenanigans of Taylor and Richard Burton on and off the set of *Cleopatra*, which was filming at Rome's Cinecittà studios. The co-stars' romance and scandalous behavior (they were both married to other partners at the time) fascinated the press and public alike, with coverage so extensive that even the Vatican commented, negatively, on the pop culture phenomenon. Life was imitating art, as the fictionalized decadence of modern Rome depicted in *La Dolce Vita* just two years earlier had now been realized by the grand soap opera of the bloated epic, complete with a cadre of image-hungry paparazzi (a term coined by the Fellini film).

As Wanger recalled, "I have been told by responsible journalists that there was more world interest in *Cleopatra* . . . and in its stars—Elizabeth Taylor, Richard Burton, and Rex Harrison—than in any event of 1962."[7] He was not exaggerating. Taylor was in the news so often that she was ranked number six in the 1962 exhibitor poll of top ten box office stars, though she didn't even have a movie in theaters that year. By the time *Cleopatra* finally opened in June 1963, it had been snidely dubbed "the romp on the Nile."

A far more modest overseas production, *Lisa*, was filmed on location in Europe and North Africa and directed by 1930s' veteran screenwriter Philip Dunne (*The Rains Came, How Green Was My Valley, The Ghost and Mrs. Muir*). His new picture was adapted from the novel *The Inspector* by Jan de Hartog. *Lisa* deals with a Holocaust survivor (Dolores Hart) aided by a Dutch police inspector (Stephen Boyd) in her efforts to emigrate to Palestine, fleeing former Nazi agents who plan to transport her to a life of prostitution in South America. *Show* magazine capsulized the "Hollywood headache" of runaway production in a favorable review, noting that unlike the "polyglot hodgepodges" that often resulted from international filmmaking, "as an example of the runaway movie, *Lisa* is the exception rather than the rule."

Lisa is most notable for a controversial marketing trend. The movie was at the center of a dispute between *New York Times* film critic Bosley Crowther and the distributor, Twentieth Century-Fox, which he accused of using an inappropriate exploitation campaign to sell the serious drama. Crowther was incensed over the "lurid" ad copy ("They Used Me Like an Animal"; "They Sold Me as Human Cargo") designed by the studio to entice ticket buyers. Crowther's objections, which he raised in his review, motivated the studio to rebut the charge. But the brouhaha forced Fox to alter its approach, highlighting the adventure and chase components of the story instead of the theme of sexual slavery. Fox's misbegotten advertising campaign for a Holocaust refugee drama like *Lisa* also illustrates that the major studios were not above using exploitation tactics to sell upmarket films. Unfortunately, the public response to the controversy and the film was general indifference, as it achieved only tepid ticket sales.

Perhaps the studio's original plan of selling *Lisa* to the masses might have been more effective, but the fact that it bowed to Crowther's indignation is telling in an era that relied heavily on reviews and newspaper advertising to market movies. Twentieth Century-Fox and every other distributor could ill afford to alienate the most powerful film critic in the country. As a major participant in that same studio's heyday, filmmaker Dunne could only reminisce about how such things were handled in bygone days. On another occasion he had offhandedly dismissed the rosy nostalgia for Hollywood's past with his observant quip, "Had I known it was the Golden Age of Hollywood, I would have enjoyed it more."[8]

Sensationalist marketing tactics continued to arouse the press. Reporting in the *New York Times,* Peter Bart, the future film producer and editor of *Variety,* took notice of the "racier" trend in advertising by pointing out the lowdown approach Columbia took in selling the already conspicuously titled melodrama, *Walk on the Wild Side.* In its review of *Days of Wine and Roses,* a sobering look at alcoholism, *Variety* cautioned Warner Bros. against the use of "superficial sordidness for its own sake" in selling the worthy drama. Even former president Eisenhower weighed in on the occasion of his presidential library opening in conservative Kansas that year, scorning the use of "filth" to sell books and motion pictures.

Inevitably all this lowbrow salesmanship, combined with some modifications of the Production Code, drew the attention of the morals police and self-
appointed moral guardians. The specter of censorship, which had seemed to
be in decline, resurfaced in the early 1960s, when city and state boards began
enforcing censorship laws that had either lain dormant or arose in new
legislation.

The stranglehold of the Production Code (aka the Hays Code), strictly
enforced in the 1930s and 1940s, had been loosening throughout the 1950s, and
the further relaxation of restrictions in October 1961 had paved the way for
exploration of more adult subject matter. The full liberalization of the screen
would occur later in the decade. In 1962 the studios were still obliged to cater
to the PCA and also sought the approval of the Legion of Decency, which had
considerable influence with its ratings classification system.

The Catholic censorship board was dismayed that of 375 films it reviewed
that year, only 20 percent were suitable for family audiences. *Long Day's Journey
into Night* (alcoholism and drug addiction), *Freud* (psychosexual neuroses),
Advise and Consent (homosexuality), and *Divorce Italian Style* (extramarital passion) were all given "Separate Classification," reserved for films that, "while not
morally offensive in themselves," required analysis and explication by mature
adults. Despite escaping the black mark of an objectionable rating, these films
were still viewed by the Legion with a skeptical eye. The potentially inflammatory *Lolita* had undergone intense scrutiny during its production by both the
PCA and the Legion, and the final release version was diluted enough for the
self-appointed moral gatekeepers that it was ultimately awarded a Code seal
and the Legion's Separate Classification compromise.

Producer James B. Harris recalls the protracted negotiations to win the
approval of the Legion of Decency after the movie had secured a Code seal.
"The Legion office was located on Madison Avenue, at the back end of St. Pat-
rick's Cathedral," Harris reports. "It's now a hotel." The man in charge of the
Catholic watchdog office, Monsignor Little, screened the picture and told Harris and director Stanley Kubrick they had a problem. As Harris explains, "If
the movie was condemned by the Legion, they would send out a letter to all the
Catholic churches in the country that their congregations should not see the
picture. And they also threatened theaters that if they ran the picture, their
theaters would be condemned for a year." Negotiations dragged on for close
to six months while Monsignor Little screened the movie for groups of priests
and nuns to solicit their opinions. "There were actually an amazing number of
cards that were favorable," Harris says. "Monsignor Little admitted that." Still,
the monsignor had the final say, and he would not relent. The scene that both-

FIGURE 6.2 Sue Lyon joins Peter Sellers at the London premiere of *Lolita*. (Photofest)

ered him most took place after Humbert (James Mason) marries Charlotte Haze (Shelley Winters) in order to get closer to her daughter. Lolita is off at summer camp, and Humbert and Charlotte are in bed together, making love— or trying to. "The way Stanley shot it," Harris states, "Humbert is continually looking at the picture of Lolita on the bedside table. Monsignor Little said, 'He is looking at the picture in order to get sexually stimulated because he can't get sexually stimulated by his wife. That's perverted.'" Kubrick wanted to retain the droll scene, but he agreed to reduce the number of shots of Humbert staring at the photograph. "That's how we got it through," Harris says in some disgust. "It's a negotiation. We also had to agree to the proviso that nobody under the age of eighteen could see the picture. That meant when we had our premieres in New York and in Beverly Hills, Sue Lyon could not watch the movie."[9]

Another drawn-out contretemps embroiled *The Connection*, the celluloid version of Jack Gelber's play (originally produced by New York's avant-garde Living Theater) about heroin-addicted, racially diverse jazz musicians, directed by pioneering maverick filmmaker Shirley Clarke. Clarke was a seminal figure in the independent film movement (the so-called New American cinema), especially as a woman director. Her documentaries *Robert Frost: A Lover's Quarrel with the World* (Academy Award winner, 1963) and *Portrait of Jason* (1967), about a gay black hustler, added to the National Film Registry in 2015, epitomize her credentials. *The Connection* was her narrative feature debut.

Although *The Connection* originally premiered at the 1961 Cannes Film Festival, its release was held up for more than a year in New York (and then shut down by the police on opening day) after the New York State Board of Regents denied it an exhibition license. The stink raised by the film's critics and censors involved the repeated use of the word "shit" (even though it was mostly used as a drug reference), along with brief glances at pornographic magazines and the speculation on one character's homosexuality. The controversy elevated the independent film's profile, earning a showing at the White House. To the relief of some conservative officials and observers, President and Mrs. Kennedy were not in residence and missed the screening. Ultimately the filmmakers prevailed when the New York State Court of Appeals ruled in the fall of 1962 that the film was not obscene. It was the first time that the court had overruled the state censor.

One enterprising exhibitor had boldly booked *The Connection* in his Scottsdale, Arizona, theater in February 1962 while the film was still being dragged through the courts in New York, and it scored at the box office. This case demonstrated the impact of the art house movement, with maverick theater owners and independent distributors circumventing established practices at the end of the studio era. Clarke expressed the independent filmmakers' point of view: "Right now I'm revolting against the convention of movies. Who says a film has to cost a million dollars, and be safe and innocuous enough to satisfy every 12-year-old in America?" She asserted, "I want to break away from other conventions, the idea of heavy production, artificial lighting, all the slickness that plagues the movies. I want to just pick up a camera and go out and shoot the world as it really is."[10] When *The Connection* finally opened unimpeded in New York on October 4, 1962, Bosley Crowther gave it an unfavorable notice. But he did appreciate the film's "nervous tension" generated by Clarke's "bold direction."

Clarke would make only one more narrative feature, *The Cool World* (1963), before returning to documentaries; she finished her career as she had begun, directing short films. Many of Clarke's methods were commercially realized by another nonconformist filmmaker, John Cassavetes, who had the distinct advantage of working within the Hollywood system as an actor when his funds ran low.[11] Clarke remained an outsider, and as a woman director who challenged conventions, she was clearly ahead of her time.

While independent films generally did not have the studios' muscle behind them to combat local restrictions, studio releases had their own obstacles to overcome. The de facto censors, the PCA and Legion of Decency, had heretofore played their hands most effectively behind the scenes, starting at script stage before a studio property was ever filmed. Just as the movie versions of *Lolita, Cape Fear,* and *Walk on the Wild Side* were altered to secure Code approval, Tennessee Williams's play *Sweet Bird of Youth* fell victim to scissors and blue pencil. Williams, recognized as one of greatest playwrights of the twentieth century, had seen virtually all of his lauded stage dramas (e.g., *A Streetcar Named Desire, The Rose Tattoo, Cat on a Hot Tin Roof, Suddenly Last Summer*) reworked when they were transferred to the screen. But the commercial and critical success of those films presumably helped soothe the wounds of the Code's eviscerations.

The screen adaptation of *Sweet Bird of Youth,* written and directed by Richard Brooks (*Blackboard Jungle, Cat on a Hot Tin Roof, Elmer Gantry*), was produced by Golden Age studio veteran Pandro S. Berman (*Top Hat, Father of the Bride*) at MGM and therefore was subject to Code modifications. Brooks bowed to the Code and painted over the dark themes of decay and degeneration that dominated the play. He also took a more realistic approach to the material that differed from the stylizations of the play as staged by Elia Kazan, where the lead female character, the Princess, broke the fourth wall and addressed the audience directly.

Sweet Bird of Youth further exhibits the dominance of the male-star-appeal mentality of the studios. Paul Newman, who had costarred on Broadway along with Geraldine Page in 1959, now got top billing in the film version, and the movie's screenplay was refashioned to showcase his character. The film's trailer and advertising were built around Newman, selling the movie with the tagline "He used love like most men use money." Newman plays Chance Wayne, an opportunistic gigolo attending to washed-up movie star Alexandra Del Lago (the Princess), played by Page, and described by Chance as a "nice monster." She offers him the dream of Hollywood stardom, while battling her own fears of losing her grip on her career. He also seeks to reclaim his first love, Heavenly (Shirley Knight), the daughter of a southern coastal town's corrupt Boss Finley (Ed Begley), but must overcome the hostility of both Finley and his son (Rip Torn).

The considerable alterations to the story, including the substitution of an aborted pregnancy instead of a venereal disease–induced hysterectomy for Heavenly and a disfiguring beating rather than castration for Chance, were designed to appease the stringent Code. In retaliation, Brooks and Williams took a jab at the PCA by giving Page a line that had not been used in the play. The Princess tells Chance, "Besides, a movie starring your special talents would be banned in all fifty states, censored worldwide," which suggests tantalizingly the film they knew they couldn't make under the Code.

Despite its compromises, the film emerged as a provocative depiction of a frankly sexual liaison, the type of unabashedly carnal relationship rarely depicted in American movies of the era. Of course there had been films about men cavorting with prostitutes or dance hall "hostesses," as in *From Here to Eternity*. But Williams's scrutiny of a male prostitute or "stud" was novel movie material in 1962. When Chance seeks to pressure the Princess to provide him with money and career opportunities, she considers his demands, then replies bluntly, "My interest always increases with satisfaction." As he closes the drapes in preparation for providing satisfaction, he asks, "Aren't you ashamed a little?" She concedes the point, but the night proceeds as she desires.

The next morning is Easter Sunday, and the Princess declares brazenly, "I feel absolutely reborn." Despite his confession of shame, Chance delivers his own carnal credo: "The big difference between people is not between rich and poor or good and evil—the biggest of all differences between people is between those that have had pleasure in love and those that haven't." That line is vintage Tennessee Williams, and such an unapologetic ode to sexual pleasure would certainly have been excised if the film had been made just a few years earlier.

Beyond the author's provocative themes, what distinguishes the movie is first-class acting by the cast, with Page's celebrated stage performance gratifyingly preserved on film when she won out over more bankable movie stars Susan Hayward, Ava Gardner, and Deborah Kerr, who had all been considered for the part. Page acknowledged the play's modifications in an interview at the time: "There's been a change of emphasis in the movie. The play wasn't clearly about anyone, and the Princess ended by dominating it. Of course, it makes me sad in a way, but the movie is clearly about Chance, and I'm just one of the people in his life. Still, you can't forget the Princess; she's vibrant and alive, and above all, funny."[12] Page made certain that no one forgot her character. The highlight of the film, taken right from the play, is the Princess's telephone conversation with columnist Walter Winchell, in which he tells her that her latest screen performance, which she feared was a disaster, had turned out to be a triumph. The one-sided conversation (Winchell is never heard), a breathtaking display of maudlin self-pity turning into egotistical bravado, is a hilarious tour de force. In this scene and many others, Page commands the screen, evoking memories of Bette Davis in her studio queen prime. Williams allegedly first wrote the role with Davis in mind. The connection was solidified when Page was instructed by Brooks to watch *A Stolen Life* and emulate Davis descending a staircase "like a movie star" for one scene in the film—a flashback that had not been included in the play. Page's portrayal of an aging screen star was particularly timely in 1962, considering the difficulties that older actresses had in securing roles. The comeback success of the fictional Princess in *Sweet Bird of Youth* was not shared by most of her real-life counterparts in Hollywood.

For those studio executives dubious of Page's marquee appeal, Berman and Brooks had box office insurance in Paul Newman, who had risen to full-blown stardom in *Cat on a Hot Tin Roof* (1958), also based on a Williams play and also directed by Brooks. Newman was at his physical peak in the early 1960s, and although he was thirty-seven at the time he made *Sweet Bird of Youth,* he probably looked a mite too young to do full justice to the author's theme, as suggested in the title. Near the end of the film, the Princess offers a scathing criticism of Chance when she says, "You have gone past something you couldn't afford to go past—your youth," hinting that his days as a stud are coming to an end. Newman had no trouble playing the character onstage, but movie close-ups of his baby blues, along with frequent shirtless scenes exposing his lean figure and washboard abs, made the Princess's lament for his lost youth seem somewhat bewildering. As a result of these confusions, *Sweet Bird* turned out to be one of the actor's less rewarding performances on-screen.

But Newman's movie star wattage proved invaluable at the box office, and the film's other performances resonated enough to be remembered a full year after its March 1962 release. Page, Knight, and Begley all received Academy Award nominations for their stellar efforts. Knight and Begley, unlike other principal cast members Newman, Page, and Torn, had not originated their roles on the stage. By building up the role of Boss Finley, Brooks was able to strengthen the film's social commentary. Shots of Confederate flags and a flamboyant political rally at the climax heightened the critique of the racist South. Begley's ferocious turn as Finley was duly rewarded when he unexpectedly emerged victorious at the Oscars. It was a moment of sweet triumph for the character actor, who began an informal tradition when he was the first winner to thank his agent in his acceptance speech. Later that night he reminisced, "I go a long way back. I learned a lot from that dear and most wonderful of actresses, Barbara Stanwyck."[13]

Shirley Knight had received an Oscar nomination in 1960 for one of her very first films, *The Dark at the Top of the Stairs,* and she received a second for *Sweet Bird of Youth.* The Warner Bros. contract player had been loaned to MGM for the Williams film, which suited Knight just fine, since she felt misused by her home studio. As a contract player, she was expected to appear in the studio's TV series as well as in movies. If she had a few days off on filming a movie, she was rushed into a small role on *Maverick* or *Surfside 6*. And her two other films in 1962, both for Warner Bros., were lesser efforts, *The Couch* and *House of Women*. When Knight went to Jack Warner's office to complain about her roles, Warner chastised her: "Young lady, I do not need another Bette Davis!" "I just stood there for a minute," Knight recalls, "and then he said, 'You're cute.'"[14]

Her experience at MGM was more satisfying. She enjoyed her collaboration with Newman, though she was taken aback when she first met him on the set. Knight recalls, "Paul came over and said, 'Shirley, I think we should go behind the set and smooch a bit, because the next scene we have to do is a love scene.' I turned scarlet. And Joanne [Woodward] said to him, 'She's only just met you, and she doesn't understand your warped sense of humor. So apologize.' We had so much fun making the film. He was always so generous." She developed a strong friendship with Newman and Woodward that continued long after the completion of the film. In fact, she acted in the theater several times with Woodward.

Still, there were surreal aspects to her work at MGM. As Knight recalls, "The first time I was going to have my hair done by Sydney Guilaroff, another woman was lying there with a towel over her face. Sydney said to me, 'That's Jayne Mansfield. She comes in every morning at four so I can dye her roots. She lies there and goes to sleep.' That was one of those moments when I thought, they do weird things here. But Sydney Guilaroff was a very interesting man. He was a gay man who adopted two boys."[15] Guilaroff, the chief hair stylist at MGM for more than forty years, played a crucial role in creating the glamorous image of many of the studio's top stars. But he was also one of the first single men ever to adopt a son. The state of California fought him, but he ultimately prevailed.

When Knight returned to Warner Bros., she realized that she would never fit comfortably into the studio system. "I asked to be released from my contract," she reports, and Jack Warner agreed (in January 1962). As one of the last of the contract players, her departure, in its way, signified the unraveling of the studio system. The actress may have lost her studio ties, but she gained an invaluable artistic alliance when she established a lifelong friendship with Tennessee Williams and starred in several of his late plays. Knight has no regrets about her decision to move to New York and concentrate on theater.

Regarding *Sweet Bird of Youth*, although Williams had to contend with having his stage drama modified, he did not seem bothered, at least in public,

FIGURE 6.3 Paul Newman and Shirley Knight in a publicity shot for *Sweet Bird of Youth*. (Photofest)

noting the film "was probably better than the play."[16] His assessment is telling in that the movie version of *Sweet Bird* satisfied the upscale, literate moviegoer as well as the regular public drawn by the suggestive ads and Newman's star power. Although the downbeat stage drama had been somewhat pasteurized for the screen, there was still enough of Williams's indelible characterizations and incisive dialogue to pass muster. Whether a more faithful adaptation of the play, with its grim ending, would have proved successful at the box office is a moot point. In the context of a changing society in 1962, which was shaking off the constricting sensibilities of the conformist 1950s, *Sweet Bird of Youth* remains just what was promised in the original advertising materials, "Provocative Adult Entertainment."   ˇ

That film was not Newman's only screen venture in 1962. A few months later, he appeared in *Hemingway's Adventures of a Young Man,* an ambitious but flawed adaptation of several of Hemingway's Nick Adams stories, mixed in with episodes from the author's life. The film was directed by Newman's most frequent cinematic collaborator, Martin Ritt, who also made *The Long Hot Summer, Paris Blues, Hud,* and *Hombre.* It was produced by Jerry Wald, who died prematurely right before the release, and was written by Hemingway biographer A. E. Hotchner, with an all-star cast that included Jessica Tandy, Arthur Kennedy, Dan Dailey, Ricardo Montalban, and Susan Strasberg, with Richard Beymer in the lead. The film probably tried to cram too much into its 145-minute running time, even including a compressed version of Hemingway's novel *A Farewell to Arms.* And it was weakened by the Freudian simplifications that also permeated several other movies of 1962. Once again the villain of the piece is an overbearing mother (Tandy), in this case a religious fanatic who drives her sensitive husband to suicide.

But there are vivid sections in the movie, and the best of these, faithfully adapted from a Hemingway story called "The Battler," features an almost unrecognizable Newman as a punch-drunk fighter whom Nick encounters on his journey across America. Newman did not change his appearance very often during the course of his long career, but his scenes in the Hemingway film represent a startling achievement. The makeup helps, of course, but this is more than a stunt performance. Newman movingly captures the confusion of a completely broken man, and he has a fine partner in Juano Hernandez (*Intruder in the Dust, The Pawnbroker*) as his loyal, wise coach and unselfish friend (one of the notable roles for a black actor that year). Whatever their flaws, the prominence of these two Newman films in a single year—one adapted from the work of a great American playwright, the other from the fiction of a great American novelist—illustrates the reverence for literature that enriched the cinema of 1962.

7 · BLACK AND WHITE TO TECHNICOLOR

Some prominent film adaptations in 1962 proved to be a mixed bag. *Five Finger Exercise*, a London and Broadway stage hit written by Peter Shaffer (*Equus, Amadeus*), failed as a movie, despite an impressive cast headed by Rosalind Russell, Maximilian Schell, Jack Hawkins, and the star of the Hemingway film, Richard Beymer (who enjoyed a brief moment in the sun after the enormous success of 1961's *West Side Story*). Tyro film director Ralph Nelson rebuked his own film of *Requiem for a Heavyweight*, originally a lauded teleplay by Rod Serling. Nelson, who directed both versions, candidly revealed to the press his disagreement with the film's lead (Anthony Quinn) over his brutish interpretation of the aging boxer. (Jack Palance had won an Emmy for his more sensitive portrayal.)[1]

Both of those movie misses were filmed in black and white. Audiences in 1962 inhabited a preponderantly black-and-white movie world, and the year remains one of the artistic high-water marks for monochrome. The art of black-and-white cinematography was well represented by the film version of William Gibson's stage play *Two for the Seesaw*, a modestly successful romantic drama on Broadway. Robert Mitchum and Shirley MacLaine were cast in the movie as mismatched lovers, and even with their attractive performances and Andre Previn's evocative, bluesy score, the film is virtually forgotten. Yet it deserves rediscovery for the exquisite black-and-white cinematography of Ted McCord (*The Treasure of the Sierra Madre, East of Eden, The Sound of Music*), who began his career in the silent era. His beautiful, painterly images of Manhattan exteriors and masterfully lit interiors elevate the mundane drama. McCord also shot the low-budget *War Hunt* in monochrome that year. The

FIGURE 7.1 Black-and-white cityscape from *Two for the Seesaw,* cinematography by
Ted McCord. (Screen shot)

cinematography branch of the Academy rightfully recognized his expert work
on *Two for the Seesaw* with a nomination. But the general membership voted
The Longest Day the winner, rewarding size and scope over detailed artistry.
Since black-and-white motion picture photography is now a rare, virtually lost
art, with most modern monochrome films shot in color, then drained to appear
black and white, *Two for the Seesaw* survives as one of its underseen gems.

A more memorable black-and-white film adaptation is found in *Days of
Wine and Roses,* photographed by Philip Lathrop and directed by Blake
Edwards, who had a huge hit with *Breakfast at Tiffany's* the year before. The
original television drama by J P Miller (who also wrote the screenplay) concerned the destructive effect of alcoholism on a marriage; Cliff Robertson and
Piper Laurie portrayed the afflicted couple in the 1958 *Playhouse 90* presentation, directed by John Frankenheimer. By 1962 Frankenheimer was preoccu-
pied with his three films released that year: *All Fall Down, Birdman of Alcatraz,*
and *The Manchurian Candidate.* Robertson and Laurie were not big stars, so
Warner Bros., the studio that produced the movie, pursued better-known
names for the cast.

Jack Lemmon had risen to major stardom after his celebrated comedic performances in *Mister Roberts, Some Like It Hot,* and *The Apartment* and was
attracted to the drama as an acting challenge. Lee Remick had costarred earlier
in the year in Edwards's smoothly directed suspense thriller *Experiment in Terror* and was primed for the female lead. In a supporting role as Remick's stoic,
disapproving father, Charles Bickford was an inspired holdover from the TV
version.

Edwards, known primarily as a comedy director, and Lemmon may have
been drawn to the material because they were both heavy drinkers; they later

FIGURE 7.2 Director Blake Edwards with actors Lee Remick and Jack Lemmon relaxing on the set of *Days of Wine and Roses.* (Photofest)

admitted to recovery from alcohol abuse. Peter Bogdanovich described Lemmon's performance as "an achingly painful and moving portrayal of an upper-middle class drunk . . . a role that evidently mirrored Jack's own problems with alcohol during his life."[2] Hollywood had filmed alcoholism stories before, notably Billy Wilder's *The Lost Weekend* (1945) and the showbiz biopic *I'll Cry Tomorrow* (1955), but the studios had seldom tackled a full-scale drama about an average married couple, especially one with a child, battling the bottle.

Warner Bros. heightened the dramatic stakes by using the advertising tagline "In its own terrifying way, it is a love story." Thus, at least no one would mistake the film for a typical Jack Lemmon comedy. Critical reaction was respectfully favorable (a few reviewers preferred the teleplay) but effusive in praise of the two leads. Lemmon and Remick are unforgettable—charming in the lighter, engaging courtship scenes, when hard-drinking public relations exec Joe Clay (Lemmon) woos nondrinking secretary Kirsten Arnesen (Remick)—and memorably affecting in their portrayals of degradation and despair during their descent. Both performances were deservedly Oscar-nominated in the lead categories. The elegant title song by Henry Mancini and Johnny Mercer, which weaves an emotional thread for the characters and story and has become a standard, garnered the duo a second consecutive Academy Award, following "Moon River" from *Breakfast at Tiffany's*.

Lee Remick made her screen debut in a small supporting role in Elia Kazan's 1957 drama, *A Face in the Crowd*. Impressed by her and by her subsequent work in *The Long, Hot Summer* and *Anatomy of a Murder*, Kazan gave her the female lead in his underseen 1960 drama *Wild River* (coincidentally released to great critical acclaim in France in 1962). Kazan recalled Remick in his autobiography as "one of the finest young actresses I knew . . . at the top of her strength and confidence."[3] His assessment fit her trenchant performance in *Days of Wine and Roses*.

One of the strengths of *Days of Wine and Roses* is how the film works as a character-driven social drama, depicting how alcohol corrodes the couple's family life and economic well-being. An especially potent scene shows Joe ransacking and destroying his father-in-law's prize greenhouse in his frenzied search for a hidden bottle. Although Joe eventually helps himself through Alcoholics Anonymous while Kirsten refuses to attend meetings, the film is not specifically issue-oriented, focusing instead on the couple's deteriorating relationship. As part of its legacy, the film did help raise general awareness of AA. But more important than any message is the film's enduring emotional power. In a key late scene, a sober Joe tries to retrieve the now dipsomaniac Kirsten from the drunken squalor of a motel room. When she seduces him into taking a drink, audiences of the day gasped. Henry Hart of *Films in Review* reported, "The afternoon I saw it in Radio City Music Hall the audience's regret was audible when Kirsten succeeded in getting Joe back on booze." That scene elicited an identical audience reaction at a revival screening in Los Angeles fifty-five years later. Notably, in 2018 the film was added to the National Film Registry.

Days of Wine and Roses opened in Hollywood in December 1962, and nationwide in January 1963, as the *New York Times* dryly noted in its review, "to bring post-holiday sobriety." Producer Martin Manulis had to fight Jack Warner to preserve the teleplay's downbeat ending, in which Kirsten and Joe are separated by Kirsten's refusal to stop drinking.[4] Manulis was ultimately vindicated. The public responded by making the aptly hued black-and-white film a box office hit; audiences were undeterred by its starkly realistic, increasingly mournful tone. Unlike the hopeful conclusions of *The Lost Weekend* and most other liquor-soaked Hollywood movies, the film ends on a somber note, underscored hauntingly by Mancini's plaintive melody.

In 1962, of 300 films submitted for Academy Award consideration in the cinematography field, only 123 were photographed in color. Black-and-white movies so thoroughly dominated the nominations that year that of the 40 narrative features eventually nominated in all categories, 65 percent were photographed in black and white.[5] *Days of Wine and Roses* and *Two for the Seesaw* joined an impressive roster of black-and-white, Oscar-nominated 1962 films: *To Kill a Mockingbird, The Miracle Worker, The Manchurian Candidate, The Man Who Shot Liberty Valance,* and *Divorce Italian Style* among them. Other aesthetically striking monochrome films released that year include *Jules and Jim, A Taste of Honey, La Notte, Cape Fear,* and *The Loneliness of the Long Distance Runner.*

Black-and-white photography had been the film industry standard since its invention, as the economy of shooting in monochrome was a boon to budget-conscious producers. Filmmakers had experimented with color in the first decades of the movies, but it was not until the introduction of three-strip Technicolor cinematography in the 1930s that black-and-white and color movies coexisted comfortably. In 1939, the Academy of Motion Picture Arts and Sciences established a separate award category for color cinematography.[6] Technicolor movies, with their relative higher cost, remained a distinct minority among those produced each year. But in 1949, Eastman Kodak perfected a single-strip color negative, and the studios signed on to more economical processes (e.g., Warner Color, Ansco Color, Deluxe, Eastman). By the early 1950s, exhibitors clamored for all-color films to get the public away from their black-and-white television programs and back into movie theaters.[7] But there was no rush to convert film production to color exclusively, as black and white was still less expensive, and many top filmmakers preferred the aesthetic advantages of black and white.

John Frankenheimer, who shot all three of his 1962 releases in monochrome, told the *New York Times* in 1961, "Color generally ruins good drama. It tends to convert dramas into travelogues." He noted exceptions, especially musicals and spectaculars, yet he lamented that many moviemakers "ruin dramatic intent with their color and wide-screen processes."[8] Oscar-winning cinematographer Burnett Guffey (*From Here to Eternity,* black and white; *Bonnie and Clyde,* color) explained his predilection for black and white: "Three decades after the color revolution in motion pictures we still find ourselves too often using color for color's sake. . . . It's more of a challenge to do a good job in black and white than it is in color."[9] In 1962 he shot *Kid Galahad,* an Elvis Presley musical, in color, then nimbly returned to black and white for *Birdman of Alcatraz.* Guffey's versatility in both mediums was further demonstrated in 1962 by the work of other gifted cinematographers. Ernest Haller, for example, had been honored for the memorable color achievement of *Gone with the Wind.*

Then, in 1962, he skillfully shot two of the year's notable black-and-white movies, *Pressure Point* and *What Ever Happened to Baby Jane?*

However, despite the aesthetic preference of many filmmakers, by 1962 the monochrome era of motion pictures was coming to an end. After announcing they would convert to all-color broadcasting by the mid-1960s, the television networks partnered with television manufacturers and insisted that the motion picture industry cooperate by making only color films. The revenue of movie sales to television was too great to resist, so the studios, and eventually filmmakers worldwide, capitulated to the demand. The transformation had begun, and with it came the putative end of film noir's classical period, which had lasted for twenty years and was represented in 1962 by the monochromatic *Cape Fear* and *Experiment in Terror* and the noir-tinged *The Manchurian Candidate, Walk on the Wild Side,* and *What Ever Happened to Baby Jane?*

Filmmakers who extolled monochrome held out as long as they could. John Frankenheimer finally succumbed to the demand for color in 1966 with his car-racing spectacle, *Grand Prix,* and never returned to monochrome. In 1967 the black-and-white categories were eliminated altogether by the Academy, and virtually all films were made in color by the end of the 1960s. Except for an occasional venture into black-and-white cinema by enterprising filmmakers in subsequent decades (e.g., *The Last Picture Show, Raging Bull, Schindler's List, The Artist, Nebraska, Roma*—several of which exemplify "faux black and white," shot in color and then drained), the original hue of cinema since its birth at the dawn of the twentieth century was now a relic of that glorious past.

International cinema would follow the American industry's move into an all-color movie universe. As in Hollywood, many of the top artists resisted at first. In 1962, Ingmar Bergman's preferred cinematographer, Sven Nykvist, brought luminous black-and-white images to their art house hit *Through a Glass Darkly.* Roger Ebert was impressed by "how painstakingly the film had been made. Nykvist's lighting is essentially another character." He called the cinematographer "one of the greatest artists of his craft."[10] Bergman and Nykvist collaborated exclusively in black and white until the end of the decade, finally surrendering with *The Passion of Anna* (1969), a mix of color and monochrome; both artists finished their careers working solely in color.

Italian auteur Federico Fellini, who shot his 1950s and early 1960s masterworks *La Strada, Nights of Cabiria, La Dolce Vita,* and *8 ½* in black and white, disdained working in color. Fellini asserted, "It will never have the depth or truth of black and white. If I shoot a scene of a stormy sea in black and white, the audience can project onto it their own experience of the ocean. If I shoot it in color it's too literal and less emotional and effective."[11] Despite his affin-

FIGURE 7.3 Frequent collaborators cinematographer Sven Nykvist and director Ingmar Bergman. (Photofest)

ity for monochrome, Fellini's *8 ½* (made in 1962, released in early 1963) would be his final film in black and white. He had already conceded to the color agenda with his segment of *Boccaccio '70.* The demands of the marketplace defeated even the most defiant auteurs, whether domestic or foreign.

Fellini's black-and-white vision of a stormy sea would wash over the screen in 1962 in an artistically accomplished film adaptation, *Billy Budd.* This sea saga came from a classic literary source, Herman Melville's novella and the 1951 stage play derived from it. Actor Peter Ustinov (*Spartacus, Topkapi*), who also produced and cowrote with veteran screenwriter DeWitt Bodeen (*Cat People, I Remember Mama*), directed the international coproduction in England and off the coast of Spain. Ustinov assembled a strong, predominantly British cast with a twenty-two-year-old newcomer from the London stage, Terence Stamp, in the title role.

Billy Budd was part of a trio of films, all released in 1962, dealing with the subject of late eighteenth-century British naval insurrections, both fact and fiction, including the little-seen UK film *Damn the Defiant* (with Alec Guinness and Dirk Bogarde) and the Hollywood epic *Mutiny on the Bounty.* In *Billy Budd* director-actor Ustinov adeptly emphasized the moral struggle of his character, the principled Captain Vere, who is confronted with the abject cruelty of master-at-arms Claggart. Ustinov cast Robert Ryan as Claggart for his Hollywood star appeal to the film's financial backers, giving him top billing. Another movie star, teen heartthrob Tab Hunter, who was trying to change his image with more challenging parts, was rejected for the title role.

Ryan had lobbied Ustinov for his part, and his love of Melville's work from his college years overcame any reservations about playing yet another villain (he had been Oscar-nominated for playing a Jew-hating killer in 1947's *Crossfire*). Melville describes Claggart's evil as "born with him and innate, in short 'a depravity according to nature.'" Ryan's excellent performance suggests he succeeded in finding sufficient motivation, and he pointed justifiably with pride to his work in the film.[12] David McCallum, who would go on to an enduring career in American television (*The Man from U.N.C.L.E., NCIS*) into the twenty-first century, played Lieutenant Wyatt and echoed the praise for Ryan's work more than fifty years later. McCallum remembered Ryan as "one of the greatest actors I ever worked with . . . [while filming] it didn't look like he was doing anything at all . . . looked like he was throwing it away. Until you see the movie and see the strength of what he did."[13] Melvyn Douglas, a veteran star who had been Greta Garbo's leading man in 1939's *Ninotchka,* was also in the cast. He had been absent from the screen for a decade, partly as a result of the Hollywood blacklist, but his quiet strength in the role of the Dansker reminded audiences of his skill.

The psychological seduction of Claggart by the angelic Billy contains a homosexual subtext that is left sublimated by Ustinov and gay screenwriter Bodeen. Ustinov was attempting to make a film viewable by a general audience and therefore did not want to tangle with the Production Code office. He also found it easier to secure financing by taking a straightforward approach to the material. A homoerotic undercurrent is more blatantly on display in the Benjamin Britten opera (in turn based on the play), yet it exists subtly in the film as well. Of course this subtlety also goes back to Melville, who died before completing the manuscript. Later literary critics found homosexual undertones in *Billy Budd* (and in other Melville works as well), suggesting that Claggart's hatred of Billy grows from an attraction that he cannot admit.

Claggart's attempt to destroy the innocent Budd leads to Billy accidentally killing him while defending himself against Claggart's false charges. Vere is then forced to grapple with his conscience as he struggles to uphold the letter of maritime law. These finely rendered scenes, especially the two or three primarily dialogue-driven character set pieces, are the soul of the film. Ustinov

FIGURE 7.4 Terence Stamp and Robert Ryan in *Billy Budd*. (Screen shot)

encouraged his actors' input into their characterizations, stating that he did not want a "rigidly-directed picture," and that permissiveness paid off handsomely. In a year of so many extraordinarily acted films, the cast of *Billy Budd* never makes a false step.

Upon release in November it received a deserved chorus of approval from the critics and was designated one of the year's ten best films by *Time* magazine, the Associated Press, and the National Board of Review. Stamp's beautiful, understated performance as the tragic Billy would earn an Oscar nomination as best supporting actor, heralding the arrival of a new international star. Venerable Hollywood columnist Louella Parsons was so smitten by the handsome young actor's performance that she proclaimed him "the most important discovery of the year." Critic Michael Sragow, writing for the Library of America, offers a twenty-first-century appraisal: "With the aid of a superb cast, this 1962 adaptation wrings a lucid, sinewy narrative from the poetry and moral complexity of Herman Melville's posthumously published masterpiece."[14] However, *Billy Budd* turned out to be only a *success d'estime.*

Allied Artists, the scrappy small distributor of *Billy Budd,* was in need of some cachet. The successor to Poverty Row studio Monogram Pictures, it had survived in the era mainly with low-rent B pictures like *Attack of the 50 Foot Woman* and *House on Haunted Hill,* after scoring a financial success with the metaphorical sci-fi chiller, *Invasion of the Body Snatchers,* in 1956.

Billy Budd was purposely, and somewhat deceptively, marketed as a high seas action tale emphasizing men in mutiny, capitalizing on all the publicity surrounding another big-budget sea saga that had just set sail in theaters. But the opportunistic plan to ride the marketing crest of *Mutiny on the Bounty* proved to be all wet, as the film was swamped at the box office by the gigantic wake of the Marlon Brando juggernaut. Although the frequently performed Benjamin Britten opera perpetuates the artistic legacy of the original work, the superlative 1962 film version also warrants rediscovery by discerning audiences.

Another reason to exhume *Billy Budd* is to appreciate the black-and-white cinematography of Robert Krasker, an Australian notable for his expressionistic black-and-white achievement on *The Third Man* in 1950. Ustinov and Allied Artists had been forced to economize by filming in monochrome, and the nautical scenes stand in sharp contrast to the lavish Technicolor of *Mutiny on the Bounty*. But Krasker's expertly shot seascapes fit the smaller scale of *Billy Budd*.

Billy Budd served as a low-cost prelude to what was rapidly becoming the most expensive movie ever made, a dubious milestone that was held only briefly, until the release of *Cleopatra* the following year. After MGM had enormous success with its remake of *Ben-Hur* in 1959, it planned to repeat that payoff with a new version of 1935's best picture Oscar winner, *Mutiny on the Bounty*. It would get the same big budget and star treatment as the studio's record-setting biblical behemoth, with hoped-for similar results at the box office. This mentality was the by-product of a burst of remake fever, which had swept through Hollywood front offices in the wide-screen era of the 1950s and 1960s. The gigantic success of *Ben-Hur* and the earlier box office bonanza of Cecil B. DeMille's 1956 lavish re-creation of his own silent film, *The Ten Commandments,* had colored the moguls' judgment. These Technicolor cinematic extravaganzas seemed the best cure for the industry's ailing box office; they were designed to lure dwindling audiences away from their black-and-white television sets. MGM invested in an overseas remake of DeMille's silent *King of Kings* (1961) by European producer Samuel Bronston (*El Cid, The Fall of the Roman Empire*) and approved expensive new versions of past successes like *Cimarron* (1960) and *Four Horsemen of the Apocalypse,* among others. Only *King of Kings* proved a box office success. Instead, *Mutiny on the Bounty* (along with Twentieth Century-Fox's *Cleopatra*) would soon become the benchmark for the problems that were plaguing the industry in 1962: runaway production, escalating production costs, and temperamental star behavior.

Mutiny on the Bounty had seemed like a safe bet, as the 1935 black-and-white production had become a screen classic, showcasing the acclaimed performances of Clark Gable as mutineer Fletcher Christian and Charles Laughton as the tyrannical Captain Bligh. The 1789 mutiny aboard HMS *Bounty* in the South Pacific had been well documented and popularized in the 1932 historical novel by Charles Nordhoff and James Norman Hall. The book would also serve as the basis for the 1962 version, with an intended screenplay by Eric Ambler, the British spy novelist and screenwriter (*The Cruel Sea, A Night to Remember*).

When consensus could not be found on the numerous versions of the script, producer Aaron Rosenberg turned to Charles Lederer, cowriter of *The Front Page* (1931), Howard Hawks's gender-switching remake, *His Girl Friday* (both written with Lederer's lifelong friend Ben Hecht), *Gentlemen Prefer Blondes,* and the sci-fi classic, *The Thing from Another World.* Hecht and Billy Wilder, among others, would later lend a hand in extensive rewrites of the script. Carol Reed, the distinguished British director noted for *The Fallen Idol* and *The Third Man,* was assigned to steward the mostly British cast, with Trevor Howard (*Brief Encounter, Sons and Lovers*) as Captain Bligh and rising Irish star Richard Harris as a mutineer.

But the stellar marquee attraction was Marlon Brando, the most esteemed actor of his generation and, for many, the greatest actor in movie history, cast as Fletcher Christian. It was on his name that a nearly $14 million budget was to be lavished on the Technicolor epic, filmed in the new Ultra Panavision 70mm process. Whereas the 1935 film gave equal weight to the adversarial roles of Christian and Bligh, the 1962 version decidedly favored Christian's (i.e., Brando's) story line. Additionally, Brando's star power was such that he was able to exercise creative input and later virtual artistic control over the film. That domination would haunt the production, as Brando's unrestrained conduct on and off the set, problems with location shooting, and spiraling costs threatened to sink the film before it ever docked in theaters.

Principal Technicolor photography by Robert Surtees (*Ben-Hur, The Graduate, The Last Picture Show*) commenced in November 1960 on location in Tahiti. Although runaway production was of great concern in Hollywood, the studio had committed to extensive location shooting in the South Pacific, an enticement for Brando, who had a lifelong fascination with Tahiti. But Carol Reed's methodical and detailed direction slowed down the shoot, and he soon ran afoul of Rosenberg, who dismissed him over creative differences. The *Bounty*'s arrival in Tahiti and some other South Seas scenes directed by Reed remain in the finished film.

Lewis Milestone, who won an Oscar for directing 1930's best picture, the acclaimed antiwar film *All Quiet on the Western Front,* replaced Reed. He had just directed Rosenberg's production of the Frank Sinatra "Rat Pack" vehicle, *Ocean's 11,* also written by Lederer, the year before. In retrospect, the Russian-born Milestone was an inspired choice, as he epitomized the figure of resilient

FIGURE 7.5 Marlon Brando, director Lewis Milestone, and costar Tarita (far right), Brando's new wife, at the Tahiti airport while filming *Mutiny on the Bounty*. (Photofest)

survivor, having been blacklisted in the early 1950s for alleged Communist sympathies. He had been active in the postwar labor disputes that divided Hollywood, and that left-leaning participation sealed his fate. It was a harsh sentence for the filmmaker, who after *All Quiet on the Western Front* went on to produce and direct John Steinbeck's *Of Mice and Men,* a best picture nominee in 1939, as well as the vintage Barbara Stanwyck noir melodrama, *The Strange Love of Martha Ivers,* in 1946.

Unfortunately, Milestone's exile from moviemaking during the 1950s left him ill prepared for the vagaries of his illustrious star. During Milestone's heyday in the 1930s and 1940s, actors were all under contract to studios and were forced to do their producers' and directors' bidding. The stars chafed under that seemingly feudal system, and their liberation began through independent production deals in the late 1940s and 1950s after victory in the courts in a notable case challenging actors' contracts, first brought by Olivia de Havilland in 1943. The stars' growing clout eventually contributed to the downfall of the old system; Milestone now stepped back into this unfamiliar environment.

During *Bounty*'s filming, the western *One-Eyed Jacks* (1961), Marlon Brando's only directorial effort (he also starred), opened to lackluster reviews, and he took its subsequent commercial failure very hard. According to his friends (as related by Peter Bogdanovich), the *Jacks* experience had "soured him" on movies and the acting profession in general.[15] The prolonged shoot of *Mutiny on the Bounty* would exacerbate his disenchantment.

All this contributed to the unsettled climate on the movie set that Milestone inherited. Aside from Brando's disengaged attitude, his reliance on the Method school of acting for inspiration necessitated numerous takes and caused a rift with Milestone, who had been shooting quickly after they returned to the studio to make up for the prior location delay. Brando bridled under Milestone's authoritarian style. Hostility between the director and star reached a breaking point when Brando stopped taking Milestone's direction and instead consulted directly with Rosenberg and Lederer. Brando had been stymied by the lack of a finished script, and this would prove costly as he insisted on writing the final portion of the story about the fate of the mutineers on Pitcairn Island, where they had sought refuge.

Costs quickly mounted as a result of the stalemate between Milestone and Brando. His fellow actors, the more disciplined Brits, were aghast at what they considered a lack of professionalism on Brando's part. Costar Richard Harris told the press that Brando was "deliberately scuttling" certain scenes he didn't want to do. Brando's relationship with Trevor Howard was described by observers on the set as a "minuet of repressed hostility." Reportedly, civility between them ended after a particularly tense scene when "Marlon walked over, smirked, and mockingly gave Trevor a loud, wet smack." Howard's response to the press was terse disapproval, "The man is unprofessional and absolutely ridiculous."[16] When the production returned to Tahiti, Rosenberg indulged his idiosyncratic star by allowing him to write the final scenes, causing further delay. Finally, the exasperated producer had enough and dictated that Lederer's script revisions, with a few outside additions, be used. Milestone later vented to the press that he felt "shanghaied" by MGM management when they did not support him. Clearly frustrated, he opined, "Maybe this experience will bring our executives to their senses. They deserve what they get when they give a ham actor, a petulant child, complete control of an expensive picture."[17] Milestone left the picture in early 1962 before finishing production. Although he did not direct the final eleven days of the shoot at the studio (reportedly supervised by George Seaton), Milestone is given sole credit on the film.

By this time production costs had ballooned to nearly $20 million, and photography was not completed until August 1962. The strife on the set was widely covered by the print media, and Brando took the brunt of criticism dished out by inhospitable studio insiders and reporters. These observers were fed up with "neurotic" star antics, having witnessed the turmoil at Twentieth

Century-Fox caused by Marilyn Monroe on the set of director George Cukor's *Something's Got to Give* and Elizabeth Taylor on *Cleopatra*.

Brando was vilified as "brat or brute?," with a hostile press citing his tempestuous on-set behavior, behind-the-scenes mischief, and sexual indulgences. During production the actor divorced his second wife (Movita Castenada, coincidentally the female lead of the 1935 version of *Mutiny on the Bounty*), and consummated his romance with his twenty-year-old Tahitian costar, Tarita, eighteen years his junior, marrying her in August 1962. Veteran gossip columnist Hedda Hopper assailed Brando's escapades, questioning whether he was "sabotaging" the film, and she used his behavior to declare that out-of-control stars were "what's wrong with Hollywood."

Brando, however, was not about to roll over for his caustic critics or Hollywood harridans like Hedda Hopper. He fought back, citing the lack of a finished script as the source of all the troubles, and called upon MGM to support him. He even went so far as to sue the otherwise respectable *Saturday Evening Post* for libel over an article, "The Mutiny of Marlon Brando," which accused the actor of singlehandedly causing $6 million in extra expenses while "sulking on the set." That suit was later settled quietly. Forever the Hollywood rebel, Brando felt scapegoated by the studio for the production running over budget. He called *Mutiny on the Bounty* "perhaps my very worst experience making a motion picture" and vowed never to make another movie like it.[18] Since the film had been green-lit without a completed script, MGM president Joseph R. Vogel was compelled to defend his eccentric star. In June Vogel issued a statement that it was "gravely unfair" to blame Brando for the high production costs. The Hollywood grapevine speculated that Vogel had no other choice but to "whitewash" Brando, since the star was needed for final retakes on the still unfinished film.

Mutiny on the Bounty was finally launched on November 8, 1962, in New York as a roadshow presentation, with reserved seats and limited showings (two a day). MGM did not skimp on marketing the finished film, promising "The Mightiest Sea-Spectacle That Ever Swept Across the Screen!" As part of the million-dollar campaign, the full-size replica of the original *Bounty* built for the movie was sent on a well-attended publicity tour to major seaports around the country and Europe. The wooden ship so impressed critics that a number of them cited the vessel as the "real star" of the film.

All the expense was not entirely wasted, as critical acclaim from some camps greeted the three-hour epic. However, Brando drew further reproach for his performance, as some reviewers and industry observers castigated him for his portrayal of Fletcher Christian as an aristocratic dandy. Most of the criticism focused on his foppish affectations early in the film and on his odd British accent, with the London critics in particular mildly amused. One wag, Donald Zec of the *London Mirror,* went so far as to publicly chide him for "mincing . . . precious imitation of an Oxford accent." In these critics' eyes, he was no Clark Gable—and not a believable Brit, either. But Zec also offered perhaps the most entertaining assessment of the film, calling it "a souped-up, sex-padded remake which is a lusty mix of belly-dancing, brutality and Brando. But I wouldn't have missed this wigging epic—not for all the breadfruit in Tahiti."[19]

The vaguely transatlantic accent Brando appropriated for the role echoes one he utilized for his portrayal of Marc Antony in 1953's *Julius Caesar.* In this case he seemed to be paying the price for his widely reported irresponsible behavior while shooting the picture. But he did have *Variety* in his corner. In its review, the venerable trade paper deemed the movie "generally superior to the 1935 film" and described Brando's multifaceted work as "in many ways . . . the finest performance of his career." Kate Cameron of the *New York Daily News* called it "a magnificent film" headlining her four-star review. Unfortunately, those positive evaluations were a minority opinion among critics.

The paying public largely ignored the contretemps that had bedeviled *Mutiny on the Bounty,* making it the highest-grossing movie of December. Brando's box office power was clearly manifested after all. On that singular premise the studio honchos had at least been right. But it was too late for MGM admirals Sol Siegel and Vogel, casualties in the wake of the troubled movie vessel. Siegel had already resigned as head of production in January 1962, and Vogel followed him out the door twelve months later. Although the film would eventually rank in the top ten box office for the year, and became the third-highest-grossing film in MGM history up to that time (after *Gone with the Wind* and *Ben-Hur*), its overinflated budget sank any chances of rescuing it from the ignominious label of box office flop. MGM quickly wrote off more than $8 million in losses in the first quarter of 1963.

Historical inaccuracies and production problems aside, the 1962 version of *Mutiny on the Bounty* remains an intelligent, well-crafted high seas adventure. It is enhanced by lush, Technicolor-drenched South Seas romantic exotica. Compared with the 1935 version, the later film conveys deeper implications of class conflict, embodied by Brando's audacious characterization of the aristocratic Fletcher Christian versus Trevor Howard's sadistic, self-made commoner, Captain Bligh. Both portrayals are decidedly effective in their own right but were overshadowed at the time by the memory of Gable and Laughton. Milestone's sure directorial hand is evident at crucial moments, principally the sequences depicting the spectacular storm-tossed attempt at rounding Cape Horn and the mutiny itself. But all the adverse publicity took its toll, and *Bounty* proved to be the veteran director's final feature.

At Oscar time, the Academy readily agreed with the public and overlooked most of the controversy, nominating the film in seven categories, including a surprise best picture nod. In that era of only five nominees in the top category, the recognition was indeed unexpected, especially against such heavyweight competition that year. Since acting, writing, and directing were not among the seven nominations, omissions that also marked best picture nominees *The Longest Day* and *The Music Man,* these oversights led to speculation that the studios were pressuring their employees to vote for their most expensive movie ventures. The Academy cachet served a crucial economic purpose, designed to help recoup costs for artistically challenged or underperforming movies. This notorious practice of studio bloc voting allegedly paid off with the best picture nods. Murray Schumach of the *New York Times* raised this issue after the 1962 nominations were announced, charging behind-the-scenes chicanery in Tinseltown.[20] The Academy dismissed Schumach's accusations as unfounded.

However, these practices may well have carried other big-budget studio entries of the era to Oscar's prestigious final five. Those suspect films include *The Ten Commandments, The Alamo, Cleopatra, Doctor Dolittle, Hello Dolly!, Airport,* and *The Towering Inferno,* a dubious mix of audience favorites and expensive, bloated productions. Some of those films might have fit more comfortably in the expanded roster of up to ten nominees, a controversial change that the Academy reintroduced in 2009 after a sixty-six year hiatus. (It is gratifying to note, however, that no big-budget movie as overblown as *The Alamo* or *Doctor Dolittle* was ever nominated for best picture in later years.)

Mutiny on the Bounty's notable aesthetic accomplishments are found among the craftsmanship of MGM studio veterans John McSweeney Jr. (film editing), Robert Surtees (color cinematography), George W. Davis, J. McMillan Johnson, Henry Grace, and Hugh Hunt (color production design), and composer Bronislau Kaper (*San Francisco, Lili, Auntie Mame*) for his towering score, arguably his masterpiece. He had inherited the assignment when esteemed composer Miklos Rozsa rejected the project during the prolonged production delays. *Bounty* would be Kaper's final studio assignment. Special effects master and the "wizard of MGM," A. Arnold Gillespie (*San Francisco, The Wizard of Oz, Forbidden Planet*), who had begun his career in the silent era, had the distinction of having worked on both the 1935 and 1962 versions. The film compels because of all their contributions, experienced by audiences of the day in wide-screen 70mm splendor in the roadshow engagements.

Originally, the film was fashioned to be told in flashback, framed by a prologue and epilogue narrated by the last surviving mutineer on Pitcairn Island when discovered after a quarter century, and his narration remains throughout the film. Although these scenes added only seven minutes to the running time, they were cut from the final prints and were not shown theatrically. This decision altered the emotional effect of the finale, which is downbeat. The discarded epilogue is a beautifully rendered summation of the major themes of the movie and is more uplifting. With the downbeat denouement, audiences were trusted to support a film without the traditional "Hollywood" ending, and this abridged, official release version remains a historical curiosity. For Brando, *Mutiny on the Bounty* marked the end of the first phase of his Hollywood career as a guaranteed box office player. He would not have another substantial commercial or artistic success until his career renaissance in *The Godfather* ten years later, netting a second best actor Oscar, which he summarily refused.

As a postscript, the replica of the *Bounty* sailed on as a functioning attraction and movie prop until sunk by Superstorm Hurricane Sandy in the Atlantic Ocean on October 29, 2012, nearly fifty years to the day after the theatrical premiere. In 1962 an eerily prescient Lewis Milestone had described the tumult of making the movie "like being in a hurricane on a rudderless ship without a captain."[21] A half century later, the real-life captain went down with the ship, as he, another crew member, and the venerable wooden vessel all slipped to an undersea grave, sharing the fate of the original *Bounty*. But the 1962 adaptation of *Mutiny on the Bounty* survives as an underappreciated, maligned movie epic, a flawed but impressive relic of the studio system, now at ebb tide.

8 · THE NEW FRONTIER

John F. Kennedy's New Frontier marked a time of percolating social change that may have been less vociferous than the cultural clashes later in the decade but was striking nonetheless. Racial conflicts, antiwar protests, and the first stirrings of the gay liberation movement took place later in the 1960s and convulsed the media. But all of these movements were prefigured earlier in the decade in some landmark films of 1962.

Civil rights had of course been in the news since the Supreme Court's landmark desegregation case, *Brown v. Board of Education,* in 1954, and in protests roiling the South later in the 1950s. A few movies of the 1950s, like *The Defiant Ones* (starring Sidney Poitier) and *Odds Against Tomorrow* (with Harry Belafonte), brought these racial conflicts onto the nation's movie screens. Hollywood took up the cause off-screen as well, and many top actors joined the civil rights marches of the 1960s. Marlon Brando, for example, began to lose interest in acting after the colossal production of *Mutiny on the Bounty,* and he took time off from film projects to join the civil rights movement as well as the struggle for Native American recognition.

Gregory Peck was another leading member of Hollywood's liberal community, so it was not surprising that he was chosen to star in one of the hottest properties to reach the screen in 1962, the film version of Harper Lee's Pulitzer Prize–winning novel, *To Kill a Mockingbird.* Peck often disputed the idea that he was committed to playing nothing but morally upright heroes. It is true that one of his memorable early roles was that of a journalist battling anti-Semitism in *Gentleman's Agreement.* But Peck pointed out that he had also played a villain in David O. Selznick's lusty 1946 western, *Duel in the Sun,* and starred in adventure films, dramas, and romantic comedies in which he was not necessarily a role model. In his other 1962 release, *Cape Fear,* Peck played a morally compromised lawyer who resorts to highly questionable tactics in his battle against a vicious predator played by Robert Mitchum.

Still, Peck's portrayal of the more heroic lawyer, Atticus Finch of *To Kill a Mockingbird,* became his signature role, the one with which he would be most closely identified for the rest of his life. When the American Film Institute conducted a survey to choose the all-time favorite movie heroes, Peck's portrayal of Finch was number one in the poll. The film's presentation of Finch as a fair-minded southern lawyer defending a black man (Brock Peters) in Depression-era Alabama touched a nerve for viewers. The Hollywood community responded as well. After four previous nominations dating back to the 1940s, Peck finally won the best actor Oscar for his performance. At the Academy Awards ceremony, his victory elicited the loudest and longest ovation of the night.

To place the film in context, it may be worth recalling just a few of the racial conflicts that made headlines in 1962. Dr. Martin Luther King Jr. was arrested—not for the first time—in Albany, Georgia for marching against segregation. In September Dr. King was assaulted by a man who declared himself a member of the American Nazi Party. Probably the most significant civil rights event of the year was the fight to admit James Meredith to the University of Mississippi. When Meredith declared his intention to enroll, the university and top state officials resisted. Eventually President Kennedy ordered the National Guard out in force to defy Mississippi governor Ross Barnett. A little later in the year, partly in response to this continuing intransigence in the South, President Kennedy issued an executive order barring discrimination in any federal housing.

One other sign of racial progress was the July induction of the first African American major leaguer, Jackie Robinson, to the Baseball Hall of Fame. Another noteworthy event of the year was the story of Don Shirley, a talented black jazz pianist who hired a white bouncer from New York's Copacabana nightclub to be his driver and bodyguard for a concert tour through the segregated South in 1962. Their odyssey and eventual bonding formed the basis for the crowd-pleasing film *Green Book,* the Oscar-winning best picture of 2018.

It was against this backdrop that *To Kill a Mockingbird* opened for its Academy-qualifying run in Los Angeles in December 1962 and then went into wider release in early 1963. Although the film was set in the 1930s, it clearly evoked the conflicts of the 1960s as well. Peck's Atticus Finch provokes the ire of his racist community when he defends a black man accused of raping a white woman. The courtroom scenes are highly effective, as Atticus shrewdly

FIGURE 8.1 Gregory Peck as Atticus Finch defending Brock Peters as Tom Robinson in *To Kill a Mockingbird*. (Screen shot)

establishes that it was really the white woman who attempted to seduce a black handyman and cried rape (at the instigation of her bigoted father) when she was rebuffed. Atticus underscores these points in his summation to the jury, a superbly written speech that is also the highlight of Peck's acting career.

The scene that follows is one that has been highly debated in subsequent reevaluations of the film. Atticus's two children, Jem and Scout, have been watching the trial from the upstairs gallery where black spectators are forced to sit. As Atticus leaves the courtroom, the black minister tells Scout, "Stand up, your father's passing," and all the black people stand to pay their respects to the lawyer. Even at the time, some black activists criticized this scene for perpetuating the idea of the white savior as the hero of the civil rights movement, and this criticism has been echoed by others over the years. Of course one response would be that the film was merely reflecting the realities that existed in an earlier era of American history. And the film itself is honest about how heavily the deck was stacked against people of color throughout much of American history.

Another brief scene illustrates how racial perceptions and attitudes have changed with time. At one point Atticus drives their black housekeeper, Calpurnia (Estelle Evans), to her home, and she sits alone in the back seat of the car. This was a subtle reflection of the social norms of the period, when the races were separated by strict conventions. This segregation was slowly breaking down by 1962, but not without considerable struggle. One sign of incremental progress was the desegregation of southern movie theaters, at least in some major cities. Atlanta, emerging as the South's leading metropolis, followed an integration plan in the summer of 1962 first tested successfully in Nashville, as the old Jim Crow laws were challenged across the region.[1]

In 2018 wordmeister Aaron Sorkin (*The West Wing, The Social Network*) expanded the role of Calpurnia in his revisionist adaptation of the novel for Broadway. Sorkin gives her (and defendant Tom Robinson) agency against racial injustice that is not present in either Lee's story or the film. In the film, screenwriter Horton Foote deftly highlights her role as a surrogate mother to the Finch children, adhering closely to Lee's account. The Sorkin stage version grants Calpurnia a more prominent role as "Atticus's foil and needling conscience," giving a contemporary sensibility to the story's timeless appeal.[2]

Gregory Peck had originally provided a statement to be utilized in the film's marketing: "For my part, I am proud of this film. It is not only heart-warming entertainment, it stands up and declares itself on basic, moral principles and on the difficult racial question in this country today. I think that in its way it reaffirms our traditional faith in the fundamental Christian idea 'Love thy neighbor.'"[3] In this manifesto, Peck was echoing what motivated Atticus to handle the case. In a passage from Harper Lee's novel, Atticus explains to his young daughter, Scout, why he was defending a black man: "When you and Jem are grown, maybe you'll look back on this with some compassion, and some feeling that I didn't let you down. . . . Scout, I couldn't go to church and worship God if I didn't try to help that man." Later, Peck further reflected on the role: "I put everything I had into it. All my feelings. All I learned from forty-six years of living, about family life and fathers and children. And my feelings about racial justice and equality and opportunity."[4]

It should also be underscored that this progressive social theme wasn't the only element that made the movie memorable. *To Kill a Mockingbird* is one of the screen's most imaginative evocations of childhood, and it endures as a beautiful memory piece as well as an indictment of racial prejudice. The striking title sequence, which takes us inside a box of toys as a child hums in the background, introduces the film's distinctive point of view. Elmer Bernstein's tender score heightens the wistful emotion. The film itself begins with narration straight out of Lee's novel, eloquently delivered by actress Kim Stanley. Horton Foote's Academy Award–winning screenplay remains faithful to the book, while director Robert Mulligan (*Fear Strikes Out, Summer of '42*) uses purely cinematic techniques to retain the child's-eye point of view. In an early sequence, for example, the children are in bed talking about their dead mother as the camera pans gently from their room to Atticus sitting alone on the front porch, lost in reverie. Cinematography (by Russell Harlan, filming in black and white) and art direction enhance the film's meticulous period feel. In fact, the art directors, Alexander Golitzen and Henry Bumstead, along with set decorator, Oliver Emert, were rightly applauded for their rich set design, duplicating sections of Monroeville, Alabama (Harper Lee's home) in a fifteen-acre set built entirely on the Universal studio backlot.

Mulligan also deserves credit for his work with the child actors—Mary Badham as Scout, Oscar-nominated for her performance; Philip Alford as Jem; and John Megna as their intrusive neighbor, Dill. The character of Dill was said to be based on Lee's close friend Truman Capote. Badham later described Mulligan's gift for handling child actors. "He would basically let us have at it," she said. "He didn't want to give us too much . . . [he] wanted us to be real." Badham noted that she, Alford, and Megna were all cast because Mulligan and producer Alan Pakula "wanted children with big imaginations so their characters could live in their imaginations. That was easy for us."[5]

When the children explore the "haunted" house inhabited by the mysterious Boo Radley (Robert Duvall in his film debut), the subjective camera encourages us to share their sense of fear and wonder. Foote's screenplay retains many of the novel's sharp set pieces, including the scene when Atticus reveals surprising skill with a shotgun and another when the children shame the town bigots out of their plan to lynch the black prisoner accused of rape. Although these dramatic scenes have a potent impact, the comic scenes, like Scout's first day at school in a starched and hated pinafore, are just as vivid. The most indelibly moving scene comes at the climax: Scout's recognition of Boo Radley cowering in her bedroom after saving her life, when she approaches him and whispers warmly and welcomingly, "Hey Boo."

This scene indicates that the author's plea for tolerance extended beyond the strong racial dimension of the movie. Lee was urging compassion for all social outcasts. And it is worth noting that this message of inclusion was expressed simply but forcefully by the film's young heroine. In the following scene, when her father contemplates having Boo arrested for killing the vengeful Bob Ewell, it is Scout who sides with the sheriff in objecting to putting this mentally damaged man under public scrutiny. "It would sort of be like killing a mockingbird," she muses. Since Lee was one of the few women who played a crucial role in creating a landmark film of 1962, her decision to give the story's strongest moral voice to a young female character should not be underestimated.

It is unfortunate that Lee's legacy was tarnished shortly before her death by the publication of an earlier version of *Mockingbird, Go Set a Watchman*, which presented a more bigoted Atticus Finch late in his career. But even that

FIGURE 8.2 Robert Duvall as Boo Radley and Mary Badham as Scout in *To Kill a Mockingbird*. (Photofest)

did not dislodge *To Kill a Mockingbird* from its perch as America's most beloved novel in a 2018 PBS competition, "The Great American Read," voted by millions of viewers. The original novel and the 1962 movie—one of the most faithful and flawless literary adaptations ever to reach the screen—continue to win converts and to be honored for their crucial role in challenging America's racist history.

A lower-budget movie released in 1962 also touched on racial conflict, this time in a contemporary setting. Director Roger Corman was right in the middle of his Edgar Allan Poe series of horror movies when he decided to shift gears and tackle an explosive topic that was all over the news. *The Intruder,* based on a novel by Charles Beaumont, focused explicitly on the skirmishes over school integration that divided the country in the period. Beaumont's novel was published in 1958, when most southern states were resistant to integrating their schools. The film's release four years later happened to coincide with the high-profile battle over James Meredith's desire to enroll in the University of Mississippi. Seven Arts had bought the rights to Beaumont's novel but was not able to find any financier to back the film. Corman purchased the rights from Seven Arts in 1960, but every studio turned him down. Eventually he received some funding from Pathe Labs, but he and his brother Gene contributed most of the $80,000 budget themselves.[6] Corman later boasted that it was the only film he ever made that lost money, though he admitted that a British release and home video sales eventually turned things around. "Forty years later we broke even," Corman observed wryly in a later interview.[7]

Unlike the Meredith case, *The Intruder* focuses on the integration of a high school in a fictional southern town. The main character, Adam Cramer, is an outside agitator who comes to town to rile up the racist residents and encourage them to fight the integration that has been mandated by law. In a way Cramer is a more sinister version of Professor Harold Hill of *The Music Man,* an outsider who plays on the fears and prejudices of the gullible townspeople to advance his own agenda. Corman had seen William Shatner in the theater in New York, and the actor had a strong supporting part in Stanley Kramer's *Judgment at Nuremberg* in 1961. Although Shatner was still a few years away from *Star Trek* fame, Corman took a chance and cast him. Shatner's performance is courageous in that the actor does not make any effort to soften the character. But he does capture the charisma that encourages the ignorant residents to join his crusade.

Working on a low budget, Corman brings off vivid scenes of mass hysteria, including one in which the townspeople protest the attempt of ten black students to enroll in school and another that echoes a famous scene in *To Kill a Mockingbird,* when a huge crowd gathers in front of the courthouse to lynch a young black student falsely accused of rape. Other scenes dramatize a Ku Klux Klan cross burning, the bombing of a black church, and the killing of its minister; these scenes startlingly foreshadow events that were taking place throughout the South in that era. Such scenes give the film a gritty, "ripped-from-the-headlines" feel that was far from typical Hollywood fare during that period. The script sometimes slips into sensationalism, as in a gratuitous scene when Cramer seduces the dissatisfied wife of a traveling salesman. And it may bend over backward in striving for balance, presenting a white newspaper editor (played by Frank Maxwell) as the champion of the black students, a crusader who is brutally beaten for his attempts to intervene. Nevertheless, at a time when racial conflicts are once again inflaming the country, *The Intruder* endures as a prescient and often explosive film.

Some revisionist critics have cited *The Intruder* for its bold depiction of racial bigotry and hatred, championing it over what they term the "safer" Hollywood films of the era, including *Mockingbird.* That argument does have some merit, but that raw authenticity ultimately kept *The Intruder* from reaching a wide audience. The film's repeated use of what the *Hollywood Reporter* euphemistically termed "a vulgar colloquialism referring to a member of the Negro race" embroiled Corman in a skirmish with the Production Code Administration over the denial of a seal of approval. *Daily Variety,* by contrast, had no problem using the ugly racial epithet in its reporting. The PCA felt that the excessive use of the word "nigger" was "inflammatory." Corman appealed, arguing that it was essential to the story, and he brought testimonials from the NAACP, the Congress of Racial Equality (CORE), the Anti-Defamation League, and the Senate Subcommittee on Civil Rights, among other groups. Impressed by the level of support, the PCA not only granted the seal without making any cuts but also offered to assist in any local censorship battles.

Corman fought for the seal so vigorously because its absence would severely limit bookings and nullify the possibility of being invited to the Cannes Film Festival, whose prestige he craved. Cannes ultimately rejected the film, but it was shown at Venice. "Sending it out without the seal takes it out of the major artistic level and puts it right into the exploitation field which it does not fit," the director stated at the time.[8] Ironically, when *The Intruder* failed to attract audiences, Corman tried reissuing it, first with an exploitation title, *I Hate Your Guts,* and again in 1964–1965, as *Shame.* Each time, the movie bombed. Audiences in the 1960s simply did not want to see a racially charged "propaganda" film. Its commercial failure dissuaded Corman from ever tackling serious sociological or political subjects again.

Despite its enlightened social conscience, and somewhat tamer approach to racial issues, *To Kill a Mockingbird* was also encumbered by censorship. The PCA objected to what it considered an overuse of offensive phrases like "nigger lover" in the script, and pushed for revisions. When the Legion of Decency classified the completed film A-3 (morally unobjectionable for adults), rather than A-2 (unobjectionable for adults and adolescents), Gregory Peck wrote to the Legion's executive secretary, Monsignor Little, for reconsideration. Peck, a devout Catholic, strongly expressed his disappointment, stating how the more restrictive rating was "a personal shock to me." He was "puzzled and dismayed" that teenagers were allowed to view the war carnage in *Lawrence of Arabia,* which had been rated A-2, but not *Mockingbird,* "with its portrayal of the importance of family love, racial tolerance, and non-violence." Peck's personal plea, and a few recuts to the film, paid off; the Legion relented and revised the classification, adding a recommendation "to the patronage of adults and young people."[9]

While *The Intruder* impressed some critics for its "courageous, realistic and stirring documentary-styled story," as noted by *Cue* magazine, *To Kill a Mockingbird* had far greater impact on the national consciousness, since it was a box office smash and reaped awards. In his glowing review of the film in *Show* magazine, JFK adviser Arthur Schlesinger Jr. praised Foote and Mulligan for preserving "what Hollywood usually throws away: the soul. With uncommon simplicity they have captured the adventure of childhood, the painful discovery of innocence and evil that gave Miss Lee's work distinction." He further applauded, "Much of the picture, like the Pulitzer Prize book from which it comes, bears the mark of Twain."

Like *To Kill a Mockingbird, Pressure Point*, another 1962 movie with racial conflict at its core, is a period piece. This low-budget drama reflects the strong social conscience of its producer, Stanley Kramer, who had directed such recent films as *The Defiant Ones* and *Judgment at Nuremberg* and would go on to make the landmark film about interracial marriage, 1967's *Guess Who's Coming to Dinner. Pressure Point* was directed by Hubert Cornfield, and if it is sometimes crudely executed, it does present a fascinating portrait of a Nazi sympathizer, played by Bobby Darin. The film is told in flashback, as psychiatrist Sidney Poitier tells another doctor (played by Peter Falk) about his most difficult case, an attempt to comprehend and cure a young racist and white supremacist, whom he encountered as a prison psychiatrist during the Second World War.

Darin's character is far from a stereotypical yahoo. Highly intelligent and cunning, he makes a smooth antagonist to Poitier's psychiatrist, taunting and needling him in order to keep the doctor on edge. Eventually Poitier does relieve some of the torments that have rankled Darin, but the result of this is to make the young racist even more adept at cajoling the prison staff into engineering his release. Indeed, the film daringly suggests that these white wardens and doctors are more inclined to side with a white prisoner than with a black doctor who is alienated from most of them.

One of the other fascinating elements of the film is its depiction of the German American Bund that Darin joined to find a sense of belonging that he never achieved in his family. The film sharply conveys the personal frustrations that led many Americans to scapegoat Jews as well as blacks, whom they viewed as impeding their own success. At a time when bigotry is once again on the rise as a result of a rabble-rousing president, *Pressure Point* takes on uncomfortable timeliness. Only a few other movies have dramatized native American fascism, including *Confessions of a Nazi Spy* and Alfred Hitchcock's *Saboteur.* But those movies were made in the Second World War era to rally Americans to the anti-Nazi cause. Looking back at that era with insight, *Pressure Point* ironically takes on more universality.

FIGURE 8.3 Psychiatrist Sidney Poitier (right) and his racist patient Bobby Darin in
Pressure Point. (Screen shot)

Cornfield's movie remains a strange, almost experimental movie because
much of it is told in voice-over, either by Poitier or Darin or by the young actor,
Barry Gordon, who plays the character as a child. Many of the characters who
appear in flashbacks have no dialogue of their own; the film seems to be aim-
ing to convey the neurotic solipsism of a disturbed personality. One of these
actors who has no dialogue, and therefore no screen credit, is James Anderson, who plays Darin's brutal father; Anderson happens to be the same actor
who portrayed the villainous Bob Ewell in *To Kill a Mockingbird.* But this
attempt at stylized storytelling does not entirely succeed, sometimes seeming
overly literary. Yet the film remains fascinating because of Darin's hard-edged,
uncompromising portrayal of an unapologetic racist.

Darin had lobbied Kramer for the part and was cast only after both Paul
Newman and Warren Beatty turned down the role. While the movie was in
production, Darin told the *Los Angeles Examiner,* "An actor can get rid of a lot
of inhibitions with this kind of role. I didn't know it was such fun being this
mean."[10] Darin starred in four other movies in 1962 (*Too Late Blues, If a Man
Answers, Hell Is for Heroes, State Fair*), and he would be nominated for a supporting actor Oscar the following year for *Captain Newman, M.D.*. But the pop
singer's acting career was short-lived, and he turned primarily to political activ-
ism, recording, and his nightclub act before his untimely death in 1973 at age
thirty-seven.

The interracial casting of *Pressure Point* was the result of a concerted effort to improve the profile of blacks in the movie industry, particularly in front of the camera. The NAACP castigated the motion picture industry in 1961 for widespread employment discrimination and further implored, "All we ask is that movies show the truthful American image . . . show the Negro as he is in American life, good, bad, or indifferent."[11] The Hollywood Race Relations Bureau then organized picketing of Los Angeles theaters and the 1961 and 1962 Academy Awards to protest the unrealistic portrait of American Negroes in the movies. Writers Guild of America West (WGAW) president Charles Schnee (*Red River, The Bad and the Beautiful*) wrote a letter to the membership in November 1961 encouraging them "to write parts in their scripts that portray Negroes as they exist in the American scene." As a result, a number of films in 1962 provided increased opportunities for black actors. In addition to *Pressure Point, The Intruder,* and *To Kill a Mockingbird,* these included *The Interns, The Manchurian Candidate, Hemingway's Adventures of a Young Man, Sergeants 3, What Ever Happened to Baby Jane?, The Man Who Shot Liberty Valance,* and *Convicts Four* (with a role written for singer Sammy Davis Jr.).

Later in the year congressional hearings were held to probe discriminatory practices in the entertainment business. Although there were few blacks in any positions, it was determined that the Hollywood guilds and unions had no official barriers; any de facto segregation was self-imposed by the members. Tellingly, the only union that had any significant nonwhite representation was janitorial. In his testimony at the hearings, Sidney Poitier assailed hiring conditions. "I'm probably the only Negro who makes a living in the motion picture industry which employs 13,000 performers," he declared. "It's no joy to me to be a symbol."[12]

The psychiatrist in *Pressure Point* was originally white and Jewish (based on a real case). This casting change was suggested by Stanley Kramer, who had also substituted a black character for a Jewish one in his 1949 film, *Home of the Brave.* In an interview with *Films and Filming* magazine, Kramer explained that he made the casting change in *Pressure Point* because "in the contemporary scene it seems more pointed, valid and dramatic. Also I was anxious to show the Negro in a different position to that of the subservient, non-educated one."[13] He further elaborated to the *Hollywood Reporter,* "The film is concerned with ideas and ends in a ringing affirmation—-by the Negro—of American democracy and its ability to improve and survive extremists." In his testimony before the congressional hearings, Poitier praised Kramer for taking the lead in bringing racially tinged stories to the screen. "What particularly impressed me," Poitier added, "was his willingness to have a key role rewritten so that it could be played by a Negro actor."[14] As it happened, *Pressure Point* turned out to be the only film of 1962 that offered a leading role for a black actor.

With the casting switch, the film then presented three major issues: race prejudice, psychoanalysis, and the psychoneurotic background of fascism, which was perhaps more than it could handle comfortably. This overreach was reflected in the film's mixed reviews. Among the unfavorable notices, Stanley Kauffman (in the *New Republic*) sneered, "This film seems half cheap liberal sermon and half opportunism." Other critics praised the two leads and respected the filmmakers' attempt at raising important social issues, however mixed the results. Hollis Alpert in *Saturday Review* approved the director's effort, writing, "If the story has occasional lapses, Mr. Cornfield's technical ability does not, and he achieves several scenes of stark brilliance."

Although much of *Pressure Point* takes place in a prison where a dedicated psychiatrist matches wits with a sociopathic patient, it cannot be described primarily as a prison movie. That genre dates back to the early 1930s, when such films as *The Big House, I Am a Fugitive from a Chain Gang,* and *20,000 Years in Sing Sing* were part of a wave of gritty social protest movies exposing some of the harsh realities of Depression-era America. Over the years most of these films were testosterone-fueled action pictures about tough men behind bars, though some of them also exposed the harsh conditions that dehumanized and degraded prisoners. The genre even expanded to encompass a few notable women-in-prison movies, including *Caged* from 1950 and *I Want to Live!* from 1958.

The filmmakers behind *Birdman of Alcatraz* had loftier goals when they devised their novel addition to the genre in 1962. Although the film incorporated many familiar elements, including sadistic guards and a violent prison riot, it was primarily designed as a chronicle of the dehumanization taking place in America's penitentiaries, along with a plea for more humane efforts at rehabilitation. The prime movers behind the project were actor Burt Lancaster and his producing partner, Harold Hecht. The original director on the film was British director Charles Crichton (*The Lavender Hill Mob*), but he clashed with Lancaster and was replaced by John Frankenheimer, who had directed the actor in *The Young Savages* the previous year. *Birdman* added to Frankenheimer's remarkable output in 1962.

During the 1950s Lancaster was one of the first movie stars to try to take advantage of his high profile in order to produce high-quality films, including *Sweet Smell of Success* and an adaptation of George Bernard Shaw's *The Devil's Disciple.* Lancaster, who started out as an acrobat and action movie star, was eager to branch out and attach himself to films of social import. He won the Oscar in 1960 for playing the flamboyant huckster-preacher of Sinclair Lewis's expose of evangelical religion, *Elmer Gantry*. Although it was a prestige film, the role fit comfortably into Lancaster's most typical screen persona—the extroverted, swashbuckling rogue. But the actor was determined to demonstrate greater range, and in *Judgment at Nuremberg,* where he was cast as a Nazi judge on trial for war crimes, Lancaster played most of the film in silence, drawing the audience's attention simply in the intense way he observed the courtroom proceedings. *Birdman of Alcatraz* gave him another opportunity to play a more introverted character. Because his character, convicted murderer Robert Stroud, spent most of his prison time in solitary confinement, Lancaster had to find a way to mesmerize the audience without relying on explosive speeches or physical action, and he clearly relished the challenge, delivering an understated, compelling performance that earned him one of his four best actor nominations as well as an award at the Venice Film Festival.

Joanna Lancaster, the actor's daughter, remembers her father as a hybrid of the extrovert he played in *Elmer Gantry* and the quieter character he embodied in *Birdman.* "Dad could hype up his persona," she reports, "but he could also be very quiet when he was concentrating." Burt relished transforming himself into Stroud. Joanna recalls an incident from her childhood when her sister came running into the house in terror to announce that there was a disheveled old man at the front door. "I don't think she used the word 'homeless,'" Joanna says, "because we weren't so conscious of that issue. But she thought it was some kind of vagrant. My mother went to the door and started laughing. The old man was my dad in makeup. He also started bringing home birds. He always got into his characters, and he wanted us to get into them as well."[15]

The acting challenges of the film clearly tantalized Lancaster, and in his producer's role, he was eager to present a subtle but potent plea for prison reform. As Lancaster told the *Christian Science Monitor* in an interview during production, "Using Stroud as our example, we are trying to say that the initial concept of prisons—to send men away to be punished—is not only inhumane, but outdated and outmoded."[16] The film was adapted by Guy Trosper from a book by Thomas E. Gaddis, chronicling the remarkable life of Bob Stroud, who was first jailed in 1909 for killing a man who had beaten a prostitute in Alaska. The film does not include the information that Stroud was working as her pimp, a detail that might have made the character seem more unsavory. For that killing, Stroud was convicted of manslaughter, and he was due to be released after several years, but while in prison at Leavenworth, he killed a guard, and for that crime, he was sentenced to death. In one of the unlikely but true details included in the film, it was Stroud's mother, played by Thelma Ritter (an accomplished and popular character actress in a dramatic departure from her usual sympathetic and comedic roles), who appealed for clemency directly to President Woodrow Wilson's wife, who was essentially running the White House after her husband's debilitating stroke. Wilson commuted Stroud's sentence to life imprisonment, but the prison warden (a composite character played by Karl Malden) decides that his life in prison will be spent in solitary confinement as an added punishment for his murder of a prison official.

The movie opens effectively by highlighting Stroud's bellicose masculine swagger. On a prison transport train heading to Leavenworth, with convicts sweltering in the heat, Lancaster's Stroud takes action into his own hands by smashing the train window. This puts him on the wrong foot with the warden once they arrive at Leavenworth, and Stroud continues to demonstrate belligerence and simmering anger in his interaction with guards and other prisoners. When a cellmate tries to handle a photograph of Stroud's mother, Stroud reacts with fury. And when a surly guard refuses to allow a visit from his mother, the confrontation ends with Stroud stabbing the guard to death. It might be pointed out that the domineering mothers who appeared in Frankenheimer's two other movies of 1962, *All Fall Down* and *The Manchurian Candidate,* find another incarnation in Ritter's character in *Birdman.* As a Freudian acolyte of the era, Frankenheimer subscribed to the gospel that saw the overbearing mother as the key figure in male psychological development. Interviewed on the NBC *Today Show* in May 1962, Ritter commented that Stroud's mother was "too complex" for her to explain fully, and that Mrs. Stroud might stymie "a great many psychiatrists" as well. Ritter added that Stroud "was [his] mother's son. He was obsessed with her and she with him."[17] Later in the film, when Stroud meets and marries a widow (Betty Field) who wants to help him in his research on bird diseases, the convict's mother becomes fiercely jealous, and a power struggle ensues that ends with Stroud burning the once-precious photograph of Mama.

After Stroud is sentenced to solitary confinement, he gradually develops the interest in birds that leads to a softening of his violent persona. These scenes, beginning with his discovery of a wounded sparrow, are muted and increasingly effective. Although there are interactions with a sympathetic guard (eloquently played by veteran actor Neville Brand) and with a prisoner in the next cell (effectively played by newcomer Telly Savalas), many of these scenes are played in silence, as Stroud experiments with feeding and training his growing

FIGURE 8.4 Burt Lancaster in the title role and Thelma Ritter as his possessive mother in *Birdman of Alcatraz*. (Screen shot)

collection of birds. These essentially interior scenes are strengthened by the delicate score of Elmer Bernstein, who had three impressive credits in 1962—on *To Kill a Mockingbird* and *Walk on the Wild Side,* in addition to *Birdman.*

Later, as the birds become ill, Stroud studies medicine and eventually writes a book on bird diseases that adds to understanding of the field. He later writes another book about the history of the prison system, pleading for a less punitive approach to prisoners, with more emphasis on rehabilitation. This book angers the warden, which leads to Stroud's transfer to Alcatraz, where he is prevented from raising birds. As a few critics pointed out, the film's title is something of a misnomer, since Stroud had no birds in Alcatraz. All in all, the film, aided by Lancaster's performance, effectively captures Stroud's transformation from angry loner to a more humane and gentle prisoner. Most of the reviews lauded the picture. *Variety* called it "the finest 'prison 'picture ever made, except that it is not really a 'prison' picture in the traditional and accepted sense of the term." *Time* magazine wrote, "*Birdman of Alcatraz* argues forcefully and with eloquence that the destruction of individual dignity, the redirection of a human soul to a numbered automaton, is as great a crime as any for which men are jailed."

Some of the real inmates who knew Stroud felt the film glossed over Stroud's hard, brutal nature. At parole hearings later in his life, his appeals for release were consistently denied, and Attorney General Robert Kennedy was one of the last people who refused the request for Stroud's release. Stroud died in a prison hospital on November 21, 1963, a day before the assassination of JFK. Stroud was undoubtedly a complex personality, but considering that he had no more than a third-grade education, his achievements are impossible to deny. The film ended up contributing to the national dialogue about the failings of the prison system, dialogue that still resonates well into the twenty-first century, with many critics protesting the mass incarceration of racial and ethnic minorities.

9 · SEXUAL AND SOCIAL OUTLAWS

Another area that *Birdman of Alcatraz* whitewashed concerned the sexuality of Robert Stroud. During one of many appeals for Stroud's release, Missouri senator Edward Long, chairman of the Congressional Committee on Federal Penitentiaries, asked whether Stroud was homosexual, and the convict's attorney conceded that his client had engaged in homosexual acts while in prison. That would have been a challenging element to incorporate into a movie made in 1962, but it would not have been impossible. The restrictive Production Code of 1930 had declared, "Sex perversion or any inference of it is forbidden." But in 1961 the Code was revised to allow discreet presentation of homosexuality. Pressured by producers and directors who wanted to expand screen content, the MPAA declared on October 3, "In keeping with the culture, the mores and the values of our time, homosexuality and other sexual aberrations may now be treated with care, discretion and restraint."[1]

One of the people pushing for this change was producer Walter Mirisch. The Mirisch Company was already in production on a new movie version of *The Children's Hour,* based on Lillian Hellman's provocative 1934 play about a child who accuses two of her teachers of lesbianism. William Wyler, who directed the film, had directed an earlier film of Hellman's play in 1936, with the lesbianism changed to a heterosexual triangle. This time the original text was restored, with Audrey Hepburn and Shirley MacLaine cast in the leads, and the film earned a coveted Code seal when it was released at the end of 1961.

The year 1962 saw several other groundbreaking films with gay characters and themes. The British film *Victim* used the word "homosexual" for the first time, and this was apparently a bit too much for the MPAA to handle, for the film was denied a Code seal. However, the New York censors acceded, which was a crucial step for any film release in that era. The film also found unlikely allies in the Roman Catholic Church, with tacit approval by the Vatican (under the guidance of liberal Pope John XXIII) and the seemingly neutral stance of the Legion of Decency, which gave it "Separate Classification" rather than tagging it morally objectionable.[2] Therefore, it managed to get limited theatrical bookings when it was released in America in early 1962. *The Children's Hour* ended with MacLaine's character committing suicide after acknowledging her own lesbian desires, whereas *Victim* presented the main character played by Dirk Bogarde in a more heroic light, which might also have contributed to the MPAA's queasiness about the film. The filmmakers set out to protest English laws that declared homosexuality to be a crime, which in turn gave blackmailers an opportunity to cash in on gay men's fear of exposure.

The blackmail plot provides an engine for the film, which was written by Janet Green and John McCormick and directed by Basil Dearden. The film begins by intercutting the experiences of two men—Boyd Barrett, a working-class youth who is on the run (played by young actor Peter McEnery), and Melville Farr, a barrister played by Dirk Bogarde. The young man, targeted by blackmailers, is desperately in need of money, and he tries to contact the barrister, who refuses his calls. Eventually Barrett is arrested, and he hangs himself in his prison cell. The police contact Farr, since they found his name among the young man's effects. It turns out that Farr had befriended Barrett, but it seems that the intense attraction between the two of them was never consummated. Nevertheless, Farr is tormented by the idea that his neglect may have contributed to the young man's death, and he agrees to work with the police to track down the blackmail ring, even though this means he will have to make a public acknowledgment of his involvement with Barrett.

The blackmail plot is somewhat convoluted and lacking in suspense, but the film is nonetheless bracing in its frank exploration of a topical theme that had never been addressed in film. As Farr explores the gay demimonde, he encounters a variety of interesting characters, including a barber who had already spent time in prison for homosexual acts and a closeted actor, played by Dennis Price. When Farr meets the actor, he encourages Price to "come out" in order to set a positive example for other gay men—an argument that has been used to urge other celebrities to disclose their sexual orientation. The actor declines, as do most of the other prominent gay men depicted in the film. But Farr resolves to put himself on the line, which also means confessing his homosexual urges to his wife (Sylvia Syms), who struggles believably with the revelations.

The film also presents an interesting range of straight characters. The police officer in charge of the case seems surprisingly tolerant, whereas his assistant is contemptuous of gay men. Similarly, some of the blackmailers are completely blasé about the "crimes" they are threatening to expose, whereas a woman who works with them is an angry, moralizing harpy. Like other early films exposing a controversial social issue, *Victim* is sometimes a bit solemn and didactic, substituting good intentions for dramatic fireworks. But it is a courageous and extremely well-acted film, especially by Bogarde, who gives a remarkably nuanced performance, seething with believable and moving anguish. The film marked a turning point in the actor's career. He had been acting in films since the 1940s, but most of his movies had been light comedies, like the popular series that began with *Doctor in the House* in 1954. As Bogarde later joked, "I was the Loretta Young of England."[3] *Victim* changed his image and pushed his career to a whole new level, leading to fruitful collaborations with such top directors as Joseph Losey (with whom he made *The Servant* and *Accident*), Luchino Visconti, and Alain Resnais. The role was doubly daring because Bogarde himself was gay, and yet he did not shy away from being identified with the role. Bogarde wrote in his memoirs that taking the role "was the wisest decision I ever made in my cinematic life." He also suggested that it transformed his personal life: "This time the door I had chosen to enter was not just ajar . . . it had been [opened] wide with a blaze of light and I was not to retreat ever again."[4]

Most critics appreciated the groundbreaking nature of the film. In his review in February 1962, the *New York Times'* Bosley Crowther found the plotting contrived, but he went on to write, "But as a frank and deliberate exposition of the well-known presence and plight of the tacit homosexual in modern society it is certainly unprecedented and intellectually bold. . . . The very fact that homosexuality as a condition is presented honestly and unsensationally, with due regard for the dilemma and the pathos, makes this an extraordinary film." Crowther acknowledged that the film might be challenging for some viewers: "How much it will be appreciated and how much its pronounced sympathy for the victimized homosexual will be shared by the viewer will depend upon the individual's awareness and tolerance of the abnormality."

Crowther's description of homosexuality as an "abnormality" may strike contemporary viewers as unenlightened, but his review was much more sympathetic than others at the time. *Time* magazine wrote, "But what seems at first an attack on extortion seems at last a coyly sensational exploitation of homosexuality as a theme—and what's more, an implicit approval of homosexuality as a practice. . . . Nowhere does the film suggest that homosexuality is a serious (but often curable) neurosis that attacks the biological basis of life itself." With that review in mind, it may be easier to appreciate just how daring *Victim* was in 1962 and how much it contributed to frank discussion of an emerging social issue.

Hollywood also jumped into the fray with the first major studio picture to address male homosexuality, Otto Preminger's production of *Advise and Consent.* This was not the first time that Preminger had eagerly courted controversy. In 1953 he released *The Moon Is Blue,* a saucy romantic comedy, without a Code seal, and his 1959 best picture nominee, *Anatomy of a Murder,* was notable for using frank sexual dialogue in its courtroom scenes. Wendell Mayes, the screenwriter of *Anatomy,* also adapted Allen Drury's Pulitzer Prize–winning novel, *Advise and Consent,* a political melodrama with an impressive all-star cast.

The story centers on the confirmation hearing of a nominee for Secretary of State, Robert Leffingwell (Henry Fonda), who is accused of having been a member of the Communist Party years earlier. This political theme was still a hot potato in 1962, as the controversy over *The Manchurian Candidate* also demonstrated, and Preminger was happy to rile the conservatives. Two years earlier he had helped to break the Hollywood blacklist by granting screenplay credit to former Communist Dalton Trumbo on *Exodus.* But the sexual subplot of *Advise and Consent* was even more explosive. One of the senators hesitant to vote for confirmation of the candidate is Brigham Anderson, played by Don Murray. Some ruthless supporters of Leffingwell try to change Anderson's vote by threatening to expose a gay liaison that he had with another soldier while in the army ten years earlier. This blackmail plot links the movie to *Victim.*

The changes from novel to film reveal the different sympathies of Preminger and author Allen Drury. Drury was a political conservative who viewed Leffingwell as a subversive turncoat overly eager to appease the Communists. This point of view is expressed in the film by South Carolina senator Seab Cooley (Charles Laughton), but Preminger's liberal sympathies are more in line with Leffingwell and his supporters. Many readers of the novel compared Leffingwell to Alger Hiss, the former State Department official who had been convicted of perjury for concealing his Communist ties.[5] In the movie version Leffingwell still lies under oath about his participation in a Communist cell while teaching at the University of Chicago, but the film is more forgiving of this sin than the book had been. As Leffingwell explains to the president (Franchot Tone), he was never actually a member of the Communist Party but simply explored Communist ideas as many liberals had during the 1930s. In the film he emerges as less like Alger Hiss and more like Democratic presidential candidate Adlai Stevenson, who was derided for being an "egghead" (a term used against Leffingwell in the film). And of course the character probably seems more sympathetic because he is portrayed by Fonda, so often the screen incarnation of decency and compassion in such films as *The Grapes of Wrath* and *Mister Roberts*. Scenes with his young son (played by Eddie Hodges, who had been the juvenile lead in the original stage production of *The Music Man*) only add to Leffingwell's likability. The novel had presented him as a danger-ous figure, whereas in the film, he emerges as a flawed but sympathetic spokes-man for humane liberal values.

On the other hand, Drury had been surprisingly sympathetic to the repressed homosexual, Brig Anderson, whereas Preminger treats the charac-ter in a somewhat more hysterical manner. In the novel Anderson's wife rec-ognizes that something is amiss in her marriage before she starts receiving telephone calls from the blackmailers threatening to expose a dark secret in her husband's past. In the film the wife, touchingly played by Inga Swenson (also on screen in 1962 as Helen Keller's mother in *The Miracle Worker*), does tell her husband, "I know we haven't had an exciting marriage," perhaps a veiled reference to their sexual incompatibility. But this came through more forcefully in the novel. In the film her suspicion is that he is having an affair with another woman, and there is a compelling scene between them when he struggles to tell her the truth but ultimately is unable to confess. This scene is a powerful one that has been played out over many decades by married and closeted gay men who wrestled with the secrets they were keeping and the inner conflict that prevented them from confessing the truth. It would take another twenty years, until 1982's *Making Love,* for a closeted married man to confess his homosexuality to his wife on-screen. Murray's performance in *Advise and Consent* is subtle and moving, capturing a drama of sexual repres-sion that was all too common in that era.

After this scene, however, the film diverges from the novel by having Brig travel to New York to seek out his ex-lover, Ray. The New York scenes are what contributed to the film's later reputation as a lurid, backward depiction of the gay subculture. Brig first stops at the apartment that he thinks is Ray's home, but it is actually inhabited by Manuel, an overweight man in a caftan, who seems to rent out his apartment to men seeking sexual rendezvous. He is basi-cally a gay pimp who shares his apartment with a collection of squealing cats.

Manuel directs Brig to Ray's favorite hangout, a club that historian Vito Russo described as the first gay bar ever depicted on-screen.[6] Brig is shocked to find the club inhabited by men only. The music playing is a suggestive tune sung by Frank Sinatra: "Let me hear a voice / A secret voice / A voice that will

FIGURE 9.1 Don Murray stares in horror as he enters a gay bar in *Advise and Consent.* (Screen shot)

say / Come to me / And be what I need you to be." Brig is horrified by the scene and flees, but Ray spots him and rushes after him, explaining that a desperate need for money led him to cooperate with the blackmailers in Washington. He follows Brig to a waiting taxi, but Brig pushes him into the mud as the taxi speeds off. Later that night, back in his office at the U.S. Senate, Brig commits suicide by cutting his throat.

This plot element comes from Drury's novel, but the breathless scenes in New York were the invention of Preminger and Mayes. Probably Preminger did not intend to stigmatize gays; he simply had a taste for sensationalism that he could not restrain, and he was undoubtedly tickled by the idea of depicting a gay bar in the most shocking manner imaginable. And so although the film broke ground by introducing fresh subject matter to the screen, it didn't have the dignity that the filmmakers of *Victim* brought to their depiction of a similar milieu.

Yet it should also be noted that Brig Anderson is not the villain of the film. That role belongs to the blackmailing senator played by George Grizzard, whose own career would skyrocket a few months later, when he costarred in the world premiere of Edward Albee's play *Who's Afraid of Virginia Woolf?* He is depicted as the epitome of a new breed of politician, an ambitious hustler who will use every possible dirty trick to advance his career.

Whatever the film's limitations in terms of its depiction of homosexuality, it succeeds as a juicy if somewhat overheated melodrama of political intrigue and chicanery. And Preminger confirmed his gift for offbeat casting, just as he had done in films like *The Man with the Golden Arm*, the screen's first depiction of drug addiction, and *Anatomy of a Murder*, which scored a coup by hiring Joseph N. Welch, the real-life lawyer in the Army-McCarthy hearings, to play the judge overseeing the film's murder trial. In *Advise and Consent,* Preminger tagged some real-life congressmen and correspondents for supporting roles, and he demonstrated a shrewd eye in filling out the large cast. The gay pimp was played by Larry Tucker, who a few years later became Paul Mazursky's writing partner on such comedy classics as *I Love You, Alice B. Toklas* and *Bob & Carol & Ted & Alice.* To play a Kansas senator, Preminger gave the first screen role to Betty White, who went on to become a comedy legend on television. As the Senate minority leader, the director cast Will Geer, a formerly blacklisted actor who went on to have a distinguished career on stage and screen for the rest of his life.

Preminger also offered a role, as a senator from Georgia, to Dr. Martin Luther King Jr., at a time when there were no prospects for electing blacks to the Senate. For a short while it appeared that King might accept it, but after due consideration, he declined, stating that the role "could not be of any significance in advancing civil rights." There had been backlash from the South about the possible casting, and one former congressman called it an "insult" and "sheer fantasy." King said his decision was not based on how it would have affected the feelings of white southerners. "I wasn't worried about that," the civil rights leader asserted.[7]

Preminger demonstrated taste in casting younger actors like Murray, Grizzard, and Swenson in key roles. But he also brought back a lot of veterans, including Gene Tierney, who had starred in his first major hit, *Laura,* but who had been absent from the screen for several years before making *Advise and Consent.* Franchot Tone, married to Joan Crawford in the 1930s, gave a superb performance as the ailing but strong-willed president, and Lew Ayres made an equally vivid impression as the seemingly weak but unexpectedly decisive vice president who is thrust into the center of power in the movie's final scene. Fonda commands every scene in which he appears, and Walter Pidgeon also had his best role in years as the shrewd Senate majority leader.

But Laughton comes close to stealing the picture as the wily southern senator. After his heyday in the 1930s and 1940s, Laughton had turned to directing in the 1950s, in the theater and also creating a Gothic film masterpiece, *The Night of the Hunter.* But that film was a crushing failure at the box office, and Laughton never had a chance to direct another film. Later in the decade, he returned to screen acting and had some of his best roles ever, in Billy Wilder's *Witness for the Prosecution,* Stanley Kubrick's *Spartacus,* and finally *Advise and Consent.* It would turn out to be his final screen performance; he died of cancer just six months after completing the film.

The movie faced opposition from some politicians and commentators (both domestically and abroad), concerned about what they felt was a negative view of the inner workings of the federal government, particularly the Senate. This criticism was echoed by the Legion of Decency, which gave the picture "Separate Classification," not simply for the homosexual subplot but for the depiction of the government as a hotbed of "corruption, dishonesty and lack of integrity, both public and private." The Legion further postulated that since the film seemed like a "documentary expose," such a distorted image "may serve only to denigrate democracy itself."[8] When the film opened in June 1962, Preminger defended his endeavor to *Newsweek*, averring that it was "a realistic movie . . . in it I show democracy at its best. . . . I made it to prove there is a balance of power. There is no single hero . . . the institution of the Senate is the hero. Institutions can only last if you can criticize them."[9] The *London Sunday Express* supported Preminger and wrote, "That such a film can be made and shown as the American entry at the Cannes Film Festival does say a great deal for the democratic system."[10] After the film got mixed reviews from the American press, the moviegoing public voted at the box office and made *Advise and Consent* a summer hit.

The film does not identify which political party the characters belong to, but in the early 1960s, conservative southern senators like Seab Cooley were all Democrats, and insiders could tell that the majority party was clearly meant to be the Democratic Party. The president who chooses a left-wing, peace-loving man like Leffingwell as his Secretary of State would have to be a Democrat, and there was a definite inside joke in casting Peter Lawford (JFK's brother-in-law) as a senator from New England who is something of a ladies' man, with women sneaking in and out of his hotel suite. Preminger reveled in all these topical touches, and despite the seamy elements in the gay subplot, he clearly helped to expand the freedom of the screen by tackling this once-forbidden subject.

As *Victim* suggested, British films were a bit ahead of Hollywood in taking a more mature approach to once-taboo themes. *A Taste of Honey,* adapted from Shelagh Delaney's acclaimed play, also reached American movie theaters in 1962. More artful than *Victim* but equally compassionate, the film was the latest effort from rising British director Tony Richardson, who had directed two earlier films adapted from plays by John Osborne, *Look Back in Anger* and *The Entertainer.* Osborne was the most gifted representative of the "angry young man" school of British theater. Richardson had directed both plays on-stage and so was a natural to turn them into films.

Delaney was an even newer voice in theater, a young woman from the Midlands. She was only nineteen when *A Taste of Honey* was first performed in England; it later transferred to the West End and then to Broadway, with Joan Plowright cast as the young heroine, Jo, and Angela Lansbury as her slatternly mother, Helen. The author said that one of her motivations in writing the play was to present a less judgmental vision of homosexuality than British theater had encompassed at that moment.[11] After the success of the play, Delaney wrote the screenplay with Richardson, who wanted to make the film more cinematic than his earlier theatrical adaptations. Delaney's play had a single set, but the film version ranged all over Manchester, with vivid scenes on the docks, in seedy residential areas and dance halls, as well as a side trip to Brighton. In bringing these locations to life, Richardson was helped enormously by cinematographer Walter Lassally, one of the most gifted of a new generation of cameramen energizing European cinema. Lassally also photographed one of the foreign film Oscar nominees of 1962, *Electra,* directed by Michael Cacoyannis, and he won an Oscar two years later for photographing Cacoyannis's *Zorba the Greek;* these films were all shot in black and white.

The rest of the film's crew—including editor Antony Gibbs (*The Knack, Performance, Fiddler on the Roof*) and composer John Addison (an Oscar winner for Richardson's 1963 film, *Tom Jones*)—also helped to revitalize British cinema during this fertile period. But the primary achievements of *A Taste of Honey* lay in the casting and the performances. The star of the Broadway production, Joan Plowright, was already twenty-nine when she played the part, and for the film version, Richardson sought a younger actress who would be closer to the right age for Jo, who is a high school student at the start of the story. He selected a magnetic new actress, Rita Tushingham, just nineteen when she made her film debut in *A Taste of Honey.* Tushingham went against the grain of the typical look for movie stars. Her plain but marvelously expressive face held the camera just as potently as more glamorous actresses.

Richardson surrounded his star with more established actors like Dora Bryan and Robert Stephens, but he also used newer faces Paul Danquah as Jimmy, the sailor who impregnates Jo, and Murray Melvin as Geoff, the young gay man who becomes her flatmate and protector. The story is fairly simple. After Jo and her mother are forced to flee one apartment for nonpayment of rent, they find another place, but Helen goes off with a new husband, a younger man played by Stephens, and Jo is pretty much left to fend for herself. She has a love affair with a young black sailor, and the racial element in the romance is barely mentioned in the film. When Jimmy asks Jo if her mother will mind that he's black, Jo responds, "Whatever else she is, she's not prejudiced." The love

FIGURE 9.2 Rita Tushingham and Murray Melvin in *A Taste of Honey.* (Screen shot)

scenes between Jo and Jimmy were daring for the era, handled tenderly and unsensationally. The lovers break up not because of race but because Jimmy's ship takes him back to sea, and a haunting close-up of Jo standing on the dock and watching him depart captures the sense of loss that she feels.

When she meets Geoff, a customer in the shoe store where she works, Jo finds a nonjudgmental friend who can help her through her pregnancy. She quickly guesses his sexual orientation and cheekily offers to let him stay with her if he will tell her exactly what he does in bed. He declines to answer the question, but the scene is both funny and bold for the era. Their deepening bond is threatened by the return of Helen after her marriage falters. Helen seems unbothered by the idea that she might have a black grandchild, but she does exhibit some hostility toward Geoff, though it's left ambiguous whether this reaction grows out of homophobia or jealousy that someone else is taking her place as Jo's closest companion. In any case, Geoff decides to leave, and the scene of his departure becomes unexpectedly poignant. Richardson, a bisexual man who died of AIDS in 1991, treated Geoff with an empathy that most straight directors would probably not have matched. We feel the sharp sense of loss that stings Jo when Geoff disappears. Still, the final close-up of Jo makes it clear that she will weather any and all disappointments in her life; she is a true and defiant survivor.

At the 1962 Cannes Film Festival, Tushingham and Melvin were named best actress and actor of the year, a tribute to Richardson's superb work with these screen newcomers. American reviews also exalted the film. The *Saturday Review*'s Hollis Alpert called *A Taste of Honey* "virtually the revolutionist's handbook of non-studio moviemaking" as well as "the best English film to come along this year." Most reviews agreed that the film improved on an already excellent play. Bosley Crowther raved, "In his magnificent adaptation . . . Mr. Richardson has preserved and indeed expanded that gracious tolerance that is the keynote of the work." He went on rapturously, "Words are completely insufficient to express the true quality and extent of eloquence got into this picture by Miss Delaney and Mr. Richardson. Theirs was the rare achievement of creating poetry amid ugliness, of discerning the richness of life in squalor." When Crowther compiled the *New York Times'* ten-best movie list for 1962, he chose *A Taste of Honey* as the year's finest film.

One dissenting note was struck by the conservative publication *Films in Review,* which referred to the character of Geoff as "a male sex pervert." The magazine complained that the film reflected the "current propaganda in England, and our own country, for miscegenation and homosexuality." All of these films certainly took chances in exploring race relations and sexuality with a bracing new openness, and if their candor proved off-putting to some of the more hidebound members of the press and the public, their very existence testified to changes afoot in the world beyond the cinemas.

Social turmoil of a different kind was prefigured in another low-budget movie released in 1962, *War Hunt,* a modest American indie feature directed by Denis Sanders and produced by his brother, Terry. They started collaborating when they were film students at UCLA in the 1950s, and they won an Oscar for a short film they produced in 1954, *A Time Out of War.* Their careers advanced from there, and they had developed considerable skill by the time they made their second feature in 1962. There happened to be a number of other war movies made in 1962, and some of them—such as Don Siegel's *Hell Is for Heroes* and Samuel Fuller's *Merrill's Marauders*—expressed antiwar sentiments. But those were both World War II movies, while *War Hunt* stood out for taking place during a far more ambiguous conflict, the Korean War.

In comparison to the multitude of World War II movies, only a few films had been made about the Korean War, including *The Bridges at Toko-Ri* (1954) and *Pork Chop Hill* (1959). No doubt this is because it was a war without a clear victor; it ended in something of a stalemate, and the few films made about the conflict reflected that ambiguity. As one of the characters in *War Hunt* comments to new recruit Roy Loomis (Robert Redford), "This is a funny kind of war, a war we can't really win." This frustrating conflict precipitated a very different kind of combat film from the hundreds of movies made about the battles to defeat the tyrants of Nazi Germany and imperialist Japan. Terry Sanders says the script by Stanford Whitmore appealed to him and his brother because "it was authentic, it was original, and it wasn't guts and glory."[12] Max Youngstein, the head of United Artists at the time, decided to back a few low-budget movies that he called "idea films," and *War Hunt* fit into that category. It was made on a tight budget of $300,000, but the filmmakers enlisted veteran cinematographer Ted McCord to shoot the picture, and they hired jazz musician Bud Shank to compose the evocative score.

Because of the tight budget, most of the film was shot in Topanga Canyon outside Los Angeles, several months after a major wildfire had devastated the area. "So it felt like a war zone," Terry Sanders comments. The filmmakers originally sought cooperation from the Defense Department to secure a tank and other military equipment. "They were very friendly," Sanders recalls, "but they said we would have to rewrite the whole script. In the end we didn't get anything from them."[13] Even without these trappings, the film impressed the critics. Bosley Crowther wrote that *War Hunt* "must have been shot in a cornfield, to the tune of a dime. And most of this little picture is pure, unvarnished gold." He went on to call it "one of the most original and haunting war movies in years."

The film is set during the final days of the Korean War, in May 1953. The script centers on the moral conflict between two soldiers, the innocent Loomis and a more seasoned soldier, Ray Endore (John Saxon), who verges on being a psychopathic killer. Endore is the opposite of a team player. Every night he slips out of base camp, skulking behind enemy lines and killing enemy soldiers with a knife before returning home in the morning. The officers tolerate his behavior because he seems too defiant to discipline, and also because he does achieve results in his unconventional way. As Sanders now explains the theme of the film, he and his brother meant to say, "In war, which is an insane activity, an insane person is invisible."

But new recruit Loomis is troubled by Endore's savagery and especially by the influence he seems to have on an orphaned Korean boy who is a kind of mascot to the platoon. When a truce is finally declared at the end of the film, Endore refuses to abide by it and continues on his murderous solo missions until he is finally killed by one of his own platoon members. But the fate of the young boy is left uncertain, as he races away from his American protectors, perhaps to follow the example set by his psychotic mentor. At the end of the film, when one of the Americans asks Loomis, "You all right, soldier?" Loomis answers, "No," and that is the final word in this unsettling film.

Does this film foreshadow American involvement in another unwinnable war a decade later? Certainly the antiwar pessimism that pervades the film does give hints of the sentiments that would intensify during the Vietnam War. In 1961, when *War Hunt* was made, there were only a few American troops in Vietnam, but their numbers increased during the Kennedy era, and this film cannot help but be seen—at least in hindsight—as a warning of the dislocations that might take place in another war in Southeast Asia. And the disturbing character of Endore foreshadows some of the American soldiers who were traumatized and brutalized during the long and frustrating Vietnam conflict. Producer Terry Sanders points out that Francis Ford Coppola was a graduate student at UCLA at the time of *War Hunt* and thus was very aware of this film being made by two UCLA graduates. "*Apocalypse Now* is really a variation of *War Hunt*," Sanders suggests. "This guy [played by Brando] has to be hunted down by his own people because he's gone rogue, just like Saxon's character in *War Hunt*."[14]

Up to this point Saxon was known primarily as a lightweight romantic leading man, costarring with Sandra Dee in *The Reluctant Debutante, The Restless Years,* and *Portrait in Black,* as well as performing in early teen musicals *Rock, Pretty Baby* and *Summer Love.* In *War Hunt* he got a chance to demonstrate his acting chops and gave a dark-edged, uncompromising performance. The supporting cast was also distinctive. Future director Sydney Pollack played the grizzled sergeant of the platoon, and future movie and TV star Tom Skerritt (*M*A*S*H, The Turning Point*) also made a vivid impression. Gavin MacLeod, who became a major TV personality in *McHale's Navy* and *The Mary Tyler Moore Show,* also had a featured role. Another cast member stood out for a different reason. At the time he made the film, twenty-four-year-old actor Tony Ray was married to his onetime stepmother, actress Gloria Grahame, after reportedly having an affair with her while she was married to his father, director Nicholas Ray, a decade earlier.

But the film is most notable for marking the first screen appearance of Redford, who gives a natural and sympathetic performance that hinted at the charisma he would solidify later in the decade. MCA agent Monique James had recommended Redford to the Sanders brothers after seeing him in a few plays and TV shows. "Redford became a friend for a while," Terry Sanders reports. "I was living in Laurel Canyon, and he had a little apartment nearby, and he and his wife Lola would often have dinner at our house. I must say I was very impressed that Redford was offered the lead role in a TV series playing a psychiatrist, and they would have paid him $10,000 a week, which was a ton of money at that time. He thought about it and told his agent no. He went back to New York to try his luck in the theater."[15] Not long after that, the actor won the leading role in Neil Simon's *Barefoot in the Park* on Broadway, and his career took off. Sanders had tried to sign Redford to a five-picture contract while they were making *War Hunt,* but the deal fell through. "His lawyers were better than my lawyers," Sanders laughs.

The most important connection for Redford was that he met Pollack while making the movie, and they forged not just a friendship but a remarkable professional partnership. When he moved behind the camera, Pollack directed Redford in seven films, including box office hits *The Way We Were* and *Jeremiah Johnson* and the Oscar-winning best picture of 1985, *Out of Africa.*

There were other small, offbeat movies of 1962 that gave hints of the potent social criticism that would intensify later in the decade. One of the most intriguing of these was a modern-day western, *Lonely Are the Brave,* starring Kirk Douglas, written by Dalton Trumbo (from a novel by Edward Abbey), and directed by David Miller. Like his frequent screen costar Burt Lancaster, Douglas was one of the movie stars of the era who branched out into producing films, many of them with a social conscience, and *Lonely Are the Brave* was typical of the kind of project he favored.

The film opens strikingly, with a beautiful shot of the open prairie and a cowboy waking up next to his horse. Jack Burns (played by Douglas) looks up to see a jet streaking across the sky. This incongruity cleverly establishes the theme that the film means to explore—the plight of an anachronistic man, a rugged individualist in a technological world that would render him obsolete. When the last cowboy rides on to a New Mexico highway with trucks flying by and horns honking, the movie's drama is solidified. Jack goes to visit a friend's wife, Jerry (played by Gena Rowlands in only her second feature film), and he learns that her husband has been arrested for his role in helping to smuggle Mexicans into the United States. Jack is immediately sympathetic and tells Jerry that he and her husband "hate fences." This scene plays startlingly today and seems remarkably prophetic of a battle against illegal immigrants that would help to determine the outcome of the 2016 presidential election, some fifty-five years after the film was made.

This protest of American xenophobia is only a secondary theme in *Lonely Are the Brave,* but it adds to the film's surprising impact. After learning of his friend's arrest, Jack gets himself into a barroom brawl (in a vivid scene that director Steven Spielberg, a later champion of the film, described as one of the best fight scenes in movie history) in order to get arrested and join his friend Paul (Michael Kane) in lockup.[16] There he lets Paul know of his plan to break them both out of jail, but Paul declines; he says he is prepared to serve his two-year sentence so that he can return to his life as husband and father.

FIGURE 9.3 Modern cowboy Kirk Douglas in *Lonely Are the Brave*. (Screen shot)

But Jack does manage to escape, and this sets the police in pursuit of him, using modern technology—including radio communication and helicopter surveillance—that would not have been available to sheriffs and outlaws in an earlier era.

In one of his early film roles, Walter Matthau gives a sly, winning performance as the dogged sheriff who develops a sneaking sympathy for his quarry. This is because Jack proves to be a surprisingly adept antagonist, outwitting his high-tech pursuers at several junctures. In one scene he expertly shoots out the rear rotor of a helicopter, causing the aircraft to topple to the ground without causing serious injury to the two deputies on board. And Jack is able to lead his horse over a steep mountain pass to elude his pursuers traveling by car.

These outdoor scenes demonstrate the skill of another major contributor to the film, cinematographer Philip Lathrop, who shot three films in 1962 (Blake Edwards's *Experiment in Terror* and *Days of Wine and Roses* in addition to *Lonely Are the Brave*). His wide-screen images of the barren New Mexico terrain represent one of the high-water marks of black-and-white cinematography during a year distinguished by many other fine achievements. Lathrop went on to shoot many important color films as well (*The Pink Panther, Point Blank,* and *They Shoot Horses, Don't They?* among them), gradually gaining recognition as one of the country's best cinematographers. New film composer Jerry Goldsmith also contributed to the film's impact with a compelling score marked by a solo trumpet, a musical motif that Goldsmith would use in a number of later films, including *L.A. Confidential,* made thirty-five years later.

But the eloquence of Trumbo's screenplay, thoughtfully interpreted by director Miller and the actors, may be even more impressive than these technical achievements. One of the intriguing elements in the script, left tantalizingly ambiguous, is the relationship of Jack and Paul's wife, Jerry. There is unmistakable passion between them when they share a farewell kiss, and it seems that the two men once vied for Jerry's affections. She settled down with Paul because he was more likely to be a devoted partner than Jack, an unapologetic loner. In one wordless scene Jack slips into the bedroom where Jerry's son is sleeping, and the emotion on Douglas's face is open to more than one interpretation. It is possible that he is experiencing regret over the domestic life that he chose to flee, but the intensity of the moment suggests that he may be the child's father and that his friend Paul chose to raise the boy and marry Jerry. Douglas and especially Rowlands play these scenes with a good deal of unexpressed but intense emotion, adding a degree of sexual and emotional complexity that was not typical of American movies made in the era.

The film makes it clear that Jack's position as a rebellious loner is becoming harder to sustain in a more mechanized and conformist country. The dark ending may be a bit heavy-handed: in a bit of emphatic symbolism, Jack is run down by a huge truck carrying a load of toilets. The truck's driver is played by up-and-coming actor Carroll O'Connor, who would rise to stardom a decade later playing America's favorite bigot, Archie Bunker, on TV's *All in the Family*. But this climactic scene is effectively staged, and the mortal injury to Jack's horse is not shown overtly, achieved through sound effects and the forlorn expression in Douglas's eyes. Goldsmith had written a musical cue for this climactic scene, but the filmmakers cut it out, recognizing that the scene could be just as effective without such typical Hollywood underscoring. The film's forlorn finale definitely packs a wallop.

Unfortunately, few audiences got to see the movie in 1962. Douglas made a financial deal with Universal, which had little interest in the film and devoted scant resources to the release. Douglas groused to the *New York Times* that he was hoping the picture would get special handling. "What broke my heart was that they tossed the picture into a theater and let it die," he said. "I asked them to put the picture in an art house. I thought this was the kind of picture people would discuss. . . . What can you do? I can kill myself trying to argue. Everybody out here is so quick nowadays to blame the stars for everything. Why doesn't a studio admit it goofed?"[17]

Another interesting note about the film is that its theme of the iconoclastic individual against the establishment was also expressed that year in Ken Kesey's first novel, *One Flew over the Cuckoo's Nest*, published in 1962. Douglas was taken with the book, and he bought the film and stage rights. He starred in a Broadway adaptation of Kesey's novel in 1963. The play flopped, but Douglas still hoped to turn *Cuckoo's Nest* into a film. He struggled for more than a decade to get it made.[18] It was finally filmed in 1975, with his son Michael as

producer and Jack Nicholson playing the role of Randle McMurphy that Douglas had once hoped to immortalize on-screen. However, at least he had the
satisfaction of playing a precursor of McMurphy in *Lonely Are the Brave*, which
became Kirk's favorite of his films.

Kesey's theme of a defiant loner battling a hidebound establishment touched
a nerve not just in America but in other countries as well. Novelist Alan Sillitoe had created an equally iconoclastic character in his short story "The Loneliness of the Long Distance Runner," and the author adapted his story for
prolific director Tony Richardson in 1962. Sillitoe's protagonist, Colin Smith,
is a rebellious young working-class man who is arrested for his role in a rob-
bery and sent to a reformatory. In one scene that directly prefigures *One Flew
over the Cuckoo's Nest*, Colin mocks an earnest psychiatrist who tries to ana-
lyze his antisocial impulses.

Soon afterward, Colin is spotted by the institution's "governor" (played by
acclaimed British actor Michael Redgrave) as a talented cross-country runner,
and Redgrave hopes to utilize Colin to fulfill his own dream of scoring a victory against the track team of a posh private school in the first-ever competition between these teams from different social classes. At first Colin is tempted
by the bright future that Redgrave promises to him if he wins the race, but he
defies the governor at the film's climax, when he stops right before the finish
line and allows his aristocratic rival (played by screen newcomer James Fox,
who would go on to star in such diverse films as *The Servant, Thoroughly Modern Millie,* and *A Passage to India*) to win the race.

As Stanley Kauffmann pointed out in his *New Republic* review, the abuse
of the working class in England remained an explosive issue even as late as the
1960s. But it was not only this dissection of class warfare that made the film
resonate for American as well as British audiences. The "rebel without a cause"
of the 1950s became a more grimly determined rebel in the 1960s. Colin's final
act of defiance is prefigured earlier in the film in flashback scenes that are inter-
woven artfully throughout the movie. After his father's death, Colin's mother,
sharply played by Avis Bunnage, is pleased to receive a meager stipend from
her husband's employer, and she gives some cash to Colin. Sitting in his father's
bedroom, he burns the money, indicating his disdain for the shabby way his
father was treated in life as well as in death. His decision to throw the race at
the end of the film is therefore a consistent act of a young man who sets himself apart from all the values of his society.

The only time when Colin feels at peace is when he is running, not in a competition but by himself, when the governor allows him to leave the institution

FIGURE 9.4 Tom Courtenay in *The Loneliness of the Long Distance Runner.* (Screen shot)

to train on his own. These scenes of Colin racing through forests are the only moments of grace he is allowed. Walter Lassally's cinematography, though perhaps too prettified at times, is exceptionally vivid, and the jazz-inflected score by John Addison contributes to the rare feeling of liberation that Colin experiences.

As he did in *A Taste of Honey,* Richardson designed the film as a showcase for a gifted new actor, Tom Courtenay. Kauffmann described the star as having "the grainy look of a teen-age old man." Indeed, Courtenay was far from the Hollywood image of a leading man, but his craggy, expressive face was mesmerizing in a different way. In a glowing review of the film, the *Saturday Review* took note of Richardson's radical approach to casting. The director "is clearly a menace to the star system," the magazine wrote. "He first discovered Rita Tushingham, who in *A Taste of Honey* bore not the least resemblance to the usual pretty young movie ingénue, and now in *The Loneliness of the Long Distance Runner* he has discovered Tom Courtenay, who is the least likely looking movie star since Ernest Borgnine. Young Mr. Courtenay has what I guess would be called a homely face. . . . As an actor, however, he is devastating; he achieves expressiveness with no palpable effort, and sends you home both heartbroken and uplifted."

Richardson's assault on the star system even had an impact on Hollywood. Later in the decade, when Mike Nichols was looking for a young actor to star in *The Graduate,* he may have been influenced by Richardson and other European directors in refusing to cast a standard matinee idol. Robert Redford was considered for the part, but Nichols went in a completely different direction when he cast Dustin Hoffman instead. It could be that actors like Hoffman,

Gene Hackman, and Al Pacino would never have been given a shot at stardom if it were not for the striking examples set by these iconic British films of 1962.

Beyond the quality of Courtenay's performance, the film was one of the first to connect with the intelligent young audiences who would change the face of movies later in the 1960s and into the 1970s. *New Yorker* film critic David Denby wrote of the film's impact before a revival screening in 2007: "Of all the early-sixties films in the British kitchen-sink school, *Loneliness* . . . is perhaps the most poetically assured (Walter Lassally's black-and-white cinematography is heartbreakingly beautiful) and the most bitter in its sense of defeat."[19] Sillitoe and Richardson's tribute to the angry maverick thumbing his nose at the privileged members of society prefigured all the antiestablishment heroes who were looming just over the horizon.

10 · CROWNING ACHIEVEMENT

The character of the loner or rebel did not merely grace low-budget films from England and America. The year's most successful and most honored film, *Lawrence of Arabia,* also had at its center a defiant misfit who became a military hero despite the fact that he was an outsider in British society as well as in the Arab army he tried to lead. Many of the same antiestablishment sentiments that animated modest, black-and-white pictures like *The Loneliness of the Long Distance Runner* and *Lonely Are the Brave* also found expression in one of the year's most expensive epics.

Yet it is worth pointing out that *Lawrence of Arabia,* the masterpiece that crystallizes all of the elements that made 1962 such an extraordinary year for movies, actually had a more checkered history than today's moviegoers may realize. This is not simply because of its tremendous production obstacles. Its critical fortunes have fluctuated dramatically over the decades. This may sound strange considering that the film won seven Academy Awards in 1962, including best picture and best director. The producer, Sam Spiegel, had won two previous best picture Oscars, for *On the Waterfront* and *The Bridge on the River Kwai.* He was a master promoter, and the Academy often honored big-budget, epic-scaled movies, even when those films were inferior efforts like *The Greatest Show on Earth* or *Around the World in 80 Days.*

Of course *Lawrence* was in a very different league from those bloated spectacles. But the surprising fact is that many of the influential critics of 1962 were lukewarm on David Lean's film. It did get rave reviews from critics like James Powers of the *Hollywood Reporter* and Kate Cameron of the *New York Daily News,* but those reviewers were considered Hollywood cheerleaders. Stanley Kauffmann of the *New Republic* and the waspish John Simon, writing at the time for the *New Leader,* did praise the film. But the country's most widely read critic, Bosley Crowther of the *New York Times,* was one of the naysayers. He called *Lawrence* "just a huge, thundering camel-opera . . . exhausting and barren of humanity." Luckily for the filmmakers, because of the New York newspaper strike, his review probably had less impact than it would have had under ordinary circumstances.

Up-and-coming critic Pauline Kael praised Peter O'Toole's performance and the striking cinematography, but she also wrote, "This picture fails to give an acceptable interpretation of Lawrence, or to keep its action intelligible." Never a fan of David Lean, Kael made her prejudices clear in a later article she wrote about spectacle films: "What makes a David Lean spectacle uninteresting finally is that it's in such goddamn good taste. . . . The hero may stick his arm in blood up to the elbow but you can be assured that the composition will be academically, impeccably composed."[1] (How else should it be composed? Kael blithely overlooked the fact that art is meant to bring precision and clarity to disturbing subject matter.)

Kael's archrival in the 1960s, Andrew Sarris, was even more contemptuous of *Lawrence of Arabia.* In a shockingly insensitive review, Sarris wrote, "Perhaps *Lawrence of Arabia* is one brutal queer film too many," and he called it "simply another expensive mirage, dull, overlong, and coldly impersonal."[2] Sarris and Kael did not have major platforms in the early 1960s, so their negative reviews did not affect the box office. But as their profiles rose and these critics' acolytes took command of other publications, the film's reputation began to sink. In 1972, ten years after the film's release, when the British magazine *Sight and Sound* asked a panel of eighty international critics to list the ten greatest movies in history, Stephen Farber was the only one to include *Lawrence of Arabia* on his list.[3]

The editing of the film over the years did not help matters. It was not until the film was restored to its original length in 1989 that the critical pendulum began to swing in the opposite direction. It is now rare to find an international poll that does not include *Lawrence* among the greatest films of all time. Directors Steven Spielberg and Martin Scorsese helped to change the film's fortunes by championing it passionately. Spielberg commented, "*Lawrence of Arabia* was the first film I saw that made me want to become a moviemaker."[4] And Scorsese wrote in the foreword to a book published to celebrate the film's thirtieth anniversary in 1992, "*Lawrence* was the first grand-scale film constructed around a character who was not a traditional hero." As Scorsese observed astutely, "Lawrence is as flawed and doomed as any of the characters in the great film noir," and he concluded, "It's the first interior epic, the first film of epic scale whose true canvas is the private passion of a man in anguish."[5]

The film's journey to the screen was a kind of epic in its own right. British producer Alexander Korda contemplated a film on T. E. Lawrence's life in the 1930s, and there were other false starts before two heavyweights got involved. *Lawrence of Arabia* represented the second collaboration of producer Sam Spiegel and director David Lean, who first joined forces in 1957 to film *The Bridge on the River Kwai*. Like *Lawrence, Kwai* won seven Oscars, including best picture and best director. It also won the award for best adapted screenplay, but the credit went to novelist Pierre Boulle, who had nothing to do with the making of the film. The script was actually written by Carl Foreman (*High Noon*) and Michael Wilson (*A Place in the Sun*), but since both writers were blacklisted in the 1950s, the industry refused to award them credit. Lean was reportedly dissatisfied with Foreman's original script, but he welcomed Wilson's revisions and promised the scribe that on their next collaboration, he would receive full credit.

Lean and Spiegel were an unlikely team, but both were larger-than-life characters who epitomized the growing internationalization of cinema that was taking hold in 1962. Spiegel was born in Jaroslau, which was part of the Austro-Hungarian Empire. He traveled around Europe, worked for a time in London during the 1930s, and served a short prison term for writing phony checks.[6] When he was released, he decided to seek his fortune in Hollywood, which presented some challenges for a man with a criminal record. He eventually entered the United States illegally from Mexico (an early example of one of Donald Trump's bad hombres?) under the name of S. P. Eagle, and he formed a partnership with director John Huston. Adrian Turner, the author of a definitive book on the making of *Lawrence of Arabia*, saw Spiegel in the mold of early Hollywood moguls who desperately sought respectability. As Turner wrote, "A highly cultured man, Spiegel wanted more than mere success; he wanted prestige, and to bathe in reflected glory."[7] The same description might have been applied to a bandit like Harry Cohn, who toyed with the idea of making a film about T. E. Lawrence as early as 1952. (The studio that Cohn founded, Columbia Pictures, eventually distributed *Lawrence of Arabia*.)

Lean had a less colorful background. He came from a middle-class Quaker family in England, which he found stultifying. Against his parents' wishes, he decided to enter the film business and worked his way up to the position of film editor. Director Michael Powell (*The Red Shoes*) said of Lean, "He was the

best editor I ever worked with—or should I say, worked for."[8] Lean soon graduated to the director's chair, and he won his first Oscar nomination for a
memorable romantic drama, 1946's *Brief Encounter*. His early films (including
two superb Dickens adaptations, *Great Expectations* and *Oliver Twist*) were all
British productions, but Lean had a hankering to burst out of the confines of
English society as well as the parochial English film industry. He took the
first step when he traveled to Italy to make *Summertime* in 1955, working for the
first time with a major Hollywood star, Katharine Hepburn. Then he traveled
to Ceylon to make *The Bridge on the River Kwai*, which starred Alec Guinness (who had appeared in both *Great Expectations* and *Oliver Twist*), along
with an American star, William Holden. Lean demonstrated his taste for the
exotic and his flair for sensuous filmmaking in both of those movies.

Both Lean and Spiegel were extremely strong-willed personalities, and
clashes between them were inevitable. According to Anne V. Coates, the editor of *Lawrence of Arabia*, "They fought all the time, but Sam had some very
good ideas, and I think they really admired each other."[9] Of course Spiegel did
not have the patience to spend every day on the remote locations, so Lean com-
manded the set. Nicolas Roeg, the second-unit cameraman on *Lawrence*,
once said, "If the Martians landed they would not have needed to say, 'Take
me to your leader.' They would have picked David out from the crowd
immediately."[10]

After the international success of *Kwai*, Lean and Spiegel contemplated a
film on the life of Gandhi, but they abandoned it as too vast a subject. They
then turned to a film about T. E. Lawrence, the flamboyant British officer who
had triumphantly led the Arab armies against Turkey during World War I. Spiegel persuaded Lawrence's brother, A. W. Lawrence, the executor of his estate,
to sell him the rights to Lawrence's highly praised book about the Arabian campaign, *Seven Pillars of Wisdom*. To adapt the book, they hired the screenwriter
whom they felt had salvaged *Kwai*, Michael Wilson. But after a year of work,
Wilson felt he could not satisfy Lean, and he left the project, leaving behind a
273-page script. The filmmakers then approached Robert Bolt, a playwright
who had made a splash with his acclaimed play *A Man for All Seasons*, which
was enjoying a successful run in London. Initially Bolt was hired for a six-week
rewrite job, but he ended up throwing out most of Wilson's script and starting from scratch, ultimately spending more than a year on the project and
continuing to write after filming began.

Lean decided to film the bulk of the movie in Jordan, which had the spectacular desert vistas that he craved. Other sequences were shot in Morocco and
in Spain. King Hussein of Jordan approved the filming, with the proviso that

no Jews were to be allowed as part of the crew.[11] Sam Spiegel, of course, was Jewish, but it is unclear whether he declared himself to be a Christian, or whether the king simply looked the other way when the producer arrived on the set. The first scene shot, on May 15, 1961, was Lawrence's introduction to the desert. It showed Lawrence and his Arab guide, Tafas, riding through the spectacular landscape. It was filmed in one of the most remote areas ever caught on camera, about 250 miles east of the port of Aqaba, in an unmarked part of the desert that might have actually been over the border in Saudi Arabia. (Needless to say, there were no signs identifying the countries.) In his re-review of the film after the 1989 restoration, Stanley Kauffmann eloquently evoked the impact of this early scene, which begins with a long shot of two men on camels, specks in a vast expanse of sand. As Kauffmann wrote, "Lawrence and his Arab guide are on those camels, as we soon discover, and we are with them, are in the desert with them, as thoroughly as we have ever been in any place in any film."[12]

The technical achievements of the film were indeed astounding, but they may have meant less if they were not placed in the service of a thematically rich and complex work of art. What makes *Lawrence of Arabia* the quintessential film of 1962 is that it brought together so many of the qualities that defined this extraordinary year. It mixed veteran talents and screen newcomers. Claude Rains, who had earned an Academy Award nomination in 1939 for *Mr. Smith Goes to Washington,* was cast once again as a weary politician, this time as a cagey diplomat looking to expand British holdings in Arabia. Other performers who got their start soon afterward—Alec Guinness, Anthony Quinn, and Jack Hawkins—were also in the cast. And of course Spiegel and Lean had also been working in film since the 1930s. But the two central roles in the film went to faces new to American audiences.

Originally Spiegel and Lean hoped to cast Marlon Brando as Lawrence. Brando had starred in Spiegel's 1954 production of *On the Waterfront* and was interested in *Lawrence of Arabia.* But he was involved in his own massive production of *Mutiny on the Bounty,* and he asked that they wait for him to complete that project. That would have meant a full year's delay, and the filmmakers reluctantly decided to move on. They then settled on newcomer Albert Finney, a rising star on the London stage who was just beginning to make his mark in films. Finney made a screen test for Lean but ultimately turned down the role; he did not want to sign the long-term contract that Spiegel demanded. Instead, he decided to stick with British films, and he starred in 1963's Oscar winner, *Tom Jones.*

The defection of Finney led the filmmakers to seek even lesser-known actors. The eventual screen credits on the movie blazed, "Introducing Peter O'Toole," but like much in Hollywood, that was a bit of an exaggeration. O'Toole was not actually making his film debut, and he was not a complete unknown. Like Finney, the actor had earned strong reviews in the British theater, and various people claimed a role in "discovering" him. Katharine Hepburn claimed that she recommended him to Lean after seeing O'Toole's screen test for her 1959 movie, *Suddenly Last Summer*.[13] Lean was impressed with his supporting performance in *The Day They Robbed the Bank of England*. Even costar Anthony Quinn could testify on his behalf, since O'Toole had appeared with Quinn in Nicholas Ray's 1960 film about Eskimos, *The Savage Innocents*.

The other crucial role in *Lawrence of Arabia* was that of Lawrence's chief Arab confederate, Sherif Ali, a composite character modeled on a few tribal leaders described in *Seven Pillars of Wisdom*. Spiegel and Lean initially considered several dark-haired European actors, who would make a contrast to the blond O'Toole. Their first choice was German actor Horst Buchholz, but after securing a leading role in Billy Wilder's *One Two Three*, he had to bow out. The filmmakers then approached French actor Alain Delon, who was on screen in 1962 as Monica Vitti's love interest in *Eclipse*, but he recognized the grueling nature of the role and turned it down. Spiegel then hired Maurice Ronet, Delon's costar in the hit thriller *Purple Noon*, and Ronet actually began shooting the film with O'Toole in Jordan. But Lean was dissatisfied with his performance, mainly because his thick accent meant that he would likely have to be dubbed. Even though the film was under way, Lean asked for recommendations of Egyptian actors who spoke English. He liked the photograph of Omar Sharif, and the actor was flown to the location to meet the director.

Sharif was already something of a movie star in Egypt, but he was completely unknown to Western audiences. The gamble of centering this expensive epic on two unfamiliar actors was not lost on Lean and Spiegel. The producer, who had almost always worked with established stars, was very aware of the risk he was taking, but he and Lean also recognized that they would win acclaim if the gambit succeeded. And the director certainly felt that audiences would be more swept up in the authenticity of the adventure if there were new faces in these two crucial roles. Besides, they had some security in casting recognizable names in the supporting parts.

Some of this other casting drew criticism in later years. But the reality is that with an expensive film, the studio needed a few well-known names like Guinness, Quinn, Jose Ferrer, and Arthur Kennedy, who took on the role of the American journalist, modeled on Lowell Thomas, after Edmond O'Brien

FIGURE 10.1 Director David Lean with stars Omar Sharif and Peter O'Toole in *Lawrence of Arabia.* (Photofest)

became ill. As the years passed, many people began to chide Hollywood for its ethnically dubious casting. Perhaps one of the most notorious examples was the casting of Paul Muni and Luise Rainer as Chinese characters in *The Good Earth.* Such casting is indeed cringeworthy, but this issue becomes more complicated in the case of *Lawrence of Arabia* and its two primary Arab characters, Prince Feisal and Auda Abu Tayi. Guinness makes Feisal a complex, intelligent leader, alternately ironic and world-weary. He is the beneficiary of some of Bolt's most elegant dialogue, and it is hard to imagine many actors who could have delivered the witty lines with his subtlety and panache. Similarly, it is hard to think of many other actors who could have matched the brash, masculine energy that Quinn brought to his portrayal of Auda. The story is told that when Quinn first appeared on the set in costume and with a false nose to match the photographs of Auda, Lean—who had never met the actor—blurted out, "Cancel Quinn, and get me that actor!"[14] The story may be apocryphal, but it testifies to the star's commitment to authenticity. It is certainly true that if the film were being made today, Guinness and Quinn would never get those parts, and we might have missed two vivid, memorable performances. It should be noted that there were other Asian or Middle Eastern actors in the supporting cast. Auda's son, for example, was played by Kamal Rashid from Jordan, and there were also cast members from Morocco, India, and Pakistan.

It wasn't only the cast that represented a blend of veterans and newer faces. Freddie Young was not Lean's first choice as cinematographer. The director considered younger cameramen, but they were unavailable. He feared that Young, who was born in 1902, might be too old and stodgy. Young was already well established in 1939, when he photographed *Goodbye, Mr. Chips* with Robert Donat and Greer Garson. He shot many color spectacles in the 1950s, including *Ivanhoe, Mogambo,* and *Lust for Life.* The collaboration with Lean turned out to be rewarding for both men. Young won the Oscar for *Lawrence of Arabia*—and for his two subsequent movies with Lean, *Doctor Zhivago* and *Ryan's Daughter.*

On the other hand, production designer John Box had his very first credits in the 1950s. Lean helped to launch his career, and Box won multiple awards over the next decade. A gifted young cameraman, Nicolas Roeg, did some of the second-unit photography, graduated to cinematographer later in the 1960s, and then became an acclaimed director on such films as *Don't Look Now* and *The Man Who Fell to Earth.* To compose the score, Spiegel initially wanted a veteran like William Walton or Benjamin Britten, but they weren't available. Even Richard Rodgers was considered, but Lean vetoed him. So they chose to go with a young French composer, Maurice Jarre, whose stirring score helped to heighten the impact of the film.

Another major contributor was the editor, Anne V. Coates, who started working in the 1950s. She had worked exclusively on modest British films, including a couple for director Ronald Neame, who had collaborated with Lean on his Dickens films in the 1940s. *Lawrence of Arabia* catapulted her to international success, winning her an Oscar, and she eventually edited a wide range of British and American movies, including *Becket, Murder on the Orient Express, The Elephant Man, In the Line of Fire,* and *Erin Brockovich.* Coates was not the first woman editor to win an Academy Award. Film editing was somewhat more open to women than many other fields, but she was unquestionably a pioneer.

Her job on *Lawrence* came about because of a chance meeting. "I've been very lucky," Coates mentioned in an interview shortly before her death in 2018. "Of course it's not just luck. But you have to be in the right place at the right time—and then hopefully you've got the talent to carry you." Coates recalled that she and her husband, director Douglas Hickox, used to go to Harrods department store in London on Sunday mornings. One Sunday she ran into Ted Sturgis, an assistant director she knew who had worked on *The Bridge on the River Kwai* and was also working on David Lean's new film. He told her that Lean was looking for an editor to cut Albert Finney's screen test. "They were paying fifty pounds a week, and I wasn't working at the time," Coates said. So, in a state of agitation, she set out to meet Lean at Shepperton Studios. "I remember my legs shaking," Coates said. "I was really nervous." Lean, after all, was an internationally acclaimed director. "He was very grand at that time," she continued. "He had those piercing eyes."[15]

Finney had shot two scenes, one with Lawrence in his British uniform and one in his Arab robes. "We did the Arab scene first," Coates recalled. "We ran the dailies, and David asked how I would cut it together. I put together a rough cut, and he said one of the best things anyone has ever said to me: 'You've cut that exactly like I would.'"[16] They continued working on the two sequences, and one day Lean said to her, "Would you like to travel up to London in the Rolls with Sam and me?" When she arrived back in London, she told her husband, and he said, "Of course he's going to ask you to edit the film." There was a possible conflict, however. Stanley Kubrick had approached her to edit *Lolita*, another of the most tantalizing projects of 1962. "And they offered me more money for *Lolita*," Coates said. She was genuinely torn.

"I'll tell you something I've never told anyone," Coates confided. "A few years ago I was moving, and I came across a letter in my files addressed to Sam Spiegel. It said, 'Dear Mr. Spiegel, I'm afraid I'm going to have to turn down *Lawrence of Arabia* because I simply cannot work for that money.' Of course I never sent the letter. Otherwise I wouldn't still have it! I'm sure my husband wouldn't let me send it. I would have had a whole different life if I hadn't had that lucky meeting at Harrods. And where would I be now if I'd posted that letter?"[17]

Her collaboration with Lean was intense and rewarding for both of them. Coates began editing while they were shooting in Jordan, then continued when the company moved to Spain in December 1961. The very last sequence was shot in September 1962, and it was the very first sequence in the film— Lawrence's fatal motorcycle accident in England. After shooting was finally completed, Lean and Coates began a marathon session that lasted for the next three months. He took an apartment right above the editing room so that they could work from nine in the morning until midnight seven days a week. Because Lean had essentially been out of the country for almost two years, he had missed a revolution in filmmaking. Coates recommended that he watch some films of the French New Wave by Truffaut, Godard, and others to sample a new style in editing. According to Coates, Lean loved their approach. His previous films had depended on more traditional techniques of dissolves and

FIGURE 10.2 Oscar-winning film editor Anne V. Coates at her Moviola. (Photofest)

fades, whereas *Lawrence* employed the direct cutting popular in the new French cinema. The most striking of these cuts—and one of the most famous cuts in film history—jumped from Lawrence blowing out a match to the sun rising in the desert.

The film's cinematic triumphs inspired other filmmakers at the time. Directors like Fred Zinnemann, Billy Wilder, William Wyler, and Joseph L. Mankiewicz all saw early screenings and raved about the picture, just as directors Scorsese and Spielberg endorsed it decades later. But the subversive content of the movie was just as remarkable as its dazzling visual style.

At the time it was said that the difference in the approach of the two screenwriters was that Michael Wilson took a more political approach to the subject, whereas Robert Bolt provided a more psychological emphasis that Lean preferred. A. W. Lawrence, T. E. Lawrence's brother, granted Spiegel the rights to *Seven Pillars of Wisdom* on the basis of Wilson's detailed screen treatment. He was not pleased with Bolt's screenplay, which he felt gave too much emphasis to "psychological aberrations."[18] The truth is that the film is striking for both its psychological and its political insights, and it is probably too simplistic to divide the screenwriters' contributions in exactly this way. It is true that Wilson had been blacklisted because of his political convictions, and he was clearly interested in constructing an attack on British colonialism and a sympathetic study of the struggle for Arab independence. But Bolt, like Wilson, had been a member of the Communist Party in his youth, and he remained passionately invested in the political issues of the day. In fact, he was arrested at an antinuclear demonstration in London in September 1961, while the film was being shot in Jordan. He served fourteen days in prison and was released after Spiegel interceded and persuaded Bolt to sign a statement promising no further public protests.[19] Bolt continued to have regrets about caving in, and it has been speculated that the second half of the script of *Lawrence,* in which Lawrence sees the Arab Revolt collapse and contemplates his complicity in British treachery, could have reflected Bolt's own torment about compromising his political beliefs.

In any case, whoever provided it, the strong social criticism was one of the most provocative elements in the movie, and this theme resonated not only with the screenwriters but also with David Lean. Although his first film, *In Which We Serve,* codirected with Noel Coward, celebrated British determination during World War II, Lean's attitudes changed significantly over the years. *The Bridge on the River Kwai* created a devastating portrait of the English colonel played by Guinness; he is a man of almost superhuman fortitude but also unyielding pride, and in the film's view, he epitomizes both the strengths and the failings of the stubborn British leaders who conquered empires and left destruction in their wake. When the Japanese commander of the prison camp cries out in frustration, "I hate the British," one cannot help but suspect he is giving voice to some of the director's qualms about British intransigence. Lean's final film, *A Passage to India,* also contains a strong critique of British rulers in India. And in *Lawrence of Arabia,* Jack Hawkins's General Allenby and Claude Rains's Dryden epitomize British deviousness; they stand for the smooth-talking colonial leaders who ran roughshod over natives whose land they coveted.

Beyond this, the film was remarkably prescient in portraying the tribal conflicts that did as much to doom the Arab revolt as the duplicity of the British. Omar Sharif's Ali makes his entrance, in the film's legendary mirage sequence, by murdering Lawrence's guide, a man from a rival tribe who was forbidden to drink at his well. This act leads to Lawrence's memorable line, "Sherif Ali, so long as the Arabs fight tribe against tribe, so long will they be a little people, a silly people, greedy, barbarous, and cruel—as you are." The bitter tribal rivalries that continue to decimate the Middle East were shrewdly depicted in *Lawrence of Arabia.* Anyone well versed in the history of the region would have known that one of the rationales for the American invasion of Iraq in 2003—the myth of a unified Arab populace embracing democracy—was at best a pathetic pipe dream. The fierce hatreds among Sunni, Shiite, and Kurds that ultimately led to a virulent civil war accompanied by the rise of ISIS could have been predicted by viewers of *Lawrence of Arabia.* As one wag observed, if the teenage George W. Bush had watched *Lawrence of Arabia* instead of *The Three Stooges in Orbit*—another movie released in 1962—the tragic history of the last fifteen years might have been different.

In addition to the political chicanery depicted in the film, it contained an understated but provocative portrayal of homosexuality, a subject that surfaced for the first time in several other movies of 1962. Lawrence's sexuality was not exactly a secret. Noel Coward, who knew T. E. Lawrence, called him "strange and elusive, painfully shy, gay and loquacious."[20] For a big-budget epic made in 1962, Lawrence's sexuality would have to be treated gingerly, but there were hints. When he is speaking with his first Arab guide, the one later murdered by Ali, the guide asks if he is like other Englishmen, and Lawrence replies, "I'm different," a line that is of course open to multiple interpretations, one of which could refer to his somewhat ambiguous sexuality. The casting of O'Toole was crucial in highlighting this aspect of Lawrence's character, and the actor fearlessly highlighted the feminine side of Lawrence, in scenes when he practically flounces in his beautiful Arab robes.

It is also worth noting that Lawrence takes as servants two boys, Daud and Farraj, who are passionately devoted to each other. Early in the writing of the script, Lean wrote to Michael Wilson to highlight the "incipient homosexuality of Daud and Farraj."[21] Daud is killed in quicksand while they are traveling across the desert toward Cairo. When Lawrence and Farraj arrive in Cairo to report the Arab conquest of the Turkish port of Aqaba, Farraj awakens from a dream and cries out, "Daud!" before realizing where he is. Maybe the relationship of these two boys is a purely platonic friendship, but there are hints of something more intense.

Lawrence's own sexuality is awakened when he is captured by the Turks in Deraa, beaten, and tortured. In *Seven Pillars,* Lawrence wrote, "A delicious warmth, probably sexual, was swelling through me."[22] In later years, it was reported that Lawrence was ritually and repeatedly flogged by a young British soldier. Of course censorship restrictions at the time prevented a completely forthright presentation of this crucial episode. The Turkish Bey, played by Jose Ferrer, is clearly lascivious in fondling Lawrence's pale white skin, which leads to Lawrence striking him in revulsion. This prompts the Bey to order calmly, "Beat him." As the guards flog Lawrence, we see the Bey in his adjoining chamber, beginning to undress. The scene is cut off at this point, and we are never clear on exactly what happened. Lean later wrote to Bolt that in their editing of the film, they had missed a crucial moment. Lean said the scene probably needed "one more beat to explain that he had been defiled by the Bey."[23] When Lawrence explains to Ali afterward that he intends to return to Allenby and ask for an "ordinary" job, Ali tries to dissuade him by saying, "A man can be anything he wants." Lawrence agrees but then adds bitterly, "But he can't *want* what he wants." That provocative but mysterious line might be interpreted to mean that Lawrence discovered his deepest desires during that traumatic beating, but the scene could have used a touch more clarity and less ambiguity.

Jose Ferrer was the last major actor cast, and he filmed his two scenes as the Bey in Spain near the end of the shooting there. Although he had won an Academy Award for *Cyrano de Bergerac* and received two other nominations, Ferrer said late in his life, "In forty years of screen acting, I've made maybe forty movies. But if I had to be judged as a film actor by only one performance, I would want to be judged by the five minutes in *Lawrence of Arabia*. I deem those five minutes to be my best work."[24]

Is it possible that Lean, a notorious womanizer who was married six times, was slightly inhibited not just by the censorship code still in effect in 1962 but by his own discomfort around the subject of homosexuality? During an interview Anne Coates told a story of one disagreement she had with Lean during the editing. Perhaps the single most brilliant sequence in the film is the rescue of an Arab tribesman, Gasim (I. S. Johar), as the army is crossing the Nefud desert to attack Aqaba from the land. Gasim has fallen off his camel, and the army does not realize it until hours later. Lawrence insists on going back to find him, to the fury of Ali, who predicts that he will kill himself in the rescue attempt. The tribesmen add that it is futile to intervene, since Gasim's death was obviously "written" by the gods. "Nothing is written," Lawrence responds defiantly, and he sets off on a possibly suicidal mission. The editing of this sequence is superlative, intercutting Gasim's desperate trek through the scorching desert heat, Lawrence's search for him, and the other Arabs waiting at the watering hole. All the elements of filmmaking—cinematography, editing, Maurice Jarre's score—come together to build suspense. The climax of the sequence is not the actual rescue of Gasim—which takes place off-screen—but the reunion of Lawrence and Ali, who finally recognizes Lawrence's heroism; the sequence solidifies their friendship, and Ali states admiringly, "For some men, truly nothing is written unless they write it."

Surprisingly, Lean and Coates had a disagreement over the final shaping of this scene. "I thought it should be much longer," Coates said, "with more reactions between Peter and Omar. They really were attracted to each other. I had lots of material, and I had made it quite an emotional scene, right on their eyes.

David didn't want anything homosexual except the later scene with Jose Ferrer, and he made me straighten it out."[25] Nevertheless, the climax of the scene comes when Sharif's Ali, who has been suspicious of Lawrence up to this point, approaches him with a canteen of water after the miraculous rescue. Lawrence has refused the offer of water from underlings, but he accepts it from Ali as a solidification of the bond between them. There is no sexual hint in the scene, but it is a very emotional moment, aided by Jarre's swelling theme music, and it may be the only scene in the history of cinema that moves audiences to tears as a result of the delivery of a canteen of water. Of course that is a tribute to the writing, the direction, the editing, and the score that all come together at this moment. The homosexual undercurrent may be missing, but the emotion underlying the rapprochement of these onetime antagonists is intense and satisfying. Thus the collaboration of Lean and Coates produced a triumphant moment that owes something to both of their talents and instincts.

It should be added that although *Lawrence of Arabia* is a virtually all-male movie, without a single line of dialogue given to a woman, women have always responded enthusiastically to this particular epic film. After its 1989 restoration, Janet Maslin wrote about it in the *New York Times:* "As a young adolescent, I became so obsessed with a certain film that I saw it over and over, spent years studying the life of its hero, regarded him as a kind of role model and even dragged my family on a long, dusty pilgrimage to a place where he had lived. If one measure of a film's greatness is its power to affect the lives of those who see it, then *Lawrence of Arabia* must be the best film I know."[26] The *Los Angeles Times* critic at the time, Sheila Benson, also described *Lawrence* as "one of the Seven Wonders of the cinematic world." When Stephen Farber wrote an article for the *New York Times* in 1971 denouncing the cuts that had been made for a reissue of the film, many of the letters he received were from women who recounted their own enthusiastic responses to *Lawrence,* very similar to the obsession described by Maslin. It could well be that Coates's contributions had an unconscious impact on these viewers. But probably the main reason for this unexpected audience response was that O'Toole's Lawrence is the most androgynous action hero in the history of cinema. Instead of the stoic (some might say wooden) demeanor of actors like John Wayne and Charlton Heston, O'Toole lets his passions spill across his remarkably mobile face. A vulnerable action hero was a novelty in 1962 and remains pretty unique today.

If psychological acuity was the hallmark of many films of 1962, none of these other movies matched the depth of *Lawrence of Arabia.* It transcends the psychoanalytic jargon that marred *Freud* and *David and Lisa,* but it definitely brings piercing psychological insight to the depiction of the hero's emotional turmoil. The very first scene, Lawrence's fatal motorcycle accident, illuminates the character. It conveys a striking incongruity between the cultivated English countryside and the driven, obsessive quality of the motorcyclist who seems to want to violate the serenity of the landscape. In this setting the speed and intensity of the cyclist have a thrilling, dangerous quality. The director seems to share his hero's sense of excitement and instability. As Lawrence speeds along, the camera encourages us to savor his exhilaration. Yet Lawrence's urge to break free of English domestic life is also demonic and self-destructive; in this scene it is quite literally suicidal.

The tensions boldly dramatized in this opening scene are then developed in much fuller detail throughout the rest of the film. Lawrence is in some ways a parody of the English gentleman—obsessively clean and fastidious, orderly and disciplined, quietly but relentlessly determined to accomplish the goals he has set for himself. Lawrence's illegitimacy is mentioned in only one scene, but it is clearly a motivating force for him. Never granted full status in British society, he is determined to remake himself; in Arabia he can satisfy the heroic image of himself that England could never encompass. Lawrence finds in the desert an opportunity to plumb his own nature, to experiment with all the extremes of which he is capable. He tests his body, believing—and almost proving—that he is invulnerable to the elements. And the illegitimate Englishman can, in Arabia, reclaim his birthright as a natural prince, a leader of men, a national hero, a sun god, "El Aurens."

After the capture of Aqaba, in an exquisite scene by the sea—a stunning visual contrast to the parched desert landscapes—Ali brings flowers and throws them at Lawrence's feet, saying, "Garlands for the conqueror, tribute for the prince, flowers for the man." "I'm none of those things," Lawrence replies with a genuine childlike innocence, awed by the possibility of what he may become. Yet the tragic irony is that in exposing himself and releasing the passion in his nature that England could not contain, he also releases a darker side of his personality—not simply an overweening pride, but, associated with it, a thrill in the power of giving and taking life, a lust for violence and murder.

A simple first viewing of the film might lead one to see Lawrence as essentially innocent and noble until his dreams for Arabia are betrayed by the machinations of English politicians and by the horror of war. That interpretation, however, ignores the true complexity of Lawrence's personality. What distinguishes him from the conventional movie warrior is that he is self-conscious about what he does, very deliberately *playing* the hero's role. This is established in an early scene, when he extinguishes a match with his fingers; it is clear that he is trying to impress the other soldiers and also testing his capacity to withstand physical pain with a relish that seems slightly masochistic. As his gestures toward superhuman endurance become grander and more astonishing, his motives remain similarly ambiguous. When he rescues Gasim in the desert, it is to prove that he is beyond the laws of men, subject only to the extravagant demands he makes on himself. Later, as a result of a tribal skirmish, he is forced to execute Gasim, and we sense a certain relish in the way he fires his pistol repeatedly before he throws it away in disgust. (When he later tells Allenby that he "enjoyed" the execution, he is only affirming what the film has already dramatized.) Lawrence's egotism muddies and undermines his heroism. Riding across Sinai to inform the English of the Arab victory at Aqaba, he compares himself to Moses; later still, when entering Deraa without a single follower, he invokes the miracles of Christ. His pride does not exactly diminish his bravery, but it makes us uncomfortable and apprehensive. With his motives more tortured than in conventional melodramas, we understand the tremendous instability of the passion that drives him.

This instability explodes in the second half of the film, in the bloodbath scene that presents the darkest expression of Lawrence's complicated character. On its way to Damascus, his army approaches a somewhat bedraggled Turkish military unit that has just laid waste to a Bedouin village. One of the tribesmen riding with Lawrence's army had family members in that village, and he wants revenge against the Turks. Ali tries to persuade Lawrence to simply ride around the Turkish unit in order to make swifter progress to Damascus, without the risk of casualties, but other soldiers urge Lawrence to strike at the Turks. Tormented by these conflicting demands, Lawrence hesitates, but he finally gives in to the sadistic side of his nature and screams "No prisoners!" as he leads the Arab army into a bloody massacre. Robert Bolt made a provocative statement about what he hoped this scene and the entire film would convey: "When men go to war their own best qualities are turned against them. Their virtues are made to serve the ends of destruction and waste. In time of war we need not look for a villain; the heroes are more than enough."[27] That is indeed part of the meaning of this potent scene, but it also illuminates the darker side of Lawrence's psychological makeup.

What makes Lawrence's fate significant and moving is his intermittent awareness of the complexity of his own motives, the furious and convoluted strategies he tries in order to maintain integrity, and his attempts—inevitably doomed—to escape what he is. At times he revels in his "extraordinary" stature; after one raid on the Turkish railways, he walks unflinchingly toward a man who is shooting at him, then parades on top of the derailed train, flinging his robes behind him like a triumphant tribal king. At other moments he recoils from his own violence and from the reminders of his vulnerability, bitterly mocking himself and seeking refuge in an "ordinary" job that will not force him to confront extremes. After his humiliation at Deraa, he attempts to transform himself into a common British soldier, archly greeting the other officers in Jerusalem as if he were one of them—a desperate and hopeless charade. Finally, though, retreat is intolerable. His "destiny" tantalizes him, and the vision of himself as god is too seductive to resist, so he constantly finds rationalizations for returning to the desert. He persuades himself of the vitality of the Arab movement, though secretly he knows that the British are merely manipulating the Arab revolt to secure their own conquests in Arabia. But by clinging to the dream that he alone can give the Arabs their freedom, he hopes to expiate his private guilt, somehow wash away all the blood and keep himself clean.

His dreams finally collapse in Damascus, in a Turkish military hospital, foul and unattended because the Arab takeover of the city has left everything in chaos. As Lawrence wanders among the dying and the dead, a British medical officer enters the hospital and, appalled by what he sees, throws Lawrence (still in his Arab robes) aside, crying, "Filthy little wog." The joke seems almost cosmic—the man who defied nature in his unsuccessful attempt to forge a new identity finally "accepted" as an Arab at this moment of humiliation—and Lawrence is too perceptive to resist it. His horribly twisted, uncontrolled but self-aware laughter brings his Arabian adventure to a shattering ironic conclusion. Stripped of all illusions, Lawrence is given the anonymity he claims to want and is sent home broken. In the final scene, back in his British uniform, he rides in a jeep, his face obscured behind a dusty windshield. As he passes some Arabs on camels, he rises for a moment to see if he recognizes them. But they are unfamiliar, and he sits back down, lost and forlorn.

This scene echoes another scene near the end of the film's first half, when Lawrence and his surviving companion, Farraj, are riding toward the Suez Canal. In one of the film's most striking images, a giant ship suddenly appears on the horizon, quite out of place in the desert. As they ride closer, however, they see that the ship is actually gliding across the Suez Canal. A motorcycle rider on the other side of the canal calls out to Lawrence: "Who are you?" It was David Lean himself who dubbed the voice of this motorcyclist. "Who are you?," he cries out again to a bewildered Lawrence. That is the most elemental question raised in *Lawrence of Arabia*. Not many intimate dramas have ever matched the complexity of this big-budget epic in probing the profound mystery of human character. And O'Toole's brilliant performance brings this character fully to life.

Despite the lack of major marquee stars, *Lawrence of Arabia* was a box office bonanza. The Super Panavision, 70mm presentation opened in December 1962 as a roadshow attraction and played in major cities in that format until October 1963, when a shortened 35mm version went into wide release; that version then played into 1964. It was formally reissued in 1971 in an even shorter version, and reissued again after the 1989 restoration. A 4K digital version of that restoration prompted another reissue in 2012 to coincide with the film's fiftieth anniversary. That restored version is revived regularly in special screenings, enduring as one of the most popular staples in repertory programs.

The uncompromising vision of Lean and Bolt was rewarded at the Oscar ceremony when the film swept key categories. Accepting the best picture award, Spiegel gave a gracious speech. "Ladies and gentlemen," he began, "there is no magic formula for creating good pictures. They are made with assiduous, concerted hard work by everyone connected with making them. The writer, the director, technicians, the actors, thousands of employees on the picture during the making of it. On their behalf, and on the behalf of those who sweated months in the desert to create this picture, I deeply, sincerely thank the voters of the Academy and proudly accept this honor on their behalf. Proudly and humbly." To some of the film's award-winning artisans, however, this speech had a slightly dubious quality because the producer and the studio refused to pay to bring them to Hollywood from Europe. Freddie Young, John Box, Maurice Jarre, and Anne V. Coates all claimed their Oscars weeks after the ceremony.

For David Lean, an even greater triumph came a quarter century later, when the original version of the film was restored by Robert A. Harris and James Painten. Bits of film that were believed lost over the years were rediscovered. Anne Coates took particular pleasure in replacing a shot that had been removed just five weeks after the film's premiere—a shot of Lawrence's goggles hanging on a tree after his motorcycle careened off the road and crashed. Most of the actors were still alive and redubbed dialogue that had faded in the intervening decades. "I remember thinking how fat Alec Guinness had become," Coates said with a laugh.

The reviews that greeted this reissue were stronger than the original reviews from 1962. Of course there were still a few curmudgeons—die-hard auteurists and Andrew Sarris disciples who refused to recognize Lean's achievement. And there were some thoughtful political critiques. Arab scholar Edward Said,

writing in the *Wall Street Journal,* objected to the portrayal of the Arab characters; he was especially critical of the scene of the Arab Council meeting in
Damascus near the end of the film, where the tribesmen's petty rivalries
reemerge and prevent them from taking charge of the city. Said wrote, "Mr. Lean
wants us to understand that serious rule was never meant for such lesser species, only for the white man."[28] This seems to be an overly simplistic reading
of the film, for most of the Arab characters come across as far more sympathetic than the British politicians who have nothing but conquest on their
mind.

The majority of critics in 1989, however, recognized that they were in the
presence of a masterpiece, one that seemed to loom even larger in the twenty-
seven years that had elapsed since the film's release. Alexander Walker of the
London Evening Standard wrote, "*Lawrence of Arabia* was a marvel when it
opened in 1962. Nowadays, because we know what it would take to make a
movie like it, it seems almost a miracle." On the other side of the pond, Roger
Ebert made a similar argument: "It is a great experience to see it in 1989 as Lean
intended it in 1962—and also a humbling one, to realize how the motion picture industry is losing the vision to make epic films like this and settling for
safe narrative formulas instead."[29]

All of the collaborators whom Spiegel had praised in his Oscar acceptance
speech contributed to the film's stunning impact. But there is no question that
Lean, aided enormously by Bolt's screenplay, had the vision to meld all the dis-
parate elements into one of the screen's authentic epics. The scale of the film
is inseparable from its meaning, for this is one of the few films to treat the idea
of military heroism seriously and intelligently. Lean and his crew created a
visual setting for Lawrence's story magnificent enough to allow everyone in
the audience to entertain the possibility of transcendence. Lawrence's audacity seems to be sanctioned by the awesome surroundings; this is truly a setting for the gods. A philosophical man of action, he tries to play out an exalted
dramatic adventure that he has written across the sands. He pushes himself to
almost superhuman limits, but the energy generated in the effort may be more
diabolical than divine. Comparisons to Homeric epics and classical Shakespearean tragedy are not out of place. Because Lawrence reaches so high, his
fall is all the more devastating. One critic who praised the film on its initial
release, Donald W. Labadie of *Show* magazine, aptly drew comparison to the
classics: "Lean has maintained a remarkable balance between action and intro-
spection, between visual splendor and simplicity, psychological and physical
excitement, which turns *Lawrence of Arabia* into the rare movie that, like the
theater of Shakespeare, includes all audiences in its appeal."

EPILOGUE

Mariette Hartley, who made her film debut in Sam Peckinpah's *Ride the High Country,* remembers going to visit the director a decade later. In 1972 Peckinpah was working on *The Getaway,* a heist movie with Steve McQueen and Ali MacGraw. Although the film turned out to be a box office hit, it did not enjoy the same critical endorsements as *Ride the High Country* or *The Wild Bunch* or even the controversial *Straw Dogs,* which Peckinpah had made a year earlier. "I walked into his beautiful office at Goldwyn Studios," Hartley recalls, "and he had changed so much. I think I said to him, 'Sam, you don't have to do this to yourself.' He was drinking and taking drugs, and he had gone downhill."[1] Peckinpah's later films were all troubled and sometimes incoherent. The director never again enjoyed the same critical acclaim that he had experienced in the 1960s. He died in 1984, at the age of fifty-nine.

Other up-and-coming directors of 1962 experienced a similar decline in the 1970s, though perhaps not as dramatic as Peckinpah's. John Frankenheimer, who made an astonishing three movies in 1962 (including *The Manchurian Candidate,* which was reissued to tremendous acclaim in 1987), saw his career fizzle in the 1970s. At a time when sequels were just beginning to be coveted by greedy Hollywood producers, Frankenheimer directed *French Connection II* in 1975, which did not achieve anywhere near the success of the Oscar-winning thriller made by director William Friedkin in 1971. Frankenheimer earned better reviews for a filmed play he directed, *The Iceman Cometh,* which was part of an experimental series of filmed theater events presented by Ely Landau, the producer of 1962's *Long Day's Journey into Night.* But these attempts to bring highbrow theatrical fare to local movie theaters never really caught on. Frankenheimer concluded the decade with one of the most maligned movies of the era, the misconceived ecological horror film *Prophecy,* in 1979. Ironically,

Frankenheimer saw his career salvaged thanks to the revival of the prestigious television dramas that he had helped to pioneer back in the 1950s. In the 1990s he won several awards for directing cable TV movies about the Attica prison riots, the notorious Andersonville prison of the Civil War era, and racist politician George Wallace. In a sense his career went full circle, but his feature film output never matched the promise he demonstrated in 1962.

Arthur Penn earned two more Oscar nominations after his 1962 drama *The Miracle Worker;* he was recognized both for the landmark 1967 film, *Bonnie and Clyde,* and for *Alice's Restaurant,* made two years later. But in the 1970s he endured a series of flops; the most notorious was his 1976 western, *The Missouri Breaks,* which teamed Marlon Brando, the greatest actor of the 1950s, with Jack Nicholson, the greatest actor of the 1970s. What sounded intriguing on paper turned out to be a disaster on film. Leonard Maltin called it "a great director's worst film and one of the worst 'big' movies ever made." Although Penn kept working during the next two decades, he never really recovered his cachet.

Of course the older directors who were still working in 1962 were nearing the end of their lives by the 1970s. John Ford, who had made *The Man Who Shot Liberty Valance* in 1962 and had won four Oscars for directing (still the most awarded to any director), received the very first Life Achievement Award from the American Film Institute in 1973, at a ceremony attended by President Richard Nixon. Ford ended his speech by declaring, "God bless Richard Nixon," an embarrassing valedictory note for his career, since Congress was already conducting the Watergate hearings, and Nixon would be forced to resign a year later. Ford himself died a few months after the AFI award, in August 1973. Ford's good friend Howard Hawks, who made *Hatari!* in 1962, died in 1977.

Some of the foreign masters who had movies on-screen in 1962 continued to thrive in the 1970s and even the 1980s, but others went into a precipitous decline. The acclaimed French director Serge Bourguignon, who had won the foreign language Oscar in 1962 for *Sundays and Cybele,* tried making movies in Hollywood, with lackluster results. His countryman Jacques Demy, who launched his career with *Lola* in 1962, had his biggest success two years later, *The Umbrellas of Cherbourg.* But when he came to Los Angeles in 1969 to make *The Model Shop* with his *Lola* star, Anouk Aimee, he had a resounding failure.

Michelangelo Antonioni, who had a hand in redefining cinematic language in the 1960s, scored a triumph with his English-language debut, *Blow-Up,* in 1966. Then he traveled to America in 1969 to make *Zabriskie Point,* which was widely derided; he recovered somewhat with *The Passenger,* starring Jack Nicholson, in 1975, but he never fully regained his footing. Other international auteurs who tried making films in English (including Ingmar Bergman and François Truffaut) were not successful in these ventures. They quickly returned to filmmaking in their native languages and found renewed acclaim. Other foreign auteurs active in 1962, including Akira Kurosawa, Federico Fellini, Luis Buñuel, and Satyajit Ray, never succumbed to Tinseltown's temptations.

Even when these foreign filmmakers kept working in peak form, the level of success they had enjoyed in the United States in the 1960s was fading. After the Production Code collapsed in 1966–1967 (replaced by the MPAA rating system in 1968), American directors were freed to explore the mature subject matter that had been primarily available in European movies in 1962. Revenue for foreign films, which had peaked at 7 percent of total U.S. box office in the 1950s and early 1960s, declined to 2 percent by the 1970s.[2] The *New York Times'* chief film critic, Bosley Crowther, who had championed foreign cinema, departed that post in 1967 after he repeatedly attacked Arthur Penn's *Bonnie and Clyde,* one of the seminal films of the rising New Hollywood. Crowther now seemed out of touch with the times, and he stepped down after a twenty-seven-year tenure as a film maven. The film culture that had flourished in major cities and on college campuses found new idols and icons to venerate, and they were now based in Hollywood. A good number of specialty theaters closed. The golden age of the art house was over.

The 1970s saw the emergence of a new wave of American directors, including William Friedkin, Peter Bogdanovich, Francis Ford Coppola, Martin Scorsese, Robert Altman, Hal Ashby, Michael Cimino, and Steven Spielberg. But several of them fell victim to the same kind of personal excesses that bedeviled Peckinpah. Scorsese, Ashby, and Coppola all had issues with drugs during the 1970s.[3] After his two superb *Godfather* movies, Coppola went to the Philippines to make what he hoped would be the greatest Vietnam movie, *Apocalypse Now.* But as his wife, Eleanor, recounted in her book about the making of that film, the set was riddled with drugs, and the production went way over budget and schedule. The definitive Vietnam movie turned out to be Cimino's 1978 Oscar winner, *The Deer Hunter.* But Cimino also went out of control after that movie's success. He basically bankrupted United Artists in attempting an epic western, *Heaven's Gate,* which became almost a synonym for directorial excess. It may be that the American directors working in 1962 benefited from making movies before auteurs were worshipped as gods and given unchecked power to indulge their fantasies. The discipline imposed on them probably turned out to be more creatively stimulating than the carte blanche granted to people like Cimino, Friedkin, and Coppola after their early successes.

The 1970s also happened to be an unfortunate decade for the Oscar-winning best director of 1962, David Lean. After *Lawrence of Arabia,* Lean worked with many of the same crew members—along with actors Omar Sharif and Alec Guinness—to translate Boris Pasternak's romantic novel, *Doctor Zhivago,* to the screen. In filling out the movie's cast, Lean turned to two of the young British actors, Rita Tushingham and Tom Courtenay, who had emerged in 1962. *Doctor Zhivago* turned out to be an even bigger commercial blockbuster than *Lawrence.* Although it eventually won five Oscars, including one for screenwriter Robert Bolt, it missed out on the top awards for best picture and best director. And the film received far more mixed reviews than *Lawrence.* Still, Lean was riding high until he made *Ryan's Daughter* in 1970. This wispy romance set in Ireland during the period of the 1916 rebellion against England was written by Bolt as a vehicle for his wife, Sarah Miles. Reviews were scathing. Pauline Kael, never a Lean champion and now ensconced in a privileged position as the critic at the *New Yorker,* went out of her way to attack the film. She called it "gush made respectable by millions of dollars tastefully wasted."

In 1970 Lean made the mistake of attending a reception held by the National Society of Film Critics at the Algonquin Hotel in New York, where Kael led the charge against the director and encouraged other critics to lay into him as well. Richard Schickel asked how the man who had made the romantic classic *Brief Encounter* could turn out "a piece of shit" like *Ryan's Daughter.*[4] Lean was devastated by the critical drubbing and by the financial failure of the film. He lost the motivation to go back to work. Anne Coates told the authors, "I heard it was a vicious write-up by Pauline Kael that got to David. He felt that he was so little respected, and it just took the wind out of his sails. I can't believe it was only that, but I never heard what the real reason was."[5]

In any case, Lean was paralyzed by the poor reactions to *Ryan's Daughter,* and for a while, he retreated from filmmaking altogether. Late in the 1970s he proposed doing a new version of *Mutiny on the Bounty*—the Marlon Brando version was one of the films that had competed against *Lawrence* for best picture in 1962—that would be divided into two separate films. Dino De Laurentiis was planning to produce but could never get the financing together. That kind of ambitious historical epic was no longer in fashion in Hollywood. It would be fourteen years before Lean made another movie. *A Passage to India* was highly acclaimed on its release in 1984, and Lean received his seventh Oscar nomination as best director, though he lost to Milos Forman for *Amadeus.* In 1990, after the triumphant restoration of *Lawrence of Arabia,* Lean received the AFI Life Achievement Award, and at the award ceremony, he criticized the filmmakers in the room for relying on sequels and remakes. He lamented the fact that there were so many "Parts I, II, III, and IV . . . don't make them a sta-ple diet. We'll sink if we do."[6] Of course this trend has only intensified in the years since Lean's death in 1991.

Partly because of this dependence on franchise filmmaking, it seems depress-ingly clear that we will never again experience a year with the cinematic riches of 1962. Adult drama, a genre that was the hallmark of mainstream films that year, has mostly shifted to television (found on dozens of cable networks and streaming services). Prestige adaptations that enjoyed wide release, such as *To Kill a Mockingbird, Lolita,* and *The Miracle Worker,* would either be designated as specialized theatrical fare or relegated to other platforms. In 1962 these films all benefited from the elaborate advertising campaigns designed by the major studios that released them. And the big-budget movies made today are not intelligent epics like *Lawrence of Arabia* but comic book adventures or high-concept retreads like *Blade Runner 2049.* In a memorial tribute to Anne V. Coates at the end of 2018, *New York Times* critic Wesley Morris wrote, "There are any number of reasons movies no longer look or feel the way they used to. But one really good one is that Anne Coates is not cutting them anymore."[7] Morris is only one of the astute critics who has acknowledged the decline in the quality of films in recent decades.

Of course, 1962 was not the last interesting year for movies. Critic Mark Har-ris wrote a well-received book about the films of 1967, including *Bonnie and Clyde* and *The Graduate,* which marked an intriguing transitional moment in Hollywood. In 1984, the year when Lean's *A Passage to India* competed against *Amadeus,* other fine films included *The Killing Fields* and Robert Benton's *Places in the Heart,* not to mention the comic blockbuster *Ghostbusters.* Still, none of these years produced the wide range of extraordinary films that tantalized audi-ences in 1962.

There were a lot of things going on outside the cinemas that may have con-tributed to the creative ferment of that landmark year. The sexual revolution did not explode until later in the decade, but the sexual audacity of many films made in 1962 prefigured a new openness surrounding hitherto taboo subjects. American movies like *Lolita, Sweet Bird of Youth, Freud, Advise and Consent,* and even less successful films like *The Chapman Report* broached adult themes for the very first time. But of course most of the sexual exploration took place in foreign films like *Jules and Jim, Boccaccio '70, Viridiana, A Taste of Honey, Vic-tim,* and *Through a Glass Darkly,* and audacious European moviemakers inspired American writers and directors to take more chances in the coming years.

More significantly, 1962 was perhaps the last hopeful year for American society, before all the violent upheavals that began with the murder of civil rights leader Medgar Evers in June 1963 and then the assassination of President Kennedy later that year. Assassinations and violent protests continued in the 1960s and well into the next decade, as the Vietnam War divided the country. Corruption scandals that began with Watergate soured Americans on the chances of seeking change through normal political channels.

This is not intended to idealize or whitewash the Kennedy era. We now know that Kennedy contributed to the buildup of American troops in Vietnam, and the Cuban missile crisis of 1962 reminded the country of the dangerous world we inhabited during the Cold War. But Kennedy and his team managed to defuse the missile crisis without violence, which encouraged people to believe that his administration had the capacity to respond sensibly and sanely to threatening world events. On the domestic front, Kennedy's New Frontier gave some hope that the civil rights movement would finally help to tamp down the racism in American society, and Kennedy's pragmatic stand against censorship promised an enlightened new era for civil liberties as well.

In February 1962 American astronaut John Glenn orbited the earth three times, a milestone in the space race with the Soviet Union. In April President and Mrs. Kennedy hosted Glenn, forty-nine Nobel Prize winners, and several other prominent writers, artists, and scientists at a White House dinner, celebrating intellectual discourse and divergent viewpoints that were held in esteem by an enlightened administration.

Recognizing the watershed nature of the social, cultural, and political events of the year, a number of filmmakers in the ensuing decades would set their movies in 1962. Some of these were comic films celebrating American innocence, such as *American Graffiti* (1973), *National Lampoon's Animal House* (1978), and *Hairspray* (1988), though the latter film did touch on socially provocative themes of racial harmony and female empowerment. Both of those themes reappeared in an Oscar-nominated drama from 2016, *Hidden Figures,* which called attention to the hitherto neglected role of black women mathematicians who contributed to the space program in 1962. Notably, the next two Academy Award–winning best pictures, the romantic fantasy *The Shape of Water* (2017) and the true account *Green Book* (2018), are both set in 1962. The director of *Hidden Figures,* Theodore Melfi, recently explained his interest in that particular year: "It's like the country is in a sea of change and '62 is the high tide."[8]

The American movies produced and released in 1962 reflected the youthful, optimistic spirit of the Kennedy administration. Even when these movies ended on a downbeat note, as many of them did, they expressed a passionate belief in the possibility of social justice and the value of community involvement. The black man defended by Atticus Finch in *To Kill a Mockingbird* ends up convicted of the false charge against him and dies attempting to escape from a corrupt penal system. Yet we are encouraged to believe that the example set by Atticus can have a positive impact on his children, through whose eyes the story is told. Moral values are reaffirmed at the end of *Ride the High Country*, even if the man who embodies those values has to die to inspire his friends. And one of the more purely uplifting films of the year, *The Miracle Worker*, celebrates the triumph of education against the most formidable odds.

Seeing these movies today, one can at least entertain the possibility that a world mired in moral compromise and prejudice might be able to change for the better. We can be touched by the spirit of commitment that shone through many of the emblematic films of a more idealistic era. Beyond that, however, we can simply watch these movies and revel in the breadth and depth of the startling achievements of this one exhilarating year.

APPENDIX A:
OTHER FILMS OF 1962

Not all the surviving stars and filmmakers from the studio era of the 1930s, 1940s, and 1950s were fortunate enough to be in critical or box office hits in 1962. Nor did all of the emerging filmmaking talent experience success that year. John Cassavetes, who began his career as an actor, made his directorial debut in 1959 with *Shadows,* a largely improvised film that presaged the American independent movement. Hollywood took notice, and Paramount signed him to a five-picture deal. *Too Late Blues,* a gritty drama about jazz musicians starring Bobby Darin and Stella Stevens, released in February 1962, was the first effort from that arrangement. It was not in tune with the ticket-buying public, however, and the film flopped.

Cassavetes retrenched as an actor and reemerged as a director with the independently made hit *Faces* (1968). He went on to become the most acclaimed indie filmmaker of his generation (*A Woman under the Influence, Husbands, Opening Night*). *Cinema* magazine, a new publication devoted to the rising film culture, speculated on Cassavetes's future in its first issue (January 1962): "We will see if his tide is coming in or going out, whether the young men hungrily waiting for their chance can ride in on his swell, whether Hollywood will be flooded with the new talent its heritage demands." (Unfortunately, the magazine ignored the possibility of young female filmmakers.)

SOMETHING FOR THE BABY BOOMERS

For the baby boomer generation, those born between 1946 and 1964, as part of the post–World War II "boom" of American confidence and productivity, going to the movies in 1962 meant a visit to the local single-screen theater. There were no multiplexes or other viewing platforms yet, and the movies on television were edited for content and interrupted with commercials, shown years after they premiered theatrically. By the twenty-first century, via multiple platforms (broadcast, cable, satellite, digital video disc, streaming), the majority of Americans (well over 70 percent) preferred to watch movies at home. Accessibility and convenience had supplanted the theatrical experience. The following is a compendium of the popular personalities, film fads, venues, hits and misses that made going out to the movies the top-rated entertainment experience of 1962.

QUICK CUTS

There were plenty of movies that suffered artistic and box office woes, illustrating the pitfalls of overt commercial calculations. Oscar-winning director Vincente Minnelli made two of the year's biggest stinkers, *The Four Horsemen of the Apocalypse* and *Two Weeks in Another Town,* which didn't help the careers of Glenn Ford, Charles Boyer, and Paul Henreid (in the former) and Kirk Douglas, Edward G. Robinson, Claire Trevor, and Cyd Charisse (in the latter). Golden Age "woman's director" George Cukor was foiled by the censored adaptation of a sizzling best seller, *The Chapman Report,* which explored female sexuality; the talented cast of Shelley Winters, Claire Bloom, Glynis Johns, and newcomer Jane Fonda sank along with him. Rock Hudson, Gena Rowlands, and Burl Ives got lost on *The Spiral Road.* William Holden and Clifton Webb were squandered in director Leo McCarey's misstep *Satan Never Sleeps* (the swan song for both Webb and McCarey). Yul Brynner and Tony Curtis floundered in the historical misfire *Taras Bulba,* ludicrous except for Franz Waxman's excellent score. As film historian Gary Giddins wrote in *Film Comment* in 2018, "Franz Waxman's score for the woeful Cossack epic *Taras Bulba* gallops joyously past the movie's mess."

Dana Andrews, Eleanor Parker, and Jeanne Crain slogged through a bargain-basement *Madison Avenue.* *The Happy Thieves* with Rex Harrison and Rita Hayworth passed unnoticed. Lana Turner and Dean Martin went looking for an audience in *Who's Got the Action?;* Fred Astaire, Jack Lemmon, and Kim Novak slummed in the moderately charming trifle *The Notorious Landlady,* while Novak, James Garner, and Tony Randall fizzled in *Boys' Night Out.* Judy Garland (voice only) was hidden in the animated musical *Gay Purr-ee.* Shirley MacLaine had little more than a lavish wardrobe in the threadbare *My Gei-*

sha. Susan Hayward and Peter Finch had no one else to blame for *I Thank a Fool.* Frank Sinatra and his Rat Pack cronies starred in the popular (but critical flop) *Sergeants 3,* a western remake of *Gunga Din.* Two movies starring famous funnymen targeted 38 million school-age baby boomers and their parents; Jackie Gleason's sentimental drama *Gigot* had critical endorsement, while Jerry Lewis continued his winning streak at the box office with the comedy *It's Only Money.* And influential silent-era comedian Harold Lloyd had an unexpected success with his compilation film, *Harold Lloyd's World of Comedy.*

INTERNATIONAL HODGEPODGES

Overseas filmmakers and their collaborators were not immune to high-concept failure. A few prime examples include *Phaedra,* a misconceived modern updating of Euripides's Greek tragedy, with director-writer Jules Dassin and his actress wife, Melina Mercouri, following up their international hit, *Never on Sunday. Jessica* saw glamorous American star Angie Dickinson and French icon Maurice Chevalier sidetracked in Italy. William Holden made the family drama *The Lion* in Kenya and then became a tax refugee by moving there. Audiences could not claim the same relief from most of these films. The film *7 Capital Sins* (aka *Seven Deadly Sins*) looked appetizing on paper, with prominent and rising international directors (including Jean-Luc Godard, Roger Vadim, Edouard Molinaro, Philippe de Broca, Claude Chabrol, and Jacques Demy) taking on the seven cardinal sins in fifteen-minute modern parables. But this anthology movie bouillabaisse turned out to be a not-so-tasty stew.

WALT DISNEY REIGNS

Disney, the impresario of popular family entertainment, enjoyed tremendous box office success by catering to the baby boom generation. Along with a reissue of 1940's *Pinocchio,* he released six new films in 1962: *Moon Pilot* (look fast for a teenage Sally Field), *Big Red, Bon Voyage, Almost Angels, The Legend of Lobo,* and the year-end smash hit *In Search of the Castaways.* Disney was foremost a savvy businessman and, looking to save production costs, filmed *Angels* and *Castaways* entirely overseas. As an avatar of the mid-twentieth-century American ethos, Disney also acknowledged self-imposed limitations. Although he admired *To Kill a Mockingbird,* calling it "one hell of a picture," he recognized his inability to attempt social or political issues, lamenting, "I wish I could make a picture like that."

RETURN OF THE THREE STOOGES

The trio of former vaudevillians who relied on slapstick for comic effect enjoyed a resurgence in popularity after their theatrical shorts from the 1930s, 1940s, and 1950s were shown on television. Although diminished from their 1940s heyday, they still had enough gas in the tank for six new family feature films. The two released in 1962 were among the most popular: *The Three Stooges Meet Hercules* (a spoof of ancient-world musclemen movies) and *The Three Stooges in Orbit* (capitalizing on the historic space flight of astronaut John Glenn).

PINSTRIPES ON THE SILVER SCREEN

Professional baseball figured in two films, both involving the reigning world champion New York Yankees. *Safe at Home,* released by Columbia at the start of the baseball season in April, featured Yankee greats Mickey Mantle and Roger Maris. Along with Yogi Berra, they would also pop up in the smash hit *That Touch of Mink* in July. Time out for filming did not hamper the Yankees' performance on the field; they repeated as World Series victors in October.

ELVIS AND THE INVASION OF THE TEEN POP IDOLS

Male pop singing stars, a draw with teenage movie fans, were in a number of major (and minor) movies in 1962. Fabian, under contract to Twentieth Century-Fox, was in three films: 5 *Weeks in a Balloon, Mr. Hobbs Takes a Vacation,* and *The Longest Day.* Frankie Avalon costarred in the postapocalyptic *Panic in Year Zero.* He found more lasting movie fame one year later in *Beach Party* and its slew of sequels. Fifties star Pat Boone was top billed in the misconceived remake of 1945's *State Fair,* with Ann-Margret, fellow singer-actor Bobby Darin, and 1940s star Alice Faye. Troy Donahue (*Rome Adventure*) and Michael Callan (*Bon Voyage, The Interns*), two dreamboat actors not known for singing, also flourished as teen favorites.

The greatest box office draw of all was Elvis Presley, the king of rock 'n' roll. Elvis starred in three popular musicals: *Follow That Dream, Kid Galahad,* and

Girls! Girls! Girls! Unlike all these other teen "fave raves," whose careers declined later in the sixties, Elvis held on as a movie star for the remainder of the decade. An attempt to put him in more serious roles, like *Walk on the Wild Side,* was quashed by Colonel Parker, his controlling manager; but the banal mediocrity of his movies eventually wore out his maturing audience. When his movie career collapsed, he made a recording comeback at the top of the pop charts in 1969.

MUSCLES IN TUNICS

Former Mr. America Steve Reeves starred in *The Trojan Horse,* sharing the marquee with *Son of Samson* and *Damon and Pythias* (all examples of the "peplum" male tunic, ancient-movie genre). *The 300 Spartans, Cleopatra's Daughter, Sword of the Conqueror,* and *Fury of the Pagans* (all filmed overseas) were all sword-and-sandal costumers. In a sign of racial awareness, American bodybuilder Leroy Colbert was announced as the first "Negro muscleman" to sign up for the Italian beefcake pix. Reeves, star of 1959's *Hercules,* a massive hit that sparked the muscleman movie craze that lasted into the mid-1960s, may have overworked, as the *Hollywood Reporter* noted in June 1962 when he was "hospitalized in Rome for too much muscle-flexing."

TAKE ME OUT TO THE DRIVE-IN

Hollywood was keen on getting the audience away from their television sets, if not at the 14,500 regular theaters ("hardtops" in industry jargon), then at least outdoors at the 4,800 drive-ins that were an integral part of warm weather moviegoing in 1962. Although watching a giant screen from your automobile with tinny metal speakers attached to the car windows was hardly the most optimal viewing experience, it was economical. Because children under twelve were admitted free, families piled in for "carload" nights, and teenagers discovered budding romance in the popular passion pits.

Although the label "drive-in movie" would later signify a low-budget picture of little artistic merit (comparable to the straight-to-video stigma of a later era), regular commercially released movies, whether studio or independent, played the local drive-ins on double or triple bills. They shared outdoor space with B westerns and war movies, teen romps like *Hey! Let's Twist* and *Ring-A-Ding Rhythm,* and a mix of low-rent imports such as the Japanese sci-fi horror flicks *Mothra* and *The Manster,* in dubbed versions so as not to be confused with art films. Ditto for the 1960 French chiller *Eyes without a Face,* making its belated American debut retitled as *The Horror Chamber of Dr. Faustus.* You could see international remakes of *The Cabinet of Caligari, Beauty and the Beast, The Phantom of the Opera,* and an above-average British sci-fi drama, *The Day the Earth Caught Fire.*

Drive-in capacities ranged from the tiny fifty-car Bramberg in South Carolina to the nation's largest, the Twin Drive-In of Cincinnati, Ohio (2,800 spaces). After peaking in popularity in the late 1950s and early 1960s, the "ozoners" survived for the remainder of the decade. But the land they occupied became too valuable, and drive-ins fell victim to suburban sprawl and real estate development by the 1970s, going into irreversible decline as movie viewing habits shifted.

KING OF THE B PICTURES

Producer-director Roger Corman craved respectability along with financial success. While he was based at low-rent American-International Pictures in the 1960s, his frugal but stylish adaptations of the works of the nineteenth-century master of the macabre, Edgar Allan Poe, appealed to teenagers lured by the horror content and to literate moviegoers who had actually read Poe. The profitable 1962 entries in Corman's Poe series (*The Premature Burial, Tales of Terror*) offered refuge for several actors from 1939 who were still on the scene: Ray Milland, Basil Rathbone, Peter Lorre, and horrormeister Vincent Price. Corman remained a purveyor of bargain-basement movies (and distributor of art house films in the 1970s), while launching the careers of several icons of the New Hollywood (Jack Nicholson, Francis Ford Coppola, Martin Scorsese, et al.); he was awarded an Honorary Oscar in 2009.

CARNIVAL OF SOULS

The American horror indie *Carnival of Souls* was made in Kansas and Utah on a $30,000 budget. It opened with little fanfare in 1962, noted by *Variety* as a "creditable can of film." The thin story involves an enigmatic blonde (Candace Hilligoss) who emerges from a car-off-a-bridge accident mysteriously unscathed and is drawn to a pavilion haunted by the dead. At the time the Midwest regional theater chain Commonwealth gambled on booking the locally produced picture; *Variety* quoted one of that company execs: "We have played lots worse lots of times." The minimalist black-and white creepie gained a cult following through late night TV showings and a major reissue in 1989, garnering positive reviews from the likes of Roger Ebert and the *Washington Post*.

SINNERS AND SAINTS

Adventurous moviegoers in the big cities could find lurid and salacious titles like *Satan in High Heels, The World's Greatest Sinner,* and *Scanty Panties* playing the downtown grindhouses. *Peeping Tom,* which shocked the United Kingdom in 1960, did not find an American distributor until 1962 and was dumped into these big-city fleapits after it flopped as an art film. Several years later this thriller from *Red Shoes* director Michael Powell was rediscovered and acclaimed as a psychologically astute study of voyeurism turned deadly.

The two films of director Edward Dmytryk illustrate the dichotomy of secular and spiritual values—*Walk on the Wild Side* looked at the demimonde, while *The Reluctant Saint,* with Maximilian Schell, was an international effort about the seventeenth-century cleric Saint Joseph of Cupertino. *Mother Joan of the Angels* from Poland straddled both worlds, as a tale of demonic possession set in a convent. (It was promptly condemned by the Legion of Decency.) Other religious films ranged from *Constantine and the Cross* to the European imports *The Story of Joseph and His Brethren* and *Bernadette of Lourdes.* The biblical opus *Barabbas,* starring Anthony Quinn, morphed from a gladiator movie to a tale of spiritual redemption. Religious-themed films, which had been a staple in the 1940s and 1950s, fell out of favor later in the 1960s. Hollywood rediscovered their appeal in the twenty-first century, and "faith-based" films could be found once again at the multiplexes.

ART HOUSES THEN AND NOW

Discriminating audiences in major metropolitan areas, including the expanding college crowd, patronized their local art houses (500-plus single-screen theaters) from coast to coast in such venues as the Music Hall (Los Angeles), Clay (San Francisco), Esquire (Denver), Downer (Milwaukee), Charles (Baltimore), and Guild 45th (Seattle), all of which survived into the twenty-first century. Other specialty theaters of the era such as the Copley (Boston), Suburban World (Minneapolis), Trans-Lux (Philadelphia), Surf (Chicago), Beverly

Canon (Los Angeles), Coronet (Dallas), Peachtree (Atlanta), and Apex (Washington, DC) have all closed.

These specialized theaters offered a cornucopia of contemporary international fare, and some of these films capitalized on recognizable talent in front of and behind the camera. Select examples included the Italian films *La Viaccia* starring Jean-Paul Belmondo and Claudia Cardinale and *The Big Night* (*La Notte Brava*) with Elsa Martinelli (costar of *Hatari!*). France offered *A Very Private Affair,* directed by Louis Malle and starring Brigitte Bardot and Marcello Mastroianni, the omnibus *Tales of Paris* featuring a teenage Catherine Deneuve, *Back Streets of Paris* starring Simone Signoret, and Jean Cocteau's *Testament of Orpheus.* Cold War adversary the Soviet Union found cultural détente with the well-reviewed *Lady and the Dog,* adapted from a Chekhov story, and *Apartment in Moscow.* The Mexican western *The Important Man* top-billed Japanese star Toshiro Mifune, demonstrating incipient cinematic globalization. Japan, in turn, provided *The Island* (aka *The Naked Island*), one of the year's acclaimed foreign dramas.

Enterprising distributors rummaged international film vaults and found titles by renowned global artists that had not played domestically. Among these films were Kurosawa's *Hidden Fortress* (1958), Bergman's *The Devil's Wanton* (aka *Prison,* 1949), and the American premiere of Orson Welles's European production, *Mr. Arkadin* (aka *Confidential Report,* 1955). On the flip side, notable films debuting internationally in 1962 that did not get stateside distribution until later years included Buñuel's *The Exterminating Angel,* Jean-Luc Godard's *Vivre Sa Vie,* Orson Welles's *The Trial,* and Roman Polanski's *Knife in the Water.*

CINERAMA APEX/TWILIGHT OF THE MOVIE PALACES

Cinerama was a popular wide-screen format that flourished with travelogues and documentaries in the 1950s. These spectacles were exhibited at major metropolitan, grand showplaces that survived from the golden age of theater construction in the 1920s, such as the Boyd (Philadelphia) and the Palace (Cleveland). The use of three cameras filming simultaneously, with the finished product projected on a giant curved screen, put the audience "in the picture." *The Wonderful World of the Brothers Grimm,* the first narrative Cinerama film, proved a substantial family hit in the fall of 1962 as a roadshow attraction, followed by the box office bonanza *How the West Was Won.* But the expensive process was jettisoned after that epic western in favor of 70mm films shown on the curved screens and advertised as Cinerama presentations (e.g., *It's a Mad Mad Mad Mad World; The Greatest Story Ever Told; 2001: A Space Odyssey*) later in the 1960s. The president of Cinerama, Nicholas Reisini, vowed to keep the spectacular theatrical process reserved for family films only, declaring that none of those "bosomy gals" would sprawl across the giant Cinerama screens. The "miracle of Cinerama" ceased to be economically viable when this diet of family-friendly flicks could no longer fill the downtown theaters in the major cities. The demise of both the format and the roadshow era by the early 1970s coincided with demographic shifts to the suburbs and the decline of the urban downtowns. Decades later, IMAX theaters and other technical innovations with digital projection attempted to re-create the Cinerama experience but only achieved mixed results.

APPENDIX B: ACCOLADES AND BOX OFFICE FOR 1962

ACADEMY AWARD NOMINEES AND *WINNERS

Nominations were announced February 25, 1963; Oscars were bestowed on April 8.

Best Picture

Lawrence of Arabia (Columbia, Sam Spiegel)
The Longest Day (Twentieth Century-Fox, Darryl F. Zanuck)
The Music Man (Warner Bros., Morton DaCosta)
Mutiny on the Bounty (MGM, Aaron Rosenberg)
To Kill a Mockingbird (Universal–International, Alan J. Pakula)

Notable omissions: *The Manchurian Candidate, The Miracle Worker, Jules and Jim, Days of Wine and Roses, The Man Who Shot Liberty Valance, Ride the High Country, Divorce Italian Style, A Taste of Honey, Billy Budd, Long Day's Journey into Night.*

Best Actor

Burt Lancaster, *Birdman of Alcatraz*
Jack Lemmon, *Days of Wine and Roses*
Marcello Mastroianni, *Divorce Italian Style*
Peter O'Toole, *Lawrence of Arabia*
*Gregory Peck, *To Kill a Mockingbird*

Notable omissions: James Mason, *Lolita;* Tom Courtenay, *The Loneliness of the Long Distance Runner;* Robert Mitchum, *Cape Fear;* Robert Preston, *The Music Man;* Dirk Bogarde, *Victim;* Kirk Douglas, *Lonely Are the Brave;* Keir Dullea, *David and Lisa.*

Best Actress

*Anne Bancroft, *The Miracle Worker*
Bette Davis, *What Ever Happened to Baby Jane?*
Katharine Hepburn, *Long Day's Journey into Night*
Geraldine Page, *Sweet Bird of Youth*
Lee Remick, *Days of Wine and Roses*

Notable omissions: Harriet Andersson, *Through a Glass Darkly;* Jeanne Moreau, *Jules and Jim;* Rita Tushingham, *A Taste of Honey;* Rosalind Russell, *Gypsy;* Eva Marie Saint, *All Fall Down;* Joan Crawford, *What Ever Happened to Baby Jane?*

Supporting Actor

*Ed Begley, *Sweet Bird of Youth*
Victor Buono, *What Ever Happened to Baby Jane?*
Telly Savalas, *Birdman of Alcatraz*
Omar Sharif, *Lawrence of Arabia*
Terence Stamp, *Billy Budd*

Notable omissions: Peter Sellers, *Lolita;* Robert Ryan, *Billy Budd;* Murray Melvin, *A Taste of Honey;* Lee Marvin, *The Man Who Shot Liberty Valance;* Charles Laughton, *Advise and Consent;* Jason Robards Jr., *Long Day's Journey into Night;* Brock Peters, *To Kill a Mockingbird.*

Supporting Actress

Mary Badham, *To Kill a Mockingbird*
*Patty Duke, *The Miracle Worker*
Shirley Knight, *Sweet Bird of Youth*
Angela Lansbury, *The Manchurian Candidate*
Thelma Ritter, *Birdman of Alcatraz*

Notable omissions: Shelley Winters, *Lolita;* Barbara Stanwyck, *Walk on the Wild Side;* Gena Rowlands, *Lonely Are the Brave;* Daniela Rocca, *Divorce Ital-*

ian Style; Patricia Gozzi, *Sundays and Cybele*; Susannah York, *Freud*; Mariette Hartley, *Ride the High Country*.

Director

Pietro Germi, *Divorce Italian Style*
*David Lean, *Lawrence of Arabia*
Robert Mulligan, *To Kill a Mockingbird*
Arthur Penn, *The Miracle Worker*
Frank Perry, *David and Lisa*

Notable omissions: François Truffaut, Ingmar Bergman, John Ford, Tony Richardson, John Frankenheimer, Stanley Kubrick, Sam Peckinpah.

Story and Screenplay (Written Directly for the Screen)

**Divorce Italian Style*—Ennio de Concini, Alfredo Giannetti, and Pietro Germi
Freud—Charles Kaufman and Wolfgang Reinhardt
Last Year at Marienbad—Alain Robbe-Grillet
That Touch of Mink—Stanley Shapiro and Nate Monaster
Through a Glass Darkly—Ingmar Bergman

Screenplay (Based on Material from Another Medium)

David and Lisa—Eleanor Perry
Lawrence of Arabia—Robert Bolt
Lolita—Vladimir Nabokov
The Miracle Worker—William Gibson
**To Kill a Mockingbird*—Horton Foote

Foreign-Language Film

Electra (Greece)
The Four Days of Naples (Italy)
Keeper of Promises (Brazil)
**Sundays and Cybele* (France)
Tlayucan (Mexico)

Cinematography (Black and White)

Birdman of Alcatraz—Burnett Guffey
**The Longest Day*—Jean Bourgoin, Walter Wottitz, Henri Persin
To Kill a Mockingbird—Russell Harlan

Two for the Seesaw—Ted McCord
What Ever Happened to Baby Jane?—Ernest Haller

Cinematography (Color)

Gypsy—Harry Stradling Sr.
Hatari!—Russell Harlan
Lawrence of Arabia—Fred A. Young
Mutiny on the Bounty—Robert Surtees
The Wonderful World of the Brothers Grimm—Paul C. Vogel

Song

*Days of Wine and Roses (title song)—Henry Mancini and Johnny
   Mercer

Music Score (Substantially Original)

Lawrence of Arabia—Maurice Jarre

Scoring of Music (Adaptation or Treatment)

The Music Man—Ray Heindorf

Film Editing

Lawrence of Arabia—Anne Coates

Art Direction and Set Decoration (Black and White)

To Kill a Mockingbird—Alexander Golitzen and Henry Bumstead; Oliver
   Emert

Art Direction and Set Decoration (Color)

Lawrence of Arabia—John Box and John Stoll; Dario Simoni

Costume Design (Black and White)

What Ever Happened to Baby Jane?—Norma Koch

Costume Design (Color)

The Wonderful World of the Brothers Grimm—Mary Wills

Sound

Lawrence of Arabia, John Cox

Special Effects

The Longest Day—Robert MacDonald and Jacques Maumont

Documentary (Feature)

Black Fox: The True Story of Adolf Hitler—Louis Clyde Stoumen, producer

Academy membership totaled 2,424. By 2020 voting membership increased to over 9,000.

Number of male nominees in 1962: 108; Oscar winners: 17.

Number of female nominees in 1962: 18; Oscar winners: 5.

NEW YORK TIMES: TOP FILMS (ALPHABETICAL) FOR 1962

Divorce Italian Style, Electra, Freud, Last Year at Marienbad, Long Day's Journey into Night, The Longest Day, Lover Come Back, Sundays and Cybele, A Taste of Honey, Whistle Down the Wind

LOS ANGELES TIMES: TOP FILMS (ALPHABETICAL) FOR 1962

English Language

Birdman of Alcatraz, Freud, Jumbo, Lawrence of Arabia, Lolita, Long Day's Journey into Night, The Longest Day, The Manchurian Candidate, The Miracle Worker, The Music Man, Mutiny on the Bounty, To Kill a Mockingbird

Foreign Language

Boccaccio '70, Divorce Italian Style, Electra, La Notte, Throne of Blood (1957 film that opened in the United States in 1961, Los Angeles in 1962)

NATIONAL BOARD OF REVIEW: TOP TEN

The Longest Day (Best Picture), *Billy Budd, The Miracle Worker, Lawrence of Arabia, Long Day's Journey into Night, Whistle Down the Wind, Requiem for a Heavyweight, A Taste of Honey, Birdman of Alcatraz, War Hunt*

FILM DAILY: ANNUAL POLL OF MOTION PICTURE CRITICS (TOTAL VOTES)

The Manchurian Candidate (193), *The Music Man* (177), *The Miracle Worker* (174), *The Longest Day* (163), *To Kill a Mockingbird* (154), *Requiem for a Heavyweight* (150), *Birdman of Alcatraz* (128), *Lawrence of Arabia* (122), *Billy Budd* (117), *A Taste of Honey* (111), *Advise and Consent* (81), *Gigot* (78), *What Ever Happened to Baby Jane?* (68), *Lolita* (67), *Sweet Bird of Youth* (65), *That Touch of Mink* (63), *Flower Drum Song* (62 [1961]), *Hatari!* (59), *Lover Come Back* (58 [1961]), *Divorce Italian Style* (54)

DIRECTORS GUILD OF AMERICA: FINALISTS

John Frankenheimer, *The Manchurian Candidate*
Pietro Germi, *Divorce Italian Style*
John Huston, *Freud*
Stanley Kubrick, *Lolita*
*David Lean, *Lawrence of Arabia*
Sidney Lumet, *Long Day's Journey into Night*
Peter Ustinov, *Billy Budd*
Bernard Wicki, Ken Annakin, Andrew Marton, *The Longest Day*

WRITERS GUILD OF AMERICA

Best Written Drama—*To Kill a Mockingbird,* Horton Foote, based on the novel by Harper Lee
Best Written Comedy—*That Touch of Mink,* Stanley Shapiro, Nate Manaster
Best Written Musical—*The Music Man,* Marion Hargrove, based on the musical by Meredith Willson from a story by Meredith Willson and Franklin Lacey

HOLLYWOOD FOREIGN PRESS (GOLDEN GLOBE AWARDS)

Best Drama Picture—*Lawrence of Arabia*
Best Comedy Picture—*That Touch of Mink*

Best Musical Picture—*The Music Man*

Best Director—David Lean, *Lawrence of Arabia*

Best Actor (Drama)—Gregory Peck, *To Kill a Mockingbird*

Best Actress (Drama)—Geraldine Page, *Sweet Bird of Youth*

Best Actor (Comedy or Musical)—Marcello Mastroianni, *Divorce Italian Style*

Best Actress (Comedy or Musical)—Rosalind Russell, *Gypsy*

Best Supporting Actor—Omar Sharif, *Lawrence of Arabia*

Best Supporting Actress—Angela Lansbury, *The Manchurian Candidate*

Best Foreign Language Film (tie)—*Best of Enemies, Divorce Italian Style* (both Italy)

Best Motion Picture Promoting International Understanding—*To Kill a Mockingbird*

Samuel Goldwyn International Award—*Sundays and Cybele* (France)

World Film Favorites—Doris Day and Rock Hudson

Cecil B. DeMille Award—Bob Hope

CAHIERS DU CINEMA TOP TEN LIST (DIRECTOR AND COUNTRY)

My Life to Live (Jean-Luc Godard, France)

Jules and Jim (François Truffaut, France)

Hatari! (Howard Hawks, U.S.)

Viridiana (Luis Buñuel, Spain)

La Signe du Lion (Eric Rohmer, France)

Wild River (Elia Kazan, U.S. [1960])

The Trial (Orson Welles, U.S./France)

Through a Glass Darkly (Ingmar Bergman, Sweden)

The Elusive Corporal (Jean Renoir, France)

Vanina Vanini (Roberto Rossellini, Italy)

Note: Producers Guild, Screen Actors Guild, National Society of Film Critics, Los Angeles Film Critics, and American Film Institute did not begin bestowing annual awards until later decades.

FILMS OF 1962 IN LIBRARY OF CONGRESS NATIONAL FILM REGISTRY (YEAR OF DESIGNATION)

Lawrence of Arabia (1991)
Ride the High Country (1992)
The Manchurian Candidate (1994)
To Kill a Mockingbird (1995)
How the West Was Won (1997)
The Music Man (2005)
The Man Who Shot Liberty Valance (2007)
Days of Wine and Roses (2018)

EXHIBITOR ANNUAL POLL OF TOP TEN MONEYMAKING STARS FOR 1962

1. Doris Day
2. Rock Hudson
3. Cary Grant
4. John Wayne
5. Elvis Presley
6. Elizabeth Taylor
7. Jerry Lewis
8. Frank Sinatra
9. Sandra Dee
10. Burt Lancaster

Source: *International Motion Picture Almanac 1964*

BOX OFFICE: TOP TWENTY HIGHEST-GROSSING MOVIES OF 1962*

1. *Lawrence of Arabia**—$45,000,000
2. *The Longest Day*—$39,100,000
3. *In Search of the Castaways*—$21,745,500
4. *That Touch of Mink*—$17,649,000
5. *The Music Man*—$14, 954,000
6. *Mutiny on the Bounty*—$13,680,000

7. *To Kill a Mockingbird*—$13,130,000
8. *Hatari!*—$12,924,000
9. *Gypsy*—$11,077,000
10. *Bon Voyage*—$11,000,000
11. *The Manchurian Candidate*—$10,474,200
12. *Lolita*—$9,250,000
13. *The Interns*—$9,232,00
14. *What Ever Happened to Baby Jane?*—$9,000,000
15. *The Wonderful World of the Brothers Grimm*—$8,920,000
16. *Days of Wine and Roses*—$8,125,000
17. *The Man Who Shot Liberty Valance*—$8,000,000
18. *State Fair*—$7,000,000
19. *Taras Bulba*—$6,8000,000
20. *The Miracle Worker*—$5,000,000

*Includes cumulative totals from later reissues; originally *The Longest Day* topped in 1962.

Source: *Variety* year-end charts for 1962–1964; "Top Grossing Movies of 1962," Listal.com. Movies in that era often played for several months (and sometimes years) in subsequent release (sub-runs), particularly if originally shown as limited roadshow engagements. Calculated in non-inflation-adjusted dollars for "domestic box office" for United States and Canada. Original *Variety* figures were film rentals (amount returned to financing studio or distributor, usually about half of total gross), with grosses listed here estimated as actual box office take. The average ticket price for a first-run movie in 1962 was $1.00.

NOTES

INTRODUCTION

1. Sophia Loren, *Yesterday, Today, Tomorrow* (New York: Atria, 2014), 161.
2. *Show,* April 1962.
3. Quendrith Johnson, "The Room Where the Industry Unspools Its Films," *Los Angeles Times,* February 25, 1994.
4. Joseph Wambaugh, "Hollywood Confidential: The Actor, the Comic and LAPD Vice," *Los Angeles Times,* December 22, 2013.

1. OVERSEAS EXPLOSION

1. Pauline Kael, *Kiss Kiss Bang Bang* (Boston: Little, Brown, 1968), 431.
2. Chas A. Alicoate, ed., *The 1963 Film Daily Year Book of Motion Pictures* (New York: Film Daily, 1963).
3. Although the French featurette *The Red Balloon* won for original screenplay in 1956, it was a thirty-five-minute short with virtually no dialogue.
4. Dale Olson, "Film Societies Become Big Business," *Daily Variety,* October 23, 1962.
5. Lenny Litman, "Even Tiny Towns Get Foreign Pix," *Variety,* May 8, 1963.
6. Eugene Archer, "Director of Enigmas," *New York Times,* March 8, 1962.
7. Roger Ebert, *Last Year at Marienbad,* May 30, 1999, rogerebert.com.
8. "Preview of *Last Year at Marienbad,*" *Show,* March 1962.
9. Archer, "Director of Enigmas."
10. Pauline Kael, *I Lost It at the Movies* (Boston: Little, Brown, 1965), 184.
11. Sheri Linden, "Stunning Return of 'La Notte,'" *Los Angeles Times,* September 16, 2016.
12. Philip Kaufman, "Adventures in Moviegoing," Video interview on FilmStruck, 2017.
13. Matilde Hochkofler, *Marcello Mastroianni: The Fun of Cinema* (Rome: Gremese International, 1992), 68.
14. Martin Scorsese, "On *Divorce Italian Style,*" essay reprinted for Criterion DVD release notes.
15. Hochkofler, *Marcello Mastroianni,* 65–66.
16. Donald Dewey, *Marcello Mastroianni: His Life and Art* (New York: Birch Lane Press, 1993), 122–124.
17. Eugene Archer, "Matinee Idol—Italian Style," *New York Times,* October 28, 1962.
18. The majority of films released in the United States in 1962 were made overseas. "55% Foreign Releases," *Hollywood Reporter,* October 8, 1962.
19. Jack Pitman, "The Saga of Joe E. Levine," *Variety,* July 4, 1962.
20. Murray Schumach, "Two Cities Face Film Censor Test," *New York Times,* August 2, 1962.
21. Manoah Bowman, *Fellini: The Sixties* (Philadelphia: Running Press, 2015), 79.

22. Bosley Crowther, "Fellini on Censors," *New York Times,* July 8, 1962.

23. "The Female Trilogy of *Boccaccio '70,*" *Cinema,* June 1962.

24. Sophia Loren, *Yesterday, Today, Tomorrow* (New York: Atria Books, 2014), 162.

25. "Congress Passes but Kennedy Vetoes Censorship Law for Capitol District," *Variety,* October 24, 1962.

26. Although *Yojimbo* was Oscar-nominated for black-and-white costume design in 1961— after playing a few West Coast engagements in specialized Japanese cinemas—the general U.S. release occurred in 1962.

27. Truffaut interview, DVD, *Shoot the Piano Player.*

28. Schiffman commentary, DVD, *Shoot the Piano Player.*

29. Aznavour commentary, DVD, *Shoot the Piano Player.*

30. Gilles Jacob and Claude de Givray, eds., *François Truffaut: Correspondence 1945–84* (New York: Noonday Press, 1988), 161.

31. "LOD Condemns *Jules and Jim,*" *Hollywood Reporter,* April 26, 1962.

32. Truffaut, *Correspondence,* 181.

33. Antoine de Baecque and Serge Toubiana, *Truffaut: A Biography* (New York: Knopf, 1999), 181.

34. de Baecque and Toubiana, 175.

35. Kael, *I Lost it at the Movies,* 219.

36. Pauline Kael, *5001 Nights at the Movies* (New York: Holt, Rinehart and Winston, 1982), 111.

37. Mike Connelly, *Hollywood Reporter,* December 20, 1962.

38. Hedda Hopper quote from her review of *Walk on the Wild Side;* "Stephen Boyd on 'Anything Goes' Sex," *Variety,* October 24, 1962; Morton Da Costa, "Movies Remain Basic Entertainment," *Hollywood Reporter,* November 20, 1962; Montgomery Clift from Mike Connelly column, *Hollywood Reporter,* August 20, 1962.

2. NEW AMERICAN AUTEURS

1. "Banner Season for Bette Davis," *Show Business Illustrated,* February 1962.

2. *Show,* April 1962.

3. Gerald Pratley, *The Films of Frankenheimer* (Bethlehem, PA: Lehigh University Press, 1998), 32.

4. Angela Lansbury, interviewed by Stephen Farber, November 9, 2018.

5. DVD interview with Frankenheimer.

6. Authors' interview with Lillian Michaelson, June 2017.

7. Pratley, *The Films of Frankenheimer,* 40.

8. Pratley, 40.

9. *Variety,* November 27, 1962.

10. *Variety,* November 27, 1962.

11. Quoted in Jack Lotto, *Los Angeles Herald-Examiner,* December 15, 1962.

12. *Variety,* October 24, 1962.

13. Charles McNulty, "The Life of a Trouper," *Los Angeles Times,* December 7, 2014.

14. Pratley, *The Films of Frankenheimer,* 38.

15. Authors' interview with James B. Harris, September 30, 2017.

16. Authors' interview with Harris.

17. Authors' interview with Harris.

18. Robert Roper, *Nabokov in America: On the Road to Lolita* (New York: Bloomsbury, 2015), 290.

19. Authors' interview with Harris.

20. Authors' interview with Harris.

21. Roper, *Nabokov in America*, 290.

22. Pauline Kael, *I Lost it at the Movies* (Boston: Little, Brown, 1965), 205.

23. "Interview with Sam Peckinpah," *Cinema* 4, no. 4 (1962).

24. Authors' interview with Mariette Hartley, July 5, 2017.

25. Authors' interview with Hartley.

26. Authors' interview with Hartley.

27. Quoted in David Weddle, *If They Move . . . Kill 'Em!: The Life and Times of Sam Peckinpah* (New York: Grove Press, 1994), 217.

28. Patty Duke and William J. Jankowski, *In the Presence of Greatness* (Albany, GA: BearManor Media, 2018).

29. Duke and Jankowski.

3. SURVIVORS: CON MEN AND HOLLYWOOD HONCHOS

1. David Weddle, *"If They Move . . . Kill 'Em!": The Life and Times of Sam Peckinpah* (New York: Grove Press, 1994), 222.

2. Quigley Poll from *Film Daily Yearbook, 1963.* Historically, Wayne finished on top five times, with the poll conducted from 1932 until 2013. Male domination of the poll continued uninterrupted from 1939 until the poll's termination.

3. "Wayne Urges Union Changes to Solve Runaway Films," *Hollywood Reporter,* February 9, 1962.

4. Andrew Sarris, "Notes on the Auteur Theory, 1962," *Film Culture,* Winter 1962–1963.

5. Peter Bogdanovich, *Who the Hell's in It: Conversations with Hollywood's Legendary Actors* (New York: Ballantine Books, 2004), 274.

6. Pauline Kael, *I Lost It at the Movies* (Boston: Little, Brown, 1965), 307.

7. George Stevens Jr., ed., *Conversations with the Great Moviemaker's of Hollywood's Golden Age at the American Film Institute* (New York: Vintage Books, 2007), 119.

8. "Interview with Howard Hawks," *Cinema* 5, no. 1 (1963).

9. Stuart Byron, "Auteurism, Hawks, Hatari! and Me," in *Favorite Movies,* ed. Philip Nobile (New York: McMillan, 1973), 267.

10. John Caps, *Henry Mancini: Reinventing Film Music* (Chicago: University of Illinois Press, 2012), 88.

11. Kenneth Turan, *Not to Be Missed: Fifty-Four Favorites from a Lifetime of Film* (Philadelphia: Public Affairs, 2014), 184.

12. Roger Ebert, "Great Movie: *The Man Who Shot Liberty Valance,*" December 28, 2011, Rogerebert.com.

13. Edward Buscombe, ed., *The British Film Institute Companion to the Western* (New York: Atheneum, 1988), 426.

14. Rudy Behlmer, , ed., *Memo from Darryl F. Zanuck* (New York: Grove Press, 1993), 260.

15. Darryl F. Zanuck letter of appreciation to cast and crew of *The Longest Day. Variety,* October 10, 1962.

16. William J. Mann, *Behind the Screen: How Gays and Lesbians Shaped Hollywood* (New York: Penguin, 2001), 296-302.

17. These later films include best picture Oscar winner *Schindler's List* (1993) and nominees *The Darkest Hour* and *Dunkirk,* both in 2017.

18. For further box office information, see appendix B.

19. "Zanuck Pledges Hollywood Filming," *Hollywood Reporter,* January 23, 1963.

20. Meredith Willson letter to Jack L. Warner, *Hollywood Reporter,* July 25, 1962.

21. Pauline Kael, *5001 Nights at the Movies* (New York: Holt, Rinehart and Winston, 1982), 397.

22. James Bawden and Ron Miller, *Conversations with Classic Film Stars: Interviews from Hollywood's Golden Era* (Lexington: University Press of Kentucky, 2016), 203.

23. Robert D. McFadden, "Bosley Crowther, 27 Years a Critic of Films for Times, Is Dead at 75," *New York Times,* March 8, 1981.

4. GRANDE DAMES AND A BOX OFFICE QUEEN

1. Doris Day and A. E. Hotchner, *Doris Day: Her Own Story* (New York: William Morrow, 1975), 187, 199.

2. Al Capp, "The Day Dream," *Show,* December 1962.

3. Doris Day on the *Tonight Show* with Johnny Carson, January 1976.

4. Robert J. Wagner with Scott Eyman, *Pieces of My Heart* (New York: Harper Entertainment, 2008), 133.

5. Alicia Malone, video introduction to *Gypsy* on TCM.

6. Angela Lansbury, who played Rose in a 1974 Broadway revival of *Gypsy,* commented on Merman's legacy in the 2014 interview with the *Los Angeles Times:* "She was it, even though she really couldn't act her way out of a paper bag. But boy, could she sing."

7. Joe Baltake, "There's Nothing Wrong with '62 'Gypsy,'" *Los Angeles Times,* December 27, 1993.

8. Eddie Muller, *Dark City: The Lost World of Film Noir* (New York: St. Martin's Press, 1998), 66.

9. Foreign censors report, Production Code Administration papers, Margaret Herrick Library, Academy of Motion Picture Arts and Sciences (AMPAS), Los Angeles.

10. David Shipman, *The Great Movie Stars: The International Years* (New York: Hill and Wang, 1980), 305.

11. Hedda Hopper, "Bette and Joan: No Collision Course for Hollywood Stars," *Los Angeles Times,* September 16, 1962.

12. Bette Davis on the Jack Paar *Tonight Show,* November 16, 1962.

13. Richard Schickel and George Perry, *Bette Davis: Larger Than Life* (Philadelphia: Running Press, 2009), 12.

14. David Shipman, *The Great Movie Stars: The Golden Years* (New York: Hill and Wang), 131.

15. Authors' interview with Gina Gillespie, December 12, 2017.

16. Susan Sontag, *Against Interpretation and Other Essays* (New York: Dell, 1967), 275–291.

17. Roger Ebert, *The Great Movies III* (Chicago: University of Chicago Press, 2010), 388.

18. Andrew Sarris, *The American Cinema: Directors and Directions, 1929–1968* (New York: Da Capo Press, 1996), 84–85.

19. Army Archerd, "Oscar Sidelights," *Daily Variety,* April 9, 1963.

20. Hedda Hopper, "Bette's New Career Like Good Old Days," *Los Angeles Times,* November 20, 1962.

21. Vincent Canby, "Bette Davis, Vigor Undiminished, Loves Those Perks 'As a Star,'" *Variety,* November 14, 1962.

5. CALLING DR. FREUD

1. John Huston papers, Margaret Herrick Library, Academy of Motion Picture Arts and Sciences (AMPAS), Los Angeles.

2. Stephen Farber's interview with Sidney Lumet, Stephen Farber and Marc Green, *Hollywood on the Couch* (New York: William Morrow, 1993), 171–172.

3. John Huston, "Focus on Freud," *New York Times,* December 9, 1962.

4. Authors' interview with David McCallum, May 12, 2017.

5. Authors' interview with McCallum.

6. Authors' interview with Susan Kohner Weitz, December 2017.

7. Authors' interview with Kohner Weitz.

8. Jerry Goldsmith quoted in liner notes of *Freud* soundtrack, CD deluxe edition, 2009.

9. Stephen Farber and Marc Green, *Hollywood Dynasties* (New York: Delilah, 1984), 79.

10. Joan Fontaine, *No Bed of Roses* (New York: William Morrow, 1978), 266.

11. Stephen Farber's interview with Jason Robards, *Hollywood on the Couch,* 160.

12. Farber's interview with Robards.

13. William Trombley, *Saturday Evening Post,* March 16, 1963.

14. *Word into Image,* documentary series on screenwriters, directed by Terry Sanders and Freida Lee Mock.

15. *Word into Image.*

16. Stephen Farber's interview with Janet Margolin, *Hollywood on the Couch,* 162.

17. Eleanor Perry papers, Margaret Herrick Library, AMPAS.

18. Eleanor Perry interview, *Word into Image.*

19. Eleanor Perry interview, *New York Times,* May 6, 1962.

20. Stephen Farber's interview with Dr. Theodore Rubin, *Hollywood on the Couch,* 162–163.

21. Pauline Kael, *I Lost It at the Movies* (Boston: Little, Brown, 1965), 246.

22. Kael, *I Lost it at the Movies,* 253.

23. *By Sidney Lumet,* documentary film directed by Nancy Buirski, 2016.

24. Pauline Kael, *Kiss Kiss Bang Bang* (Boston: Little, Brown, 1968), 372.

25. David Shipman, *The Great Movie Stars: The Golden Years* (New York: Hill and Wang), 287.

26. Kael, *Kiss Kiss Bang Bang,* 372.

6. ADAPTED FOR THE SCREEN: PRESTIGE AND PROVOCATION

1. Hazel Guild, "Fritz Lang Foresees Good Future for Hollywood Films," *Daily Variety,* October 23, 1962.

2. Samuel Fuller, "The Business of Originals," *Hollywood Reporter,* November 19, 1963.

3. "Classification Plus Mutilation," *Variety,* December 19, 1962.

4. Polly Bergen, TCM commentary on *Cape Fear.*

5. Barrie Chase, interviewed by Stephen Farber, August 1, 2017.

6. Walter Wanger, "The Runaway of Necessity," *Hollywood Reporter,* November 20, 1962.

7. Walter Wanger and Joe Hyams, *My Life with Cleopatra* (New York: Bantam Books, 1963), 2.

8. Philip Dunne, *Take Two* (New York: McGraw-Hill, 1980).

9. Authors' interview with James B. Harris., September 30, 2017.

10. Eugene Archer, "Woman Director Makes the Scene," *New York Times,* August 26, 1962.

11. For more on Cassavetes, see appendix A.

12. *Show,* March 1962.

13. *Hollywood Reporter,* April 9, 1963.

14. Authors' interview with Shirley Knight, August 18, 2016.

15. Authors' interview with Knight.

16. Maurice Yacowar, ed., *Tennessee Williams and Film* (New York: Frederick Ungar, 1977), 98.

7. BLACK AND WHITE TO TECHNICOLOR

1. Ralph Nelson letter to the editors, *Life,* February 22, 1963.

2. Peter Bogdanovich, *Who the Hell's in It: Conversations with Hollywood's Legendary Actors* (New York: Ballantine Books, 2004), 125.

3. Elia Kazan, *A Life* (New York, Doubleday, 1988), 598.

4. Stephen Farber interview with Martin Manulis, September 2002.

5. Special Collections, Margaret Herrick Library, Academy of Motion Picture Arts and Sciences (AMPAS), Los Angeles.

6. Fred L. Basten, *Glorious Technicolor: The Movies' Magic Rainbow* (Burbank, CA: Technicolor, 1994), 168–170.

7. Basten, 128–131.

8. Murray Schumach, "Director Decries Color Film Glut," *New York Times,* October 6, 1961.

9. Wheeler Winston Dixon, *Black and White Cinema* (New Brunswick, NJ, Rutgers University Press, 2015), 125.

10. Roger Ebert, *Through a Glass Darkly,* rogerebert.com, July 24, 2008.

11. Manoah Bowman, *Fellini: The Sixties* (Philadelphia, Running Press, 2015), 300.

12. J. R. Jones, *The Lives of Robert Ryan* (Middleton, CT: Wesleyan University Press, 2015), 200–202.

13. Authors' interview with David McCallum, May 12, 2017.

14. Michael Sragow, "Peter Ustinov's *Billy Budd,*" Authorlink, www.loa.org, April 6, 2016.

15. Bogdanovich, *Who the Hell's in It,* 72.

16. Richard Harris quote to Hedda Hopper; Brando and Howard encounter related in "Double Trouble," *Show,* March 1963.

17. Lewis Milestone Papers, Margaret Herrick Library, AMPAS; liner notes to *Mutiny on the Bounty* soundtrack (TCM, Film Score Monthly, 2004).

18. Marlon Brando audio diary in documentary film, *Listen to Me Marlon* (2015).

19. "Mincing, Precious Oxford," *Variety,* November 28, 1962.

20. The *Hollywood Reporter* item on April 10, 1962, notes an invitation to Schumach by Publicists branch of the International Alliance of Theatrical Stage Employees (IATSE) to detail his charge of "vote swapping by Academy members, particularly press agents."

21. Murray Schumach, "Hollywood at Sea," *New York Times,* March 25, 1962.

8. THE NEW FRONTIER

1. "Atlanta to Admit Negroes," *Variety,* April 4, 1962; Robert Landry, "Dixie's Film Desegregation Pace," *Variety,* May 16, 1962.

2. Jesse Green, "A Broadway 'Mockingbird,' Elegiac and Effective," *New York Times,* December 13, 2018.

3. Gregory Peck papers, Margaret Herrick Library, Academy of Motion Picture Arts and Sciences (AMPAS), Los Angeles.

4. Gregory Peck as related by his daughter Cecilia Peck at a screening of *To Kill a Mockingbird,* the American Cinematheque, Hollywood, January 27, 2018.

5. Mary Badham at American Cinematheque screening of *To Kill a Mockingbird.*

6. Roger Corman audio commentary on *The Intruder* DVD.

7. Corman audio commentary.

8. *Variety,* March 14, 1962.

9. Gregory Peck papers.

10. George H. Jackson, "Big Year Ahead for Bobby Darin," *Los Angeles Examiner,* December 31, 1961.

11. Murray Schumach, "N.A.A.C.P. Assails the Movie Industry," *New York Times,* November 29, 1961.

12. "Showbiz Color Line Probe Opens," *Daily Variety,* October 31, 1962.

13. Stanley Kramer, "Sending Myself the Message," *Films and Filming,* February 1964.

14. Jennifer Frost, *Producer of Controversy: Stanley Kramer, Hollywood Liberalism, and the Cold War* (Lawrence: University Press of Kansas, 2017), 212.

15. Authors' interview with Joanna Lancaster, January 11, 2019.

16. John C. Waugh, "Birdman Assigns Itself Some Penological Problems," *Christian Science Monitor,* January 11, 1961.

17. "Inside Stuff-Pictures," *Variety,* June 6, 1962.

9. SEXUAL AND SOCIAL OUTLAWS

1. Vito Russo, *The Celluloid Closet* (New York: Harper and Row, 1987), 121–122.

2. "*Victim* Denied a Code Seal," *Hollywood Reporter,* February 5, 1962.

3. Pauline Kael, *5001 Nights at the Movies* (New York: Holt, Rinehart and Winston, 1982), 633.

4. Dirk Bogarde, *Snakes and Ladders* (New York: Holt, Rinehart and Winston, 1978), 201.

5. Ken Ringle, *Washington Post,* September 4, 1998.

6. Russo, *The Celluloid Closet,* 141.

7. *Los Angeles Times,* October 21, 1961.

8. *Variety,* May 30, 1962.

9. *Newsweek,* June 11, 1962.

10. *London Sunday Express* quoted in reviewing service, Harrison's Reports, June 9, 1962.

11. C. D. Innes, *Modern British Drama: The Twentieth Century* (Cambridge: Cambridge University Press, 2002), 80.

12. Authors' interview with Terry Sanders, November 9, 2017.

13. Authors' interview with Sanders.

14. Authors' interview with Sanders.

15. Authors' interview with Sanders.

16. Spielberg interview on DVD of *Lonely Are the Brave.*

17. Murray Schumach, "Hollywood Flop," *New York Times,* August 19, 1962.

18. Stephen Farber and Marc Green, *Hollywood Dynasties* (New York: Delilah, 1984), 220.

19. David Denby, *New Yorker,* July 23, 2007.

10. CROWNING ACHIEVEMENT

1. Pauline Kael, *Kiss Kiss Bang Bang* (Boston: Little, Brown, 1968), 161.

2. Andrew Sarris, *Confessions of a Cultist: On the Cinema, 1955–1969* (New York: Simon and Schuster, 1970), 65–67.

3. *Sight and Sound,* Winter 1971–1972.

4. L. Robert Morris and Lawrence Raskin, *Lawrence of Arabia* (New York: Anchor Books, 1992), 209.

5. Morris and Raskin, xiv.

6. Natasha Fraser-Cavassoni, *Sam Spiegel* (New York: Simon and Schuster, 2003), 52.

7. Adrian Turner, *The Making of David Lean's Lawrence of Arabia* (London: Dragon's World, 1994), 41.

8. Turner, 17.

9. Authors interview with Anne V. Coates, December 1, 2017.

10. Turner, *The Making of David Lean's Lawrence of Arabia,* 143.

11. Turner, 102.

12. Stanley Kauffmann, *New Republic,* February 20, 1989.

13. Turner, *The Making of David Lean's Lawrence of Arabia,* 44.

14. Turner, 44.

15. Authors' interview with Coates.

16. Authors' interview with Coates.

17. Authors' interview with Coates.

18. Turner, *The Making of David Lean's Lawrence of Arabia,* 161.

19. Turner, 87.

20. Turner, 87.

21. Turner, 73.

22. T. E. Lawrence, *Seven Pillars of Wisdom* (Ware, Hertfordshire: Wordsworth Editions Limited, 1997), 436.

23. Turner, *The Making of David Lean's Lawrence of Arabia*, 133.

24. Dennis Brown, "'Lawrence' Stars Recall Epic Adventure," *Los Angeles Times,* February 9, 1989.

25. Authors' interview with Coates.

26. Janet Maslin, "Lawrence Seen Whole," *New York Times,* January 29, 1989.

27. Robert Bolt, *Lawrence of Arabia* Souvenir Program, 1962.

28. Edward W. Said, "'Lawrence' Doesn't Do Arabs Any Favors," *Wall Street Journal,* February 21, 1989.

29. Quoted in Jeremy Arnold, *The 50th Anniversary Lawrence of Arabia* (Sony Pictures Home Entertainment, 2012), 79.

EPILOGUE

1. Authors' interview with Mariette Hartley, July 5, 2017.

2. Dan Cox and Jonathan Bing, "Overkill or Over-the-Hill?," *Variety,* October 2, 2000.

3. Peter Biskind, *Easy Riders, Raging Bulls* (New York: Simon and Schuster, 1998).

4. L. Robert Morris and Lawrence Raskin, *Lawrence of Arabia* (New York: Anchor Books, 1992), 198.

5. Authors' interview with Anne V. Coates, December 1, 2017.

6. Morris and Raskin, *Lawrence of Arabia,* 228.

7. Wesley Morris, *New York Times Magazine,* December 30, 2018.

8. Susan King, "1962 Was a Fertile Year in Filmmaking," *Los Angeles Times,* December 25, 2018.

BIBLIOGRAPHY

Aaronson, Charles S., ed. *1963: International Motion Picture Almanac.* New York: Quigley Publications, 1962.

———. *1964: International Motion Picture Almanac.* New York: Quigley Publications, 1963.

Alicoate, Chas. A., ed. *The 1963 Film Daily Year Book of Motion Pictures.* New York: Film Daily, 1963.

Balio, Tino. *The Foreign Film Renaissance on American Screens, 1946–1973.* Madison: University of Wisconsin Press, 2010.

Basinger, Jeanine. *The Star Machine.* New York: Vintage Books, 2007.

Basten, Fred L. *Glorious Technicolor: The Movies' Magic Rainbow.* Burbank, CA: Technicolor, 1994.

Bawden, James, and Ron Miller. *Conversations with Classic Film Stars: Interviews from Hollywood's Golden Era.* Lexington: University Press of Kentucky, 2016.

Behlmer, Rudy, ed. *Memo from Darryl F. Zanuck.* New York: Grove Press, 1993.

Belton, John. *Widescreen Cinema.* Cambridge, MA: Harvard University Press, 1992.

Biskind, Peter. *Easy Riders, Raging Bulls.* New York: Simon and Schuster, 1998.

Blum, Daniel, ed. *Screen World: 1963.* New York: Biblo and Tannen, 1983.

Bogarde, Dirk. *Snakes and Ladders.* New York: Holt, Rinehart, and Winston, 1978.

Bogdanovich, Peter. *Who the Hell's in It: Conversations with Hollywood's Legendary Actors.* New York: Ballantine Books, 2004.

Bowman, Manoah. *Fellini: The Sixties.* Philadelphia: Running Press, 2015.

Brown, Gene, ed. *The New York Times Encyclopedia of Film, 1958–1963.* New York: New York Times Book Company, 1984.

Buhle, Paul, and Dave Wagner. *Radical Hollywood.* New York: New Press, 2002.

Buscombe, Edward, ed. *The British Film Institute Companion to the Western.* New York: Atheneum, 1988.

Caps, John. *Henry Mancini: Reinventing Film Music.* Chicago: University of Illinois Press, 2012.

Casper, Drew. *Postwar Hollywood 1946–1962.* Malden, MA: Blackwell, 2007.

Chapman, David. *Retro Stud.* Portland, OR: Collector's Press, 2002.

Coldstream, John. *Dirk Bogarde: The Authorised Biography.* London: Weidenfeld and Nicolson, 2004.

Couvares, Francis G., ed. *Movie Censorship and American Culture.* Washington, DC: Smithsonian Institution Press, 1996.

Cowie, Peter, ed. *International Film Guide 1964.* London: Tantivy Press, 1964.

Day, Doris, and A. E. Hotchner. *Doris Day: Her Own Story.* New York: William Morrow, 1975.

De Baecque, Antoine, and Serge Toubiana. *Truffaut: A Biography.* New York: Alfred A. Knopf, 1999.

Denby, David, ed. *Awake in the Dark: An Anthology of Film Criticism.* New York: Vintage Books, 1977.

Dewey, Donald. *Marcello Mastroianni: His Life and Art.* New York: Birch Lane Press, 1993.

Dixon, Wheeler Winston. *Black and White Cinema.* New Brunswick, NJ: Rutgers University Press, 2015.

Duke, Patty, and William J. Jankowski. *In the Presence of Greatness.* Albany, GA: BearManor Media, 2018.

Ebert, Roger. *The Great Movies III.* Chicago: University of Chicago Press, 2010.

Esposito, Joseph A. *Dinner in Camelot.* Lebanon, NH: University Press of New England, 2018.

Farber, Stephen, and Marc Green. *Hollywood Dynasties.* New York: Delilah, 1984.

———. *Hollywood on the Couch.* New York: William Morrow, 1993.

Finder, Henry, ed. *The 60s: The Story of a Decade/The New Yorker.* New York: Random House, 2016.

Fordin, Hugh. *The World of Entertainment: Hollywood's Greatest Musicals.* New York: Doubleday, 1975.

Fraser-Cavassoni, Natasha. *Sam Spiegel.* New York: Simon and Schuster, 2003.

Frost, Jennifer. *Producer of Controversy: Stanley Kramer, Hollywood Liberalism, and the Cold War.* Lawrence: University Press of Kansas, 2017.

Gabbard, Glen O., and Krin Gabbard. *Psychiatry and the Cinema.* Washington, DC: American Psychiatric Press, 1990.

Gomery, Douglas. *Shared Pleasures: A History of Movie Presentation in the United States.* Madison: University of Wisconsin Press, 1992.

Grant, Barry Keith, ed. *American Cinema of the 1960s.* New Brunswick, NJ: Rutgers University Press, 2008.

Hamilton, Ian. *Writers in Hollywood, 1915–1951.* New York: Edward Burlingame, 1990.

Harris, Mark. *Pictures at a Revolution: Five Movies and the Birth of the New Hollywood.* New York: Penguin, 2008.

Hepburn, Katharine. *Me: Stories of My Life.* New York: Alfred A. Knopf, 1991.

Hirschhorn, Clive. *The Universal Story.* New York: Crown, 1983.

———. *The Warner Bros. Story.* New York: Crown, 1979.

Hochkofler, Matilde. *Marcello Mastroianni: The Fun of Cinema.* Rome: Gremese International, 1992.

Hunter, Tab, and Eddie Muller. *Tab Hunter Confidential.* Chapel Hill, NC: Algonquin Books of Chapel Hill, 2005.

Huston, John. *An Open Book.* New York: Alfred A. Knopf, 1980.

Jacob, Gilles, and Claude de Givray, eds. *François Truffaut: Correspondence 1945–1984.* New York: Noonday Press, 1988.

Jones, J. R. *The Lives of Robert Ryan.* Middleton, CT: Wesleyan University Press, 2015.

Kael, Pauline. *5001 Nights at the Movies.* New York: Holt, Rinehart and Winston, 1982.

———. *I Lost It at the Movies.* Boston: Little, Brown, 1965.

———. *Kiss Kiss Bang Bang.* Boston: Little, Brown, 1968.

Kaminsky, Stuart M., ed. *Ingmar Bergman: Essays in Criticism.* London: Oxford University Press, 1975.

Kashner, Sam, and Jennifer MacNair. *The Bad and the Beautiful: Hollywood in the Fifties.* New York: W. W. Norton, 2002.

Kauffmann, Stanley. *A World on Film.* New York: Dell, 1966.

Kazan, Elia. *A Life.* New York: Doubleday, 1988.

Kennedy, Matthew. *Roadshow: The Fall of Film Musicals in the 1960s.* New York: Oxford University Press, 2014.

Lawrence, T. E. *Seven Pillars of Wisdom.* Ware, Hertfordshire: Wordsworth Editions Limited, 1997.

Lee, Harper. *To Kill a Mockingbird.* New York: Hachette Book Group, 1988.

Leff, Leonard F., and Jerold L. Simmons. *The Dame in the Kimono: Hollywood, Censorship, and the Production Code from the 1920s to the 1960s.* New York: Grove Wiedenfeld, 1990.

Levy, Emanuel. *Small-Town America in Film.* New York: Continuum, 1991.

Loren, Sophia. *Yesterday, Today, Tomorrow.* New York: Atria, 2014.

Madsen, Axel. *Stanwyck.* New York: HarperCollins, 1994.

Maltin, Leonard. *Classic Movie Guide.* New York: Plume, 2015.

———. *2015 Movie Guide: The Modern Era.* New York: Plume, 2014.

Mancini, Henry, and Gene Lees. *Did They Mention the Music?* New York: Rowman and Littlefield, 1989.

Mann, William J. *Behind the Screen: How Gays and Lesbians Shaped Hollywood.* New York: Penguin, 2001.

———. *Kate: The Woman Who Was Hepburn.* New York: Henry Holt, 2006.

Mordden, Ethan. *Medium Cool: The Movies of the 1960s.* New York: Alfred A. Knopf, 1990.

———. *Movie Star: A Look at the Women Who Made Hollywood.* New York: St. Martin's Press, 1985.

Morris, L. Robert, and Lawrence Raskin. *Lawrence of Arabia.* New York: Anchor Books, 1992.

Muller, Eddie. *Dark City: The Lost World of Film Noir.* New York: St. Martin's Press, 1998.

Muller, Jurgen, ed. *Movies of the 60s.* Cologne: Taschen, 2004.

Nashawaty, Chris. *Crab Monsters, Teenage Cavemen, and Candy Stripe Nurses.* New York: Abrams Books, 2013.

Nichols, Peter M., ed. *The New York Times Guide to the Best 1,000 Movies Ever Made.* New York: St. Martin's Press, 2004.

Nobile, Philip, ed. *Favorite Movies.* New York: Macmillan, 1973.

Nourmand, Tony, and Graham Marsh. *Film Posters of the 60s.* Cologne: Evergreen/Taschen, 2005.

O'Neil, Tom. *Movie Awards.* New York: Perigree Books, 2003.

Pratley, Gerald. *The Films of Frankenheimer.* Bethlehem, PA: Lehigh University Press, 1998.

Reich, Jacqueline. *Beyond the Latin Lover: Marcello Mastroianni, Masculinity, and Italian Cinema.* Bloomington: Indiana University Press, 2004.

Riese, Randall. *All about Bette.* Chicago: Contemporary Books, 1993.

Roper, Robert. *Nabokov in America: On the Road to Lolita.* New York: Bloomsbury, 2015.

Russo, Vito. *The Celluloid Closet.* New York: Harper and Row, 1987.

Sarris, Andrew. *The American Cinema: Directors and Directions, 1929–1968.* New York: Da Capo Press, 1996.

Schatz, Thomas. *The Genius of the System: Hollywood Filmmaking in the Studio Era.* New York: Metropolitan Books, 1996.

Schickel, Richard. *Keepers.* New York: Alfred A. Knopf, 2015.

Schickel, Richard, and George Perry. *Bette Davis: Larger Than Life.* Philadelphia: Running Press, 2009.

Sennett, Ted. *Hollywood's Golden Year: 1939—A Fiftieth Anniversary Celebration.* New York: St. Martin's Press, 1989.

Shipman, David. *The Great Movie Stars: The Golden Years.* New York: Hill and Wang, 1979.

———. *The Great Movie Stars: The International Years.* New York: Hill and Wang, 1980.

Sikov, Ed. *Dark Victory: The Life of Bette Davis.* New York: Henry Holt, 2007.

Sklar, Robert. *Movie-Made America.* New York: Vintage Books, 1994.

Slotkin, Richard. *Gunfighter Nation: The Myth of the Frontier in Twentieth-Century America.* Norman: University of Oklahoma Press, 1998.

Sontag, Susan. *Against Interpretation and Other Essays.* New York: Dell, 1967.

Sova, Dawn B. *Forbidden Films.* New York: Checkmark Books, 2001.

Stevens, George, Jr. *Conversations with the Great Moviemakers of Hollywood's Golden Age at the American Film Institute.* New York: Vintage Books, 2007.

Stevenson, Jack. *Land of a Thousand Balconies.* Manchester: Critical Vision/Headpress, 2003.

Stine, Whitney. *"I'd Love to Kiss You . . .": Conversations with Bette Davis.* New York: Pocket Books, 1990.

Sylbert, Richard, and Sylvia Townsend. *Designing Movies: Portrait of a Hollywood Artist.* Westport, CT: Praeger, 2008.

Taylor, Charles. *Opening Wednesday at a Theater or Drive-In Near You.* New York: Bloomsbury, 2017.

Thomson, David. *The Big Screen: The Story of the Movies.* New York: Farrar, Straus and Giroux, 2012.

Truffaut, François. *Hitchcock.* New York: Simon and Schuster, 1984.

Turan, Kenneth. *Not to Be Missed: Fifty-Four Favorites from a Lifetime of Film.* Philadelphia: Public Affairs, 2014.

Turner, Adrian. *The Making of David Lean's Lawrence of Arabia.* London: Dragon's World, 1994.

Various authors. *The New York Times Film Reviews.* Vol. 5, *1959–1968.* New York: New York Times and Arno Press, 1970.

Various authors. *Variety Film Reviews.* Vol. 10, *1959–1963.* New York: Garland, 1983.

Wanger, Walter, and Joe Hyams. *My Life with Cleopatra.* New York: Bantam Books, 1963.

Weddle, David. *If They Move . . . Kill 'Em!: The Life and Times of Sam Peckinpah.* New York: Grove Press, 1994.

Weis, Elizabeth, ed. *The Movie Star.* New York: Viking Press, 1981.

Whitburn, Joel. *The Billboard Book of Top 40 Hits.* New York: Billboard Books, 2010.

Wiley, Mason, and Damien Bona. *Inside Oscar.* New York: Ballantine Books, 1993.

Yacowar, Maurice. *Tennessee Williams and Film.* New York: Frederick Ungar, 1977.

INDEX

ABOUT THE AUTHORS

STEPHEN FARBER, president of the Los Angeles Film Critics Association from 2012 to 2016, has written for the *New York Times, Los Angeles Times, Hollywood Reporter,* and many other publications. He has written or co-written four previous books: *The Movie Rating Game* (1972); *Hollywood Dynasties* (1984); *Outrageous Conduct: Art, Ego, and the Twilight Zone Case* (1988); and *Hollywood on the Couch* (1993). He is on the faculty at UCLA, teaching film criticism.

MICHAEL MCCLELLAN is the co-producer of a classic film series in Los Angeles. He is the past senior vice president and head film buyer for Landmark Theatres and served on the board of appeals of the Classification and Ratings Administration of the MPAA. A graduate of Rutgers University–Camden and Villanova University, he resides in Los Angeles.